DATE DUE

Brodart Co.   Cat. # 55 137 001   Printed in USA

MAKING SPACE ON THE
WESTERN FRONTIER

W. PAUL REEVE

Making Space on the Western Frontier

MORMONS, MINERS, AND SOUTHERN PAIUTES

UNIVERSITY OF ILLINOIS PRESS

URBANA AND CHICAGO

Library of Congress Cataloging-in-Publication Data
Reeve, W. Paul.
Making space on the Western frontier : Mormons,
miners, and southern Paiutes / W. Paul Reeve.
p.   cm.
Includes bibliographical references and index.
ISBN-13: 978-0-252-03126-7 (cloth : alk. paper)
ISBN-10: 0-252-03126-1 (cloth : alk. paper)
1. Frontier and pioneer life—West (U.S.)
2. West (U.S.)—Ethnic relations—History—19th century.
3. West (U.S.)—Social conditions—19th century.
4. Great Basin—History—19th century.
5. Mormon pioneers—West (U.S.)—History—19th century.
6. Miners—West (U.S.)—History—19th century.
7. Southern Paiute Indians—History—19th century.
8. Group identity—West (U.S.)—History—19th century.
9. Social conflict—West (U.S.)—History—19th century.
10. Intercultural communication—West (U.S.)—History—19th century.
I. Title.
F596.R413   2006
978'.034—dc22   2006029374

For Beth

for making space for me.

Contents

Acknowledgments

I am grateful to a variety of individuals who helped with different aspects of this project. I had the good fortune of meeting Peter Kraus, the government-documents specialist at the University of Utah's Marriott Library, early on in the project. He proved a valuable resource who frequently went beyond the call of duty to locate obscure items for me, including one document at Yale's Beinecke Library. He has continued to be a support and a friend. Paul Mogren at the Marriott Library's special collections was also helpful and always friendly. Mark A. Scherer at the Community of Christ archives, Ronald Watt at the LDS archives, Eric Moody at the Nevada Historical Society, and the special collections staff at the University of Nevada at Las Vegas were generous with their time and resources. Janet Burton Seegmiller at Southern Utah University's special collections was enthusiastic, knowledgeable, and always quick to respond. Floyd A. O'Neil offered helpful suggestions and frequent encouragement. William P. MacKinnon shared his research and wisdom with me. I had rare luck one day to be in the right place at the right time to make the acquaintance of Ardis E. Parshall, an extraordinarily talented and thorough researcher who shared her ideas and findings with me and helped tie down a few loose ends. She continues to be generous with her time, talents, and hard work. Thank you, Ardis.

I am grateful to Elliot West, whose work I admire and whose feedback I prize. Fran MacDonnell, a mentor, colleague, and friend, read the manuscript and offered insightful comments, encouragement, and vision that helped me think about the work in new ways. Bob Goldberg read and reread the manuscript several times. He always strengthened it and greatly influenced its final form. He helped me to stretch my capabilities, cheered my successes, and offered counsel and concern that reached beyond the academic relationship. He stepped in to fill the void that Dean left and guided me through the completion of this project. I am grateful he chose to be a teacher.

My family, of course, endured the most during the preparation of this manuscript. Porter, Eliza, Emma, and Hunter made it worthwhile. Beth, most especially, deserves credit. She sacrificed the most to allow me to chase my dream. Her confidence, companionship, and love carry me.

Dean May left suddenly and far too soon. I will spend my career attempting to repay my debt to him. I feel lost without his gentle guidance. He was my mentor and friend who never doubted, even when I did, that this project is worthwhile and significant. The many times we shared lunch he always paid, promising that once I landed a tenure-track position, it would be my turn to treat. We planned to share that lunch at the Mormon History Association conference at Kirtland, Ohio, in May 2003, but Dean didn't show. I'll savor that lunch all the more when we finally sit down together to eat it. My treat, Dean.

1 Intersections

In March 1866, the southwest fringe of Utah Territory simmered in a stew of mistrust and anxiety. Euro-American Mormons and non-Mormon miners had come to the southern edge of the Escalante Desert seeking very different gods through very different means. In the process they disrupted the region's long-term inhabitants, the Southern Paiutes. These three disparate communities, thrown together by a variety of forces, quickly found themselves in competition over the area's natural resources. It was a "convergence of diverse people," which in this case proved difficult for all and deadly for some.[1]

In late March, the murder of George Rogers, a lone miner from Kentucky, brought the three groups together in a tragic episode. The events that unfolded highlight each group's ideas about community and how they separately set out to define and defend their differing notions. According to Mormon accounts, an expedition from Panaca, a Mormon town in present-day southeastern Nevada, captured a Paiute named Okus, who upon interrogation confessed to killing Rogers. Okus admitted that he had lain in wait "for five days to kill a man, 'Mormon or gentile,' and get his outfit." He then volunteered to show where he had committed the murder.[2]

As a company of men from Panaca escorted Okus to the murder scene, things grew increasingly complicated. Fifteen armed miners riding toward Panaca, intent upon taking "vengeance on the Mormons for suffering their friend, Rogers, to be killed by Danites," came upon the Mormon group outside of town.[3] Upon learning the nature of the Mormon excursion, the hostile miners joined the entourage in traveling to the place of Rogers's death. After surveying the scene and hearing Okus confess, the miners felt satisfied that it was an "Indian murder" and fixed their anger upon Okus. They forced him from the wagon where he was being held, wrapped one end of a chain around his neck, and secured the other end to a saddle horn. The miners "set off at full speed for Meadow Valley," ten miles distant, with Okus literally in tow. They arrived one hour and ten minutes later, Okus no doubt battered and "quite exhausted through traveling so far at such a speed."

At Meadow Valley, Okus gave the names of two other Indians indirectly involved in the murder, as well as implicating Bush-head, another Native American who reportedly instigated the whole thing. The miners, still bent upon revenge, tracked down the two Indians that Okus named at a nearby Paiute camp and murdered them along with another luckless Paiute who happened to be there.

The entourage returned to Panaca, where the miners prepared to kill Okus. With his death imminent, Okus declared that "he knew he had bad blood in him and that it ought to be poured out but, he asked to be shot instead of hanged." The miners refused. They hanged him, and he "died without a struggle." Still not satisfied, the miners set out for Clover Valley, a Mormon ranching outpost, in quest of Bush-head, whom they "hanged in the presence of [Mormon] settlers and Indians."[4]

Clearly, prejudice on all sides shaped this sad series of events. Beyond its tragic nature, the episode raises intriguing questions concerning nineteenth-century frontier interactions. The death of Rogers forced Mormons, miners, and Southern Paiutes into a three-headed confrontation that encompassed far more than this single episode; it stretched through space to envelop much of Paiute traditional lands and through time to the beginning of the twentieth century. Rogers's death is symbolic of that larger confrontation because it illuminates key reasons for interactions between the three groups and underscores several points: the way each community viewed its neighbors, the way each group defended differing spatial constructs, each group's contrasting economic identity, and even differing ritualistic notions of death.

This study explores these themes. While ethnographers, anthropologists, historians, and cultural geographers tend to separate the groups of people they study, this work attempts to bring them back together and find meaning at the points where their lives intersected. Mormons, miners, and Southern Paiutes carved a world for themselves, an intercultural space that each group defined and defended for itself. Those defenses varied in intensity and lacked consistency but persisted for nearly forty years.

The story that follows is therefore complicated and messy. It rethinks the early version of America's frontier experience, which emphasized progress and triumph, while it simultaneously moves beyond newer ideas about the West as a place of declension, conquest, or dependence. There is no frontier line or successive waves of civilization here[5] but rather a meeting place where three worlds collided and struggled to coexist.[6] It is a story of interethnic[7] and cross-cultural connections viewed through the lenses of power, space, and place. Nineteenth-century Mormons, miners, and Southern Paiutes came together in the 1860s on the southern rim of the Great Basin. Over the ensuing four decades they fashioned a world-between-worlds where they acted out the "drama of life on the edges."[8] An integral part of that drama was the way in which each group shaped its own identity in part as a response to its interactions with the other two groups.

As the historian Richard White notes, western communities, try as they might to live by their own values and customs, were "always being flooded by a larger governmental and economic sea or invaded by members of adjoining communities." "Members of any communities," White contends, "inevitably had to embark upon the sea surrounding their neighborhood, village, or township. And at sea, the rules that obtained within island communities proved inappropriate."[9] In keeping with White's metaphor, the myriad of interactions between Mormons, miners, and Southern Paiutes chronicled here are episodes at sea. They teach important lessons about how each group viewed the other as well as the identity each invented for itself.

To understand why Mormons, miners, and Paiutes left the boundaries of their communities in the first place, it is essential to ascertain the nature of those boundaries, how they were formed, and the meaning they embodied for each group. What cultural notions of land and space were the three groups so intent upon defending? What significance did the parched land on the southern rim of the Great Basin hold for each community, and why were its members willing to kill and be killed for this desert soil? The answer has less to do with the actual dirt itself than with the three very different worldviews that dug, plowed, grazed, and mined that dirt with symbolism.

The task, therefore, is to catch that symbolism and decipher its message for each community. Certainly a crash of economies occurred when Mormons, miners, and Southern Paiutes met, but the nature of the contest between them reaches beyond the economic to the sacred. The Paiutes were more than simply economic beings intent upon protecting traditional hunting, gathering, and farming places; they were spiritual beings with distinct notions of their privileged spot in the universe. When the Mormons and miners invaded that spot, it was more than an affront to the Paiute economy; it was a shaking of the Paiute cosmos.

The Paiutes first began defining their space around AD 1300. Then, in 1862, a group of Mormon ranchers invaded that space and later built Hebron, an outpost on the Mormon fringe but at the Paiute center. Finally, in 1864, restless prospectors, pushing east from the California gold fields, poured into that same space and eventually founded Pioche, Nevada, an 1870s mining boomtown (see figure 1). Each arrival marked a transition in meaning for the land.

The real significance of the story, however, is the rich cross-fertilization that took place, as each group found ways to adjust to the other two while simultaneously clinging to core aspects of their respective cultural identities. As their lives increasingly intersected, it is clear that the story of any one of these three groups cannot be fully understood without the other two. It is also evident that each group's cosmology shaped its exchanges with the others so that the contest over resources and land that ensued was physical as well as spiritual.

In that light, sacred notions of space for these three groups serve as bookends (chapters 2 and 7) for the story told here. It begins as each group came to the same geographic place, worldview in tow. Upon arrival, the Mormons, miners, and Southern Paiutes each followed rituals of possession designed to claim the land and reorient it toward respective notions of sacredness. Those starkly different ideas about sacred space drove the ensuing conflict. This point becomes abundantly clear by the end as we witness other rituals, this time of sickness, death, and dying, that highlight in haunting ways the deep cultural and spiritual divides that separated the three groups.

In between those bookends, the story also underscores lessons about power and the making of space, especially as the federal government intervened to muscle borders in heavy-handed attempts to push American progress. Federal power notwithstanding, the resilience of the three communities is striking as each one shaped its own world in meaningful ways. The three central chapters (4, 5, and 6) focus upon the dynamics of the interaction between the Mormons, miners, and Southern Paiutes. Each chapter seeks to understand how each group viewed the other two through time and space, with the Southern Paiutes, Mormons, and miners, respectively, serving as lenses into the other two. A hierarchy of Americanness emerged that favored the miners as the embodiment of American progress, industry, and quest for wealth. Mormons and Southern Paiutes, however, valued community over individualism and celestial

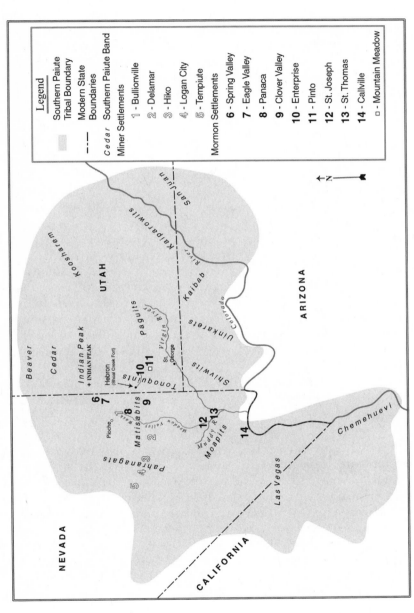

Figure 1. *Geographic Space Shared by Mormons, Miners, and Southern Paiutes.*

rewards over material gain, ideals that placed them well outside prevailing standards of what it meant to be an American.

By 1902, when an earthquake hit the region, it symbolized a rumbling of change that was already pulling the three groups in different directions. By then, the intensity of the competition for land had diminished, and the Mormons, miners, and Southern Paiutes had reinvented their space, to varying degrees, in ways that reflected the new realities of each group's vastly altered world.

———————

Shifting relationships of power played a significant role in the way that this story unfolded, as did its timing. The first consequential three-headed interaction between Mormons, miners, and Southern Paiutes took place in 1864, during the Civil War, which virtually guaranteed that the federal government would become a power broker in the ensuing drama. Union policy during the war "embodied a spirit of national economic activism unprecedented in the antebellum years." The power and role of the federal government mushroomed to include a national paper currency, an enormous debt, a banking system, a consolidated telegraph industry, and land grants to railroads and settlers, as well as a greatly expanded bureaucracy and budget. It was, as the historian Eric Foner suggests, "the birth of the modern American state." The economic policies of this emerging nation-state "originated in the crucible of war" and "aimed first and foremost to mobilize the nation's resources in order to finance the conflict."[10]

By the end of 1866, Radical Republicans had solidified their control of the federal government and would spend the next eleven years attempting to define the shape of post–Civil War America—the West and all. For Republicans, the task involved not only plowing new "free soil" ideals into the former slave soil of the South but digging meaning into the semi-barren expanses of the American West. By virtue of winning the Civil War, northerners won the right to redefine the nation. "Union victory in the war," the historian James M. McPherson writes, "destroyed the southern vision of America and ensured that the northern vision would become the American vision."[11]

In the West, that vision involved solving the "Mormon Question" and the "Indian Problem." As the victorious party of the Civil War, the Republican party, especially during Radical Reconstruction (1867–77), won the right to define those two "problems" and to attempt to legislate their solutions. In doing so, Republicans created a definition of what it meant to be an American that was filtered through a predominantly northern and Protestant worldview.[12] That definition held far-reaching implications, even for the three cultural groups thousands of miles away vying for control of the southern rim of the Great Basin.

The lessons that follow, then, stretch well beyond Mormons, miners, and Southern Paiutes to encompass the nation. While the characters in this drama lived their lives in relative obscurity upon a remote geographic stage, their actions speak loudly of national trends in politics, economics, and culture during the last half of the nineteenth century. Mark Twain and Charles Dudley Warner aptly named the post–Civil War era the Gilded Age (1865–1901). Their novel of the same name chronicled and condemned the political fraud, business corruption, land speculation, jury tampering, and bribery that they witnessed permeating American society.[13] While more recently historians have somewhat tempered or even attempted to revise that vision, this study bears it out.[14] The desert expanses of southwestern Utah and southeastern Nevada form the unlikely backdrop for the weaving together of several major strands that form the broader fabric of Gilded Age America. There, among the sagebrush and cactus, nationalization and the growth of federal power, corrupt politics, no-holds-barred laissez-faire capitalism, and enforced cultural homogenization played out in sometimes exaggerated ways.

James M. Ashley, a member of the U.S. House of Representatives from Ohio and the Radical Republican who led the charge to impeach President Andrew Johnson, embodies the growth of federal power and its impact upon the West. Ashley held significant authority over the West as chairman of the House Committee on Territories. As such, he led Congress to draw political boundaries that aimed to separate Mormons from miners and later endeavored to redraw the West altogether. In a little-known episode in 1869, he even attempted to eliminate Utah from the map and thereby solve the Mormon Question for good. Radical Republicans in Congress viewed federal power as expansive and wielded it in ways that not only reconstructed the South but remodeled the West.

Fraud, greed, and corruption form integral parts of this story, too. Those forces found their way, in perhaps disproportionate doses, to the southern rim of the Great Basin in the 1860s and 1870s. The pages that follow are replete with crooked governors, Indian agents, lawyers, jurors, and local officials. Most public servants used their jobs for personal gain rather than the common good. Individualism and an attendant quest for wealth seemed to dominate public attitudes. Alexis de Tocqueville, a French observer of American life, noticed this phenomenon already at play in the early 1830s: "It is odd to watch with what feverish ardor the Americans pursue prosperity and how they are ever tormented by the shadowy suspicion that they may not have chosen the shortest route to get it. . . . [Americans] clutch everything but hold nothing fast, and so lose grip as they hurry after some new delight. Love of comfort has become the dominant national taste. The main current of human passions running in that direction sweeps everything along with it."[15] It was a trend that only accelerated over time and came to typify Gilded Age America.

Tocqueville's individualism and materialism fed and was fed by America's postwar manufacturing boom. As the historian Sean Dennis Cashman put it, during the Gilded Age "the promise of American life lay in its industrial future." America's 1876 Centennial Exhibition outside Philadelphia embodied that notion. Machinery Hall become one of its central attractions, as nearly ten million visitors awed over the giant Corliss engine housed there. The mammoth steam-driven device weighed almost 1.7 million pounds, yet ran without noise; its fourteen-hundred-horsepower capacity powered all the exhibits inside Machinery Hall, where its peaceful churning became a symbol to the crowds of the relentless march of "American industrial progress." That progress pushed America from a second-rate industrial power in 1860 to surpass Britain, France, and Germany by 1890. The number of people engaged in manufacturing more than doubled from 1870 to 1890. The same held true for people in mining, construction, transportation, and public utilities. This boom was optimistically tied to the West, where America's treasury of gold, silver, and copper lay buried, many believed, for the taking.[16]

Those who found prosperity during this period were called "Robber Barons": men such as John D. Rockefeller, Andrew Carnegie, John Pierpont Morgan, and others who amassed vast fortunes largely at the expense of disadvantaged laborers. The story told here of Pioche, Nevada, was no different. Miners there extracted wealth from the second-richest silver mines in 1870s Nevada, the proceeds from which largely wound up in the pockets of absentee capitalists. George Hearst, the father of William Randolph Hearst, engaged in courtroom mining at Pioche in a little-known court case that depicts the graft and corruption of the era. Through it all, laissez-faire capitalism held sway and played out on the national stage in economic peaks and valleys punctuated by the depressions of 1873 and 1893. Pioche itself endured an even more exaggerated boom-bust cycle.

Massive immigration was another important trend of the period, as was a corresponding nativist backlash. Between 1860 and 1914, twenty-five million people immigrated to America. While these newcomers were initially welcomed, economic fears in the form of job loss and lower wages changed the mood of many Americans. The flood tide of newcomers eventually gave rise to the exclusion of Chinese immigrants altogether and a drastic reduction in the number of outsiders allowed into the United States from southern and eastern Europe. Those "undesirable" Europeans tended to have olive skin and practice Roman Catholicism or Judaism, which set them apart from the white Protestant majority's definition of Americanness.[17] While immigration was not at the heart of the homogenization forced upon the Mormons and Southern Paiutes, the process, rhetoric, and results fit well within the larger Americanization framework of the period. The difference here is that America made outsiders out of these two inside ethnic groups. In the end, the miners in this story pushed America's destiny along; the Mormons and Southern Paiutes, however, seemed to stand in its way.

Despite the various forces at play, the experiences of the Mormons, miners, and Southern Paiutes do more than merely embody national trends; they tell a little-studied tale all their own. At its most basic level, what follows is a frontier story about what it meant to be an American during the last half of the nineteenth century. It also delves into fundamental issues governing the human condition. What does it mean to be a good neighbor, especially to peoples with drastically different values than yours? Is it possible to look past ethnic and cultural diversity to view broader commonalities? Does a people's worldview preclude acceptance of other cultures, especially if that view is linked to divinity and tied to the land? While the Mormons, miners, and Southern Paiutes studied here will not provide definitive answers to those questions, their experiences offer insights that make the journey worthwhile.

2 Making Space

Mormons, miners, and Southern Paiutes all tell stories about their coming to the land. Through those stories, we get a glimpse of the three different worldviews that brought competing meanings to the same geographic place. What follows is an exploration of those founding rituals—a Paiute origin story and settlement stories of the Mormons and miners.[1] As the religious historian Mircea Eliade contends, "[T]o settle in a territory is, in the last analysis, equivalent to consecrating it."[2]

Although Mormons, miners, and Southern Paiutes used very different means to consecrate their space, those means fall within three broad commonalities that offer room for comparison. The founding rituals of each group included the selection of space to inhabit, the naming of that space, and the ritualization of the founding experience through its retelling. In general, these founding rituals served important transtemporal functions as they positioned each group in time and space and defined its worldview. The founding experience for the miners was most complicated. It included a contest for silver that involved the Mormons and Paiutes and culminated in a court of law. The courtroom drama that ensued not only symbolizes the contested nature of mining space but also embodies the economic power structure that came to dominate the region.

The story begins, as best as historians and anthropologists can determine, around AD 1000, with the Southern Paiutes' gradual push eastward from California. Within three hundred years, the Southern Paiutes had spread to inhabit a large area extending through what would much later become southern California, southeastern Nevada, southwestern Utah, and northern Arizona.[3] Bounded on the southwest by the Colorado River, traditional Paiute lands hug the landscape and are defined by its features. To the north, small Paiute bands dominated the southern rim of the Great Basin. The largest bands, however, inhabited the Colorado Plateau, where they hunted, gathered, and farmed along the Virgin River and its major tributaries, Ash Creek, the Santa Clara River, and the Muddy River. Ethnographers have identified as many as thirty-five smaller groups, or at least sixteen larger bands of Paiutes, inhabiting this vast region in the nineteenth century. Of principal import to this study are the bands that occupied lands straddling what would become the Utah/Nevada/Arizona borders: the Moapits who occupied the banks of the Muddy River, the Pahranagats who inhabited the Pahranagat Valley, the Tonoquints or St. George band who lived along the Santa Clara, the Shivwits and Uinkarets who made a homeland bounded by the Virgin River on the north and Colorado River on the south, and the Matisabits or Panaca band who roamed at the north end of Meadow Valley Wash in Lincoln County, Nevada, near the present-day Mormon town of Panaca and the mining town of Pioche.[4]

This is the geopolitical and economic space the Paiutes constructed. It is the space that separated them from other tribes and within which the Paiutes organized themselves in small family bands. It is the space on which they hunted and gathered, the space they farmed, the space they came to know intimately as their annual cyclical journeys took them to the best springs, hunting spots, garden plots, and gathering places. Every rock, ledge, gulch, and canyon were familiar to them; it was stingy ground, but it was their homeland. "We climb the rocks and our feet are sore," one Paiute explained. "We live among rocks and they yield little food and many thorns." Nonetheless, he continued, "[T]he pines sing and we are glad. Our children play in the warm sand; we hear them sing and are glad. The seeds ripen and we have to eat and we are glad."[5]

Clearly the Paiutes built significant value into their space. Understanding the premium they placed upon their homeland, therefore, is integral to comprehending the contest that ensued between Mormons and miners.[6] For the Southern Paiutes, as with most Native Americans, land was not a commodity to be bought or sold, or even possessed in the Anglo-American sense. Billy Mike, a southern Ute, closely related in culture and language to the Paiute, recalled his people's association with the land before the white man arrived: "'No one really owned the land. It was like it owned us.'"[7] John Wesley Powell, an explorer who spent considerable time among the Paiutes in the 1870s, came to a similar conclusion: "An Indian will never ask to what nation or tribe or body of people another Indian belongs," Powell explained, "but to 'what land do you belong and how are you land named?'"[8] The Indians belonged to the land and were its caretakers.[9] One Paiute explained it to Powell this way: "'We love our country; we know not other lands. We hear that other lands are better; we do not know. . . . We do not want their good lands; we want our rocks and the great mountains where our fathers lived.'"[10]

It seems a mistake, therefore, to view Paiute space as simply geopolitical and economic. Those notions help define Paiute space, but it is necessary to understand it on a deeper, more religious level. As Powell put it, "'[T]he land belonging to an Indian clan or tribe is dear to it not only as a region from which it obtains subsistence but chiefly because it is the locus of its religion.'" "'When an Indian clan or tribe gives up its land,'" Powell added, "'it not only surrenders its home as understood by civilized people but its gods are abandoned and all its religion connected therewith.'"[11] In other words, there was more meaning dug into the Southern Paiute dirt than a simple subsistence economy.

The Piautes explain it best. One day following the creation of the world, Ocean Grandmother, carrying a heavy sack, came to where the wolf Tabuts lived. Ocean Grandmother set down her weighty load and instructed Tabuts and his younger brother, Shinangwav, a coyote, to carry the sack eastward, scattering its contents evenly across the earth. Tabuts decided to trust Shinangwav with this important task and sent him off to fulfill Ocean Grandmother's instructions. Curiosity, however, quickly overcame Shinangwav. He cut open the sack, and people fell out unevenly, in bunches all over the earth. Tabuts, seeing the carelessness of his younger brother, angrily intervened, resealing the sack. The only people left inside were the Southern Paiutes; Tabuts carried them to "the very best place," at the center of the world, on the north side of the Colorado River, and opened the sack. There they could find plenty of deer, piñon nuts, and agave to eat. The people liked their new home and decided to stay; that is where the Paiutes came from.[12]

For the Paiutes, their coming to the southern edge of the Great Basin had less to do with a centuries-long push eastward from California than with a purposeful placement by the gods. It was a placement, in the words of one Paiute, that brought them to "the very best place." Tabuts carried them to their land, placed them there, and in the process implied his divine approval. Shinangwav, the slovenly trickster that he was, haphazardly scattered all the other tribes across the land, but the Paiutes were different—their space had meaning and importance, and in the act of the gods placing them upon it, it became sacred.

The sacred nature of the Paiute existence, however, did not end there. The Southern Paiute, along with their neighbors, the Northern and Western Shoshoni, the Gosiute, and the Northern and Southern Ute, are Numic peoples, a branch of the broader Uto-Aztecan language family. The term Numic is the anglicized version of the name these tribes call themselves, simply meaning "the People." As one ethnographer put it, "As with so many other American Indian tribes, the Southern Paiutes considered themselves the only true humans on the earth."[13]

Individual bands of Southern Paiutes frequently took their names from the earth, more specifically its physical features to which they were most closely tied. They generally identified neighboring bands in a similar manner. For example, members of the Kaibab band called themselves the Mountain Lying Down People and referred to members of the adjacent Kaiparowits band as the Seed-Valley People. Members of the San Juan band were called Rock-River People; the Uinkarets, Pine-Mountain People; the Cedar group, the Hard-Rock People; the Tonoquints, Black Flowing People or Black-Rock Stream People; and the Shivwits, the Whitish Earth People.[14] These band identities were thereby not only tied to the land but often derived from it.

The Southern Paiutes sealed their founding experience through its retelling. Paiute oral tradition is rich with tales, some believed as true and others told as moral lessons. The setting for telling such stories was always winter, when the snakes and bears hibernated and could not attack the Tu-gwí-vai-gunt, or storytellers, as they performed the tales. Usually a fire flickered its light in the faces of the group, or perhaps the band listened to the tales while lying down before going to sleep. John Wesley Powell witnessed one such event and called it a "theatrical performance": men, women, and children "all intently listening, or laughing and talking by turns, their strange faces and dusky forms lit up with the glare of the pine-knot fire." The stories frequently centered around the exploits of Tabuts and Shinangwav, with the tellers sometimes punctuating the characters' actions with rhythmic singing.[15]

The Paiute creation story, told and retold in such an intimate setting, no doubt was meant to instill a sense of identity, purpose, and chosenness. As with all ritualization, these performances provided the means for future Paiute generations "to take their place in the human continuum."[16] Each telling anchored the Paiutes in time and space, reaching back to the Paiute beginning to foster a sense of the band's historical identity, including its oneness with the land, while simultaneously cultivating visions of future greatness. In the retelling, the Tu-gwí-vai-gunt essentially created Paiute sacred space anew, ritualized it, and imbued it with

meaning for all band members to share. This solidified their position at
the center of the cosmos as "the People."

Clearly, the Euro-American intrusion into Paiute space was devastating for more than its destruction of hunting, gathering, and farming
lands. It was an intrusion into god-given space and an affront to the Paiute
identity that was bound up in that space. No wonder that the Paiutes
occasionally responded with force to settlers' encroachments, including
the arrival of Mormon colonizers.

―――――――――

In March 1862, three Mormon brothers, John, Charles, and William
Pulsipher, made an exploratory trip to the southern rim of the Great Basin,
looking for good herd ground to feed the growing number of livestock ac-
cumulating in southern Utah. When the brothers rode into a mountain
valley in northwest Washington County, they found what one of their
descendants remembered as "beautiful pastureland, with its many grassy
meadow bottoms and mountains covered with scrub oak, serviceberry
bush and tall bunch grass," an ideal spot for grazing cattle.

But the land possessed more than good feed; it was occupied by the
Southern Paiutes. A camp of Paiutes situated at what the Pulsiphers came
to call "the Indian Rocks" stirred with excitement, watching intently as
the brothers approached. A dark cloud of "strong feelings" seemed to hang
over the Paiute camp with this "intrusion of the Indian domain." While
the Pulsipher brothers tried to calm the Paiutes with presents, a young
Paiute climbed up the rocks and darted over the hill north of the camp.
The remaining Paiutes, meanwhile, warmed to the Pulsipher brothers
and settled into a friendly interchange. Before long, however, the atmosphere shifted again as the missing brave returned with reinforcements,
swarming over the rocks, waving war clubs, and bows and arrows, clearly
intent upon defending Paiute space. The Paiutes who had stayed behind,
after considerable effort, prevailed upon the more hostile bunch, and "at
last a treaty of friendship was made, which to the credit of both parties
was forever kept inviolate and sacred." Even the hotheaded young Paiute
who had gone in search of reinforcements altered his outlook and, according to John Pulsipher's grandson, eventually "became grandfather's
very dear friend for life." In what must have been a sign of respect and
honor, John Pulsipher called his Paiute friend Moroni after an ancient
Book of Mormon prophet. Moroni, in turn, later named one of his sons
John. Pulsipher's grandson remembered visits from this John, his wife
Sally, and their children, recalling that they would "stop over and visit,

sometimes for several days, with us and were welcome to anything we had to eat or feed their stock."[17]

By all accounts, this invasion of Paiute space, which eventually led to the founding of the Mormon town of Hebron, proved friendly. John Pulsipher remembered that, when he and his brothers returned to Shoal Creek to settle, the Paiutes "expresst themselv[e]s well pleased with our coming to live with them."[18] More Mormons, however, would soon crowd into nearby valleys, thereby opening up new frontiers of interaction, most of which did not end so peacefully.

Mormon settlers who invaded Paiute space held notions very similar to the Paiutes regarding their chosenness and the sacred nature of their land. Mormons started to settle on Paiute land as early as 1851, with the establishment of an Iron Mission at Parowan and then Cedar City. Mormon leaders conceived of this mission as a means to mine and refine the iron necessary to help build the physical kingdom of God.[19] In 1854, Brigham Young created the Southern Indian Mission and sent twenty-three men south to establish it. Those missionaries built outposts at Harmony and along the Santa Clara River and lived peacefully among the Paiutes. Before long, however, many more Mormons were on their way south. The largest contingent of settlers came in 1861, with what was called the Cotton Mission, a further attempt by Young at achieving economic self-sufficiency. The plan was for cotton missionaries to grow cotton and other warm-climate crops throughout southwestern Utah in an effort to cut ties with eastern markets for those goods. As the principal city of the mission, St. George grew into a southern capital of sorts, where Brigham Young established a winter home and the Saints completed their first temple west of the Mississippi. It was also from St. George that the Mormon apostle and president of the Cotton Mission, Erastus Snow, directed settlement in the south. Snow, in essence, created Mormon geopolitical and economic space, both of which were bound up in Mormon notions of Zion. As with the Paiutes, to understand the culture clash that played out as Mormons attempted to plow their own sacred symbols into dirt already dug deep with meaning, it is essential to explore Mormon religiosity.

For nineteenth-century Latter-day Saints, the Great Basin represented spiritual ground; it was their refuge in the desert where they hoped to build Zion in peace. Mobs had burned, plundered, and driven them from their homes in Ohio, Missouri, and finally Illinois. The founder of their faith, Joseph Smith, died a martyr at Carthage, Illinois, in 1844. It fell to his successor, Brigham Young, to lead more than twelve thousand followers on an exodus of biblical proportions in search of new spiritual ground. Young found it in the Great Basin and quickly set to work building a western Zion. In doing so, he replicated many of Smith's notions for creating sacred space, but in the West Mormon space also evolved.

According to Richard Lyman Bushman, in Joseph Smith's attempts to create Zion in Ohio, Missouri, and Illinois, he "turned space into a funnel that collected people from the widest possible periphery and drew them like gravity into a central point."[20] That point was the city of Zion, and at its center was the temple. "The whole scheme," Bushman contends, "divided space in two, with Zion and the temple at the center emanating spiritual power, and a Babylon-like world outside, where people were to be converted and brought to Zion, the missionaries going out and the converts coming in."[21] In the West, Brigham Young followed an identical pattern in platting Salt Lake City, with the temple square at its center. As one of America's great colonizers, however, Young "flattened the [Mormon] religious landscape." Zion was no longer only one city and one temple; it encompassed the Great Basin as a whole, which Young began to fill with over three hundred satellite villages. It was at these villages that Mormons for the first time constructed chapels for worship, creating hundreds of what Bushman calls "little epicenters of religious life."[22]

Despite this leveling, Mormon notions of chosenness still shaped space on the frontier. As the historian Leonard J. Arrington noted, "[T]he Mormons were inclined to regard the Great Basin as specially ordained by God to become their home."[23] Joseph Smith had allegedly prophesied in 1842, two years before his martyrdom, that "the Saints would continue to suffer much affliction and would be driven to the Rocky Mountains."[24] Brigham Young, upon seeing the Salt Lake Valley for the first time, reportedly became wrapped in vision for a few moments and then said the words that have become immortalized into a monument and state park: "This is the right place. Drive on." And if all of that was not sufficient proof of the sacred nature of the Great Basin's semibarren expanses, then Mormons contend that the biblical prophet Isaiah foresaw this western Mecca when he prophesied, "And it shall come to pass in the last days, that the mountain of the LORD's house shall be established in the top of the mountains, and shall be exalted above the hills; and all nations shall flow unto it."[25]

The Mormon entrance into the Salt Lake Valley bore the weight of prophecy as old as Isaiah, was foretold by Joseph Smith, and was divinely confirmed to Brigham Young. Broadly speaking, it was an act of creation similar to the Paiute placement, wherein a heavenly manifestation an-

nulled the homogeneity of space and revealed a fixed point, which then
became spiritual ground.[26]

Beyond the very act of this creation, however, Mormon colonization
of space in the Great Basin, especially on the frontier, differed from the
Paiute founding in that it had as much to do with pragmatism, ritual
consecration, and the perceived threat of an ever-encroaching Babylon as
it did with given or revealed space.[27] The experience of settlers at Hebron,
a present-day Mormon ghost town in southwestern Utah, is illustrative.
Hebron was born in 1868, a bastard child of the forced merger between
two Mormon ranching outposts, Clover Valley in present-day Nevada and
Shoal Creek in southwestern Utah. Indian depredations during Utah's
Black Hawk War led to the abandonment of Clover Valley and its merger
with Shoal Creek; families from the two hamlets huddled together for
two years at a fort on Shoal Creek before it was deemed safe to abandon
the fortress and found Hebron. The four years of settlement along Shoal
Creek prior to the founding of Hebron and then the founding ritual itself
are indicative of the way these frontier Mormons conceived of, consecrated, and created spiritual ground.

John, Charles, and William Pulsipher, accompanied by their brother-
in-law David Chidester, arrived at their new home along Shoal Creek
with flocks and family in tow on 27 April 1862. John Pulsipher described
it this way: "When spring come we moved on north past the Mountain
Meadows, over the rim of the great Basin of Desert, turn[e]d west 12 m.
to Shoal Creek a small stream fed by Springs [that] runs a few miles &
sink again. This is about 45 miles from St. geo.—quite a Distance—but
the nearest suitable location for a large stock that we could find."[28] Later
in life, Pulsipher remembered this founding event in similar terms, but
added that the hand of the Lord was also at work: "We moved on til we
come to Shoal Creek, the first place we found suitable for our business,
where there was plenty of feed for our flocks so we located our selves &
. . . *gave thanks to the Lord.*"[29]

Apparently Erastus Snow sanctioned the efforts of the Pulsipher clan.
He visited the area on 18 June 1863 and pronounced divine approval of
it. According to John Pulsipher, Snow blessed "our families, our flocks
& herds—the hills Vallies—the air & Waters & all we have, he blessed in
the name of the Lord & said it was our right & Priveledge [*sic*] to enjoy
the Blessings of the Kingdom of God." He further admonished them to
"hold meetings Bless children, Baptise, Partake of the Sacrament & live
the life of Saints."[30] Snow's visit seems immensely important to the
Shoal Creek settlers. It bore the weight of Snow's apostleship, which for
Latter-day Saints implied powers as a prophet, seer, and revelator. Snow

created spiritual ground for the Shoal Creek ranchers not by means of a heavenly manifestation, as with the Paiutes, but by ritual consecration. Snow, in essence, took a portion of the land given by Tabuts to serve as the center of the Paiute world and realigned it toward the Zion head-quartered at Salt Lake City.

Such ritual detachment, however, did not provide immunity from the contest over sacred space that was playing out in the Great Basin as a whole. What would come to be called the Black Hawk War, the largest Indian uprising in Utah history, began in 1865. Prior to this conflict the spatial arrangements at Shoal Creek were scattered at best, with clusters of two or three houses spread from two to seven miles apart. By April 1866, the Shoal Creek Saints had selected a site called the "big willow patch" at the center of all the waters of Shoal Creek, laid off lots, built houses and corrals, and moved into what they called Shoal Creek Fort. In July, Erastus Snow visited and again expressed apostolic approval. He told the residents that "the protecting power of the almighty has been over you" and prophesied that "the time is near when there will be a flourishing settlement here." He complimented the fort dwellers on the good spot that they had chosen to defend and said he would instruct the residents of Clover Valley, a town thirty miles west that had been plagued by Indian troubles, to abandon their community and join Shoal Creek for mutual defense.[31]

Two years later, Snow again traveled to Shoal Creek, this time to par-ticipate in the ritual of town founding. Indian depredations had generally ceased, and Snow deemed it safe to abandon the fort and to found a proper Mormon village. Accompanied by G. A. Burgon, the county surveyor, Snow traveled to the area for that purpose. According to one resident, Orson Huntsman, when Snow arrived there was some disagreement over where the town site should be: "[S]ome wanted the town one place and some another, but the most of the brethren wanted it right where the fort was and immediately around the fort." Snow looked over the situation and counseled with the men as he inspected the land. Huntsman described the site chosen by the majority of the people as "a very nice location," but he also remembered that it "did not suit Brother Snow very well." Snow agreed that the spot was likable but claimed that it was not practi-cable. He prophetically warned the people that the locale was too remote from their water source, and it would be expensive to channel water to the town and keep it there. But the self-ruling settlers persisted, even against Snow's advice, and he gave in to their wishes.[32]

Before long the Mormon grid system scarred the earth as the surveyor laid out three streets running east and west and five north and south.

Burgon also surveyed four areas into fields for farming. Snow stayed for a week to preside over the founding, and when the surveying was done he called the people together to decide on a name for the town and to bless the land and people. In choosing a name, John Pulsipher borrowed from Old Testament scripture and suggested Hebron, after the site where the ancient prophet Abraham had tended his flocks and herds. The people voted to accept the name, and Snow then blessed and dedicated the townsite.[33] In short, it was land first born of economic necessity, frontier circumstances, and the whims of its settlers and secondly born of the spirit through ritual consecration.

If there was any lingering doubt over the chosen location, Zera Pulsipher, Hebron's oldest resident and presiding ecclesiastical authority, soon helped dispel it. Father Pulsipher, as Hebronites commonly called him, attended worship services on Sunday, 20 September 1868, and stood before the congregation to announce a dream he had had that morning. According to one resident's version, Pulsipher reported seeing "in a vision, a nice town with streets, sidewalks, shade trees, water running in nice ditches and nice dwelling houses and barns and nice fences." Another account reports that Pulsipher saw "a beautiful town built here of most elegant houses & barns—Built & Painted in the finest style. A large town in the midst of a fertile country surrounded with herds in abundance."[34] Here, finally, after the site had been selected, surveyed, and dedicated, Pulsipher's dream granted divine approval to the decisions already made.

The final element of the founding experience, naming the town, seems the most significant to the Mormons at Hebron, especially as it has become ritualized through the retelling. Record keeping is an essential part of the Latter-day Saint experience. At the official organization of the Church, Joseph Smith received a revelation wherein the Lord instructed him "that there shall be a record kept among you." Two years later Joseph Smith charged, in a letter later canonized, that "it is the duty of the Lord's clerk, whom he has appointed, to keep a history, and a general church record of all things that transpire in Zion."[35] It is no wonder that Erastus Snow gave similar advice to the Shoal Creek settlers when he visited in 1863, telling them to choose one of their number to preside and "one to keep a record."[36] The settlers selected John Pulsipher as their chronicler, and it was largely through his efforts that the Hebron founding became ritualized, passed from his account into family and local histories.

Pulsipher penned the official version this way: "Located & surveyed a town site which we named Hebron a scripture name. We read that Abraham & Lot separated & moved to get room for their large flocks &

herds—& when he came to a place suitable for his business—he located & kept his flocks there & called the place Hebron, . . . & he built an alter & offered sacrifice to the Lord. So it was with us, when Pres. Snow gave us a mission to take care of the stock of St. George . . . we located our selves & called the place Hebron & gave thanks to the Lord."[37] Here Pulsipher drew an important parallel to ancient Israel, which anchored the Hebron founding in time and place and added biblical importance to the town's frontier errand. Hebronites, in essence, reified the scriptural experience and in the process saw themselves as reliving it, thus becoming Israel.

Joseph Fish, a local historian, in his retelling of the town founding also focused upon the connection to biblical times: "It was suggested by John Pulsipher that the name of the newly surveyed town be called Hebron after the Hebron of old, where Abraham and Lot kept their flocks and herds."[38] Carrie Elizabeth Laub Hunt, a descendant of Hebron pioneers, offered a similar version. She noted that Hebron was "a scripture name" and recounted its association with Old Testament events.[39] The sacred nature of Mormon record keeping, therefore, ritualized the Hebron founding. The most important element of that founding, preserved and passed through official and family records, was the naming event that linked Hebron to Father Abraham and thereby sanctified the ranching nature of the Hebron economy.

If Paiute space was spiritual as well as economic and geopolitical, and Mormon frontier space practical, though revealed and sanctified through ritual consecration, then mining space as it came to be defined at Pioche, Nevada, was mostly economic and primarily contested. Like the Mormons and Paiutes, miners dug their earth with what the historical geographer Richard V. Francaviglia deems some of America's "deepest cultural values." To understand the miners of Pioche, therefore, it is essential to look beyond what are often considered landscapes of extraction and exploitation to understand the nineteenth-century symbolism with which the prospectors mined their space. Francaviglia observes that to Victorian-era America, the mining frontier "epitomized civilization's inevitable victory in the quest for knowledge and superiority over nature." Similarly, to the nineteenth-century capitalist, "mining was seen as an indispensable part of the mission of Western civilization." It embodied deeply held American values such as competitiveness, risk taking, individualism, industry, and progress ushered in by the market revolution and pushed to new limits during the Gilded Age.[40]

Those values certainly were not foreign to Pioche. In 1872, the town's news voice, the *Pioche Daily Record*, ran an article championing "the laboring men of Pioche." Even the lowly miners, carpenters, and blacksmiths, the newspaper insisted, "have their chances of becoming wealthy. . . . For in America, it has been proven that labor is the key which unlocks wealth's great iron safe and opens the road to honor."[41] The "hardy prospector," his "indomitable spirit" and "persevering disposition," were highly favored at Pioche, and many such men, the newspaper bragged, had already moved on "with large amounts of coin as a reward for their industry."[42]

Even though the miners' connections to Pioche were largely ephemeral, their participation in America's march forward overshadowed the need for a sense of place similar to that which tied the Paiutes and Mormons to their land. The miners' worldview made them a part of something bigger than Pioche—it made them American. As Americans, the Pioche miners were engaged in what one resident called "sacred rights," centered on the quest for wealth.[43]

Lawlessness and lawsuits were inevitable by-products of that quest and best characterize the town's early years. In January 1873, the *Pioche Record* declared: "Crime is rampant in Pioche. Law-defyers, of high and low degree, emboldened by immunity from arrest and punishment for former transgressions, are seemingly more vicious and audacious with each returning day."[44] Likewise, Rossiter W. Raymond, U.S. commissioner of mining, in his report for 1872, observed: "Two classes of persons reap a rich harvest, lawyers and 'roughs.' The former are paid to maintain the titles, and the latter to hold the ground. Pioche has been a bloody camp; but it is to be hoped that the days of violence are passing away. The lawyers, however, still have a strong hold, and the complexity of suits and cross-suits is such as no stranger can hope to unravel or comprehend."[45]

Whether through "courtroom mining," violence, or just persistent prospecting, the goal at Pioche was to strike it rich. With potential wealth at stake, it is no wonder that the founding ritual at Pioche was complicated. The founding events stretched over a six-year period and clearly illustrate the contested nature of the town's genesis. Mormons, miners, and Paiutes vied for control of what would prove to be some of Nevada's richest silver mines—second only, in the 1870s, to the more famed mines at Virginia City. Perhaps even more telling of the disputed nature of Pioche's space is the ritualization of the founding story years later in a court of law.[46]

The contest began during the fall of 1863.[47] Prior to that, only local

Paiute bands were aware of the outcropping of ore at what would become Pioche. In fact, what Pioche residents would come to call Meadow Valley Street in their town actually was a worn Paiute trail leading to the ore.[48] Moroni, John Pulsipher's Paiute friend, was well acquainted with another Mormon settler and Indian missionary, William Hamblin, and once carried a piece of "glittering ore" to Hamblin for inspection. Hamblin was a two-year veteran of the California gold fields and quickly recognized the rock's potential.[49] Moroni, however, refused to tell where the ore came from, only indicating that "for years chosen members of his tribe had resorted to and used it as a paint."[50] Moroni's dying father had warned him never to disclose the ore's location to white men, "lest they should come and drive the Indians from their hunting grounds to secure the riches thus exposed." Eventually, however, Hamblin wore down Moroni's resolve, through continued friendship and a new rifle as a gift. Moroni led Hamblin, along with William Pulsipher, to the rugged side of a mountain where "the glittering ore cropped out above the ground."[51]

The three men dug down several feet to expose a well-defined vein and then laid claim to the spot. This very act set in motion a series of events that would, by the end of 1864, drastically change the meaning of the dirt they dug. Each gouge marked the beginnings of a profound cultural transformation of a relatively small section of land away from Paiute symbolism to soil with a very different essence.

Hamblin returned home to tell others of his find. Before long, local Mormon leaders expressed interest in the claim. In January 1864, Bishop Edward Bunker, head of the Mormon settlement at Santa Clara, organized an expedition to the site. Bunker's group surveyed and outlined a square claim but did not organize a mining district or post traditional notice, thereby leaving the ore open for the taking. Bunker reported his expedition to Brigham Young and sought the prophet's advice on the matter.[52]

Young responded favorably. He not only liked the idea of claiming the ore for Zion but also wanted the surrounding valleys as good herd ground for Mormon cattle. He put it this way: "I think, all things considered, that it will be best for the brethren to branch out and occupy for their stock the valleys you mention [Clover Valley and Meadow Valley] and also to claim, survey, and stake off as soon as possible those veins or ore that br. Hamblin is aware of, . . . all that are sticking out, or likely to be easily found and profitably worked."[53]

Young also furnished Erastus Snow with copies of "the rules and regulations observed by miners in locating and working mining claims" and instructed him to file on the site.[54] However, almost before Snow had time to act, another interested group with a drastically different worldview laid claim to the same ground. This latter group's aspirations, while not as religiously grandiose, were equally compelling: to find the abundant wealth that American providence seemed to promise was hidden in the West.

Stephen Sherwood is perhaps typical of such rootless searchers. He was born in New York in 1811, but at the time of his prospecting in Utah, he made his home in Illinois. As Sherwood described it, though, it would be more accurate to call Illinois his base camp rather than his home, for he spent a great deal of time prospecting in the West. He claimed to have first passed through the Meadow Valley area in 1849 on his way to the California gold fields. If not for the lure of treasures farther west he might have stayed; instead, he looked over Meadow Valley's "rich mineral belt from a mountain, and concluded to return to it." He eventually did, fifteen years later, after trying his miner's luck in the mineral fields of California, Oregon, Idaho, and Montana. In February 1864, he found himself boarding at the Salt Lake City home of a Mormon, Thomas Box, where he encountered an old mining friend, Jacob N. Vandermark. In the course of reminiscing over old times, Sherwood recalled the "rich mineral country" in southwestern Utah that he had passed through in '49.[55] Vandermark apparently had heard of some mines in the southwestern portion of the territory too, perhaps along the Santa Clara River. Before long, the two mining friends became convinced that they should head south, especially as Box's home became the locus of swirling rumors about abundant ore deposits there. Box's son, Thomas Box Jr., and another Mormon, Peter Shirts, shared stories of mineral wealth in Utah's Dixie country. Box Jr. even bragged of finding a piece of "very rich" ore along the Santa Clara in 1860, and Shirts rumored it aloud at Box's home that there were "rich mines" down there.[56]

All of this talk soon translated into action, which, unbeknownst to Young, put in motion a contest for silver that would quickly grow to include General Patrick Edward Connor. Connor, the U.S. military commander stationed at Fort Douglas in Salt Lake City, detested Mormon dominance of Utah Territory. He saw Utah's mineral wealth as a great way to attract a large non-Mormon population to the area and thereby vote the Mormons out of office. He encouraged his soldiers to prospect for minerals and published news of Utah's riches in his newspaper, the *Union Vedette.* Although this tactic never worked the way he hoped, it did earn him acclaim as the father of Utah mining.[57] Connor supplied Sherwood with a copy of mining laws so that he could establish a proper mining district, should he discover ore on his trip south.

Sherwood, along with the two Boxes, Shirts, and Vandermark, left Salt Lake City in early 1864. They arrived in southern Utah in March and spent three or four days prospecting without any luck. Rumors of silver at Meadow Valley soon reached them and prompted the party to seek an audience with Hamblin.[58] Hamblin, however, greeted the Salt Lake group with caution. A similar experience a few months earlier made him wary of outsiders attempting to get at the newfound silver.[59] After some discussion, the prospectors led Hamblin to believe that their intentions "were honestly for the upbuilding of the Church as they claimed to be Saints."[60] Hamblin, therefore, gave them directions to the ore and agreed to meet them there in a few days. On 17 March, when the Salt Lake party arrived, they found Hamblin and another local Mormon, Daniel C. Cill, and an Indian companion, likely Moroni, already there working their earlier claims. According to Vandermark, the two Mormons had "no objection to our taking ground with them."[61]

Sherwood then began explaining miners' rules to Hamblin, who agreed to adopt those laws as long as he and Cill should have choice of ground. Hamblin clarified that he and the Bunker expedition had surveyed the site three months previous and expressed interest in protecting the rights of that earlier party. That agreed, the men began staking claims according to mining code, with Hamblin given the discovery claim. William Pulsipher's ground came next, and then Cill, followed by at least some of the other Mormons who had visited there earlier. Box laid claim for himself, his two sons, and his wife. Sherwood, Vandermark, and Shirts made strikes for themselves and friends, making around twenty names in all. The following day, the men held a miner's meeting and organized the Meadow Valley Mining District. They adopted with a few alterations the set of mining laws borrowed from Connor. The group then parted ways, with Box, Sherwood, Vandermark, and Shirts traveling to Salt Lake City for supplies, while Hamblin and Cill returned to their homes at Clover Valley.[62]

Finally, proper mining procedures redefined the ground at what would become Pioche and further shifted its cultural meaning. The organization of a mining district forever stripped the land from Paiute hands and already loosened Young's hoped-for grip upon it. Stephen Sherwood played an important role in this transformation. He and Vandermark, apparently posing as Mormons, were able to convince Hamblin not only to show them the ore but also to allow them to stake claims with him. More importantly, however, the mining rules that Sherwood carried with him became the means whereby he and Vandermark gained access to the wealth that Young wanted kept in Mormon hands. Sherwood's knowledge of mining ritual, including the proper means of establishing a district and setting up claims, ensured that Young's wish would largely go unfulfilled.

The campaign over who would control the Paiute silver intensified over the next three months. Erastus Snow sent settlers there to hold the pasture and farmland twelve miles south of the mines at Meadow Valley. The first of these Mormons arrived on 5 May 1864, and soon others followed, founding the town of Panaca, named for the Paiute word for silver.[63] In the meantime, at Salt Lake City, Patrick Connor was aware of events in the southwestern portion of the territory and quickly involved his troops. On 30 April, he issued orders to one company of soldiers to "scour the country" surrounding the "newly discovered silver mines in Washington County, . . . for the protection of miners and exploration of the resources of the country." Connor not only wanted his men to "afford protection to miners from Mormons and Indians" but also commanded, "You will thoroughly explore and prospect the country over which you travel, and if successful in finding placer diggings, you will at once report the fact to these headquarters."[64]

Those soldiers were only one of many groups headed to the mines in May 1864. On 22 May another detachment from Fort Douglas under Captain Charles Hempstead left Salt Lake City for Meadow Valley. Sherwood, Vandermark, and an expanded group of mining buddies were on their way too. They had spent the previous month gathering supplies, recording the district rules in a proper ledger, and noising news of their find around Salt Lake City. Close to the same time, Erastus Snow left St. George with a large contingent, intent upon solidifying Mormon claims to the area. All of these groups converged in late May and early June 1864 upon the once isolated land that less than a year before held meaning only to Southern Paiutes.

Snow's entourage arrived first. Convinced that by virtue of abandonment, the Sherwood group's claims were invalid, Snow organized a new mining district based upon the mining rules Young had given him. He staked new claims and placed Mormons in charge.[65] On the return trip to St. George, Snow passed several other parties in the area, including Sherwood, Vandermark, and company, as well as Hempstead and his troops from Fort Douglas. Despite such competition roaming the country, Snow seemed satisfied that "[o]ur brethren . . . had laid claim to what they supposed, the principal leads for some miles."[66]

When Hempstead arrived at the mines, he found that Snow had indeed "gone in with a vim." Hempstead and his men discovered the whole mountain "covered and spotted with stakes." "So frequently did the St. George President's name appear stuck in the stakes," Hempstead reported, "that it looked as though there had been a recent *snow* storm on that mountain." Hempstead concluded that "the whole country has gone wild over the silver mines."[67] Upon further investigation, however, he determined that the Mormon attempt to establish a competing mining district was illegal. Hempstead convinced the Mormons that this was true, and they filed their claims with Sherwood, the legal recorder of the district. Hempstead remarked, "[A]ll is harmony, peace and good will, and Saint and Gentile are at work in happy accord, on Mount Panacker."[68]

Even though gentiles and Mormons had at least temporarily worked out their differences, neither group had bothered to address the Paiutes' longer-standing claim to the area. It was the Paiutes, in June and July, who attempted to reassert their control and in the process placed themselves at the center of the contest. As Sherwood recalled, "[T]he Indians troubled us incessantly: stole and ran off our stock . . . they drew weapons on us . . . [and] threatened to kill us if we did not leave." Thomas Box Jr., who claimed to know something of the Paiute language, said that he "understood the Indians, and they said they meant war." The hostility escalated to the point that in July 1864 the miners moved to the new town at Panaca, where they huddled together with the Mormons for mutual defense.

It was at Panaca on 23 July that two Paiute men entered the tent of Mother Jane Vail Johnson Lee. They noticed some guns and asked to handle them, and when Lee refused, the Paiutes grew hostile. One Paiute even drew an arrow to his bow. Undaunted, the feisty Lee grabbed a stick of firewood and "broke the arrow and drove the Indians out of her tent." Perhaps in response, the next night Paiutes stole two oxen and further annoyed the settlers. Days later, five Paiutes harassed Box Jr., who narrowly escaped. Other settlers intervened and took the five Paiutes prisoner, but a terrible row ensued when the Paiutes attempted to flee. John N. Lee, a Mormon guard over the Indians, claimed one Indian came after him with a butcher knife, stabbing him three times. The Mormons prevailed, however, killing all five Indians. Lee recalled that "the Indians themselves said they would kill Box, and surround and massacre all of us."[69] Sherwood remembered that the miners were forced to guard "against an Indian attack" and alleged that for two years "the Indians were too hostile for us to do anything."[70] In response, the miners held a meeting to amend the district laws so that they could maintain their claims without actually working them until the Indian danger passed away.[71]

Paiute hostility put an end to mining activity at Meadow Valley for nearly six years. In the meantime, Sherwood and Vandermark spent time in Chicago and New York fruitlessly seeking investors to develop the mines or potential buyers for their claims.[72] By 1869, miners farther west at the Pahranagat mining district began to show interest in the Meadow Valley area. In March of that year, some of those miners reorganized the district. They renamed it the Ely Mining District after John H. Ely, who later was a partner in the Raymond and Ely Mine at Pioche.[73] Activity at the newly named district gathered steam, especially as excitement spilled over from the rich strike at White Pine about one hundred miles north.[74]

François Louis Alfred Pioche, a distant though wealthy observer, owned stock in mines at White Pine and sought additional investment opportunities. Born in France in 1818, Pioche immigrated to California, via Chile, in 1849 and quickly capitalized upon the gold rush. He opened a general merchandising store in San Francisco and then turned to banking, utilities, real estate, railroads, agriculture, livestock, and mining. In 1852 he carried news back to France of the prosperity to be had in the American West and thereby attracted European investors to his business ventures. By the 1860s he had built a sound reputation as a financier and leading developer of San Francisco.[75] Pioche sent his agent, Charles E. Hoffman, a mining engineer from California, to the Ely District on an exploratory mission to examine its potential and to buy up any promising claims. Hoffman did so, and shortly thereafter, in May 1869, Pioche and other high-powered partners organized the Meadow Valley Mining Company, capitalized at six million dollars.[76]

At roughly the same time, William Raymond and John Ely bought original titles to claims from Hamblin, Pulsipher, and the other early district organizers. The two investors rapidly began to develop their mines and built a mill to process the ore.[77] With this renewed interest, backed this time with San Francisco capital, the dormant strikes sprang to life. Soon a town survey haphazardly crisscrossed the mountainside, with streets intersecting at various odd angles, most leading from town to the numerous mines. Pioche's investment partner and fellow Frenchman, Louis Lacour, was honored with one of the principal streets named after him, while Pioche himself received an even higher honor: his name was selected for the town as a whole.[78]

Ironically, François Pioche never visited the town that still bears his name. In 1872, the year that the mines at Pioche reached a production peak of nearly $5.5 million, François Pioche's personal wealth had been tumbling for some time. He had financially overextended himself and was starting to feel the consequences. On a morning in May 1872, Pioche arose from bed in his opulent three-story San Francisco home and opened a mahogany case resting on a table in the center of the room. He reached inside to retrieve one of two navy pistols, walked back to bed, placed the gun to his head, and fired. While the inquest into his death advanced a variety of theories for the suicide, his financial straits remain an obvious answer and linger, perhaps, as a fitting metaphor for the roller-coaster fortunes of his mining-camp namesake.[79]

In any case, by 1870, that camp's contested founding ritual was finally complete, with a town properly surveyed and named now defining the spot. The only thing left was the equally contested retelling three years later in a court of law. The court battle centered on two competing mining claims held by the Raymond and Ely Mining Company and the Hermes Mining Company. Lawyers for Raymond and Ely contended that the Hermes Company had not only illegally filed claim on adjoining land but after digging a shaft, had struck the Ely Company's main silver-bearing ledge. The Hermes Company, an investment for George Hearst, father of the newspaper tycoon William Randolph Hearst, countered that the Ely Company's title to the Panaca ledge was "worthless." Hearst's lawyers argued that Raymond and Ely's title was based upon purchase of the original Panaca shaft from Sherwood's crew of Mormons and miners, who not only staked their claims improperly but created illegal mining laws and then voided their strikes anyway through years of abandonment.

Nine years after the fact, the courtroom became the forum for the ritualization of Pioche's founding. If lawyers for Raymond and Ely could prove the validity of the original claims, they believed they would prevail. Hermes lawyers, however, were intent upon destroying the credibility of those claims, thereby maintaining Hearst's right to continue extracting silver from his mine.

The *Pioche Daily Record* called it "The Great Mining Suit" and carried comprehensive coverage of the courtroom drama. Early on in the month-long proceedings, the *Record's* reporter noted that interest in the case ran high. Crowds gathered outside the courthouse, generally thirty minutes before the doors opened, with "men eager to get seats" blocking the sidewalk in front of the building and clogging "all the avenues leading to it." Almost instantly after the sheriff opened the courthouse doors, "every available seat was occupied."[80] After three days, the *Record* noted one side effect from the throngs of "idlers" crowding the courthouse: "[V]isitors are compelled to wade through two inches of muck which has accumulated on the floor, made up of tobacco juice, catarrh mucus, and influenza ejections."[81] Even still, engrossment in the case remained high. It seemed to some that the fate of the town hung in the balance, especially because rumors ran rampant that William Henry Raymond threatened to close the Raymond and Ely mine should his company lose the suit, thereby throwing a good portion of the town's population out of work.[82]

The list of witnesses called to testify was truly impressive and included most of the district's founders. Sherwood and Vandermark were there, Thomas Box Sr. and Jr. both testified, as did Shirts, Pulsipher, and George Hearst. A slew of expert mining witnesses also took the stand, as did a variety of Mormons peripherally involved in the case. Noticeably missing from the witness list was Moroni, the Paiute principally responsible for instigating the entire contest, and his partner William Hamblin. Moroni's absence is easily explained. It was completely outside of the Euro-American worldview to consider any alternative meaning to the land in dispute, apart from the abundant wealth at stake. As for Hamblin, it seems that his involvement in the founding ritual at Pioche cost him his life. He had been subpoenaed to testify at Pioche in a similar case the previous year. According to family legend, however, after he arrived at Pioche the litigants who stood to lose the most from his testimony poisoned his coffee before he could take the stand. Hamblin was immediately struck sick and died a few weeks later at Clover Valley. His widow, Mary, did return to the scene of Hamblin's demise, as a witness in the Raymond and Ely case.[83]

Hermes's lawyers focused their defense on the founding rituals at Pioche and claimed that they were invalid on three key grounds: Mormons corrupted the original claims, there was no Indian uprising that prevented the miners from working their claims, and the miners abandoned their strikes, leaving them open for the taking.

First, Hermes's lawyers argued that the original claims were convoluted, competing, and, worse still, heavily polluted at the hands of Brigham Young. William W. Bishop, a Hermes lawyer, maintained that "the location was not made in good faith," but instead "it was done in accordance with the policy of the Mormon Church, the members of which were opposed to mining." He went on to suggest that "it was hard to tell to which class the location belonged. If it was made by American citizens, it would be governed by the laws of the United States; if made by the Mormons, it would be for Brigham Young, and he would hold it for God Almighty." In any case, Bishop insisted, and his co-counsel Judge Pitzer concurred, that the laws of the Meadow Valley District were "Mormon mining laws" "made in the interest of the Mormon Church." If that were not enough, "[T]he locations made by Vandermark, Sherwood, and others were made for the purpose of selling and not for working"—witness their long absences to New York and Chicago attempting to peddle their claims.[84]

Judge Hardy and Mr. Wren, co-counsel for Raymond and Ely, directly attacked the Mormon argument. Hardy and Wren suggested that Hermes's lawyers were "setting up" Brigham Young as "'a man of straw.'" Hardy, for example, charged that Hermes's lawyers were attempting "to try the Mormon Church, to try Brigham Young, the authors of the Mountain Meadow massacre," and "everything in this case but the case itself." Wren added that Hermes's lawyers "have no other appeals to make to an intelligent jury than those of prejudice. Because some of the locators of the Panaca ledge were Mormons, they would have you divest them of their rights by virtue of that location."[85] Mormon involvement, in other words, was not grounds to invalidate the claims.

Hermes's lawyers offered two additional, closely related challenges: There was no Indian uprising that prevented the miners from working their claims from mid 1864 to 1870, they insisted, and because there was no uprising, the claims, invalid to begin with, were invalidated a second time through abandonment. Meadow Valley mining laws, Hermes's lawyers quickly pointed out, required that "each company must do one faithful day's work on their claim in each month." If a miner failed to do so, "the claim or claims will be subject to re-location by any other person." Raymond and Ely's lawyers countered that company rules made provision for a claimant who was "prevented from working by local insurrection or rebellion."[86]

Thus, the Paiutes indirectly played a key role in the case. Their attempts to recover the silver at Pioche became fodder for the courtroom. Raymond and Ely's attorneys played up the Paiute violence in an effort to show that a local insurrection had existed, thereby preventing work at the mines. The Hermes side poked fun at the idea of a rebellion, which they alleged was invented by the plaintiffs to hide the real reason claims went unworked for six years: abandonment.

Raymond and Ely's lawyers laid out the basis for their version of the "Indian troubles." Rather than abandonment, the locators "tenaciously clung to their claims like enthusiasts," the attorney H. I. Thornton insisted. "They stood here alone, surrounded by hostile Indians, and located the first titles to the Panaca ledge; and long after, through dangers and privations, maintained those titles—with their lives in their hands they sank shafts, excavated cuts and extracted ore." The Indian problem was so bad, Thornton contended, that Connor had to send soldiers under Captain Hempstead to protect the miners. Certainly, he admitted, Vandermark and Sherwood left the area, but for good purpose, "to enlist the aid of men of capital." Vandermark went to New York and Sherwood to Chicago, but "all without success in the final results." Their "persistent efforts" nonetheless "showed how far from the minds of these men was the thought of abandonment."[87]

Not true, the Hermes attorneys countered. "Sherwood and Vandermark left the ground for years, only to return to the district when it had become famous." As for the Indian troubles, the Hermes lawyers had a field day poking fun at the supposed "insurrection." Judge Pitzer queried, "Now, was it 'local insurrection,' or 'rebellion,' when mother Lee put the five Indians to flight with a billet of wood?" Judge Lake sarcastically called it "the Indian war in 1864–5" and suggested that it deserved "as notorious a place in the history of the country as some of the battles of the civil war." Judge Mesick then summed the Indian argument for his side: "[I]t has not been shown that there was any real danger from Indians; or, if there was, the danger existed but a few months. . . . For six years we find not a stroke of work was done on the Panaca location; it was not used; for trying to sell it in Chicago or New York was not making use of it. . . . So the Panaca location was abandoned."[88]

With all the arguments made, the Pioche founding story told and retold and then contested again and again, the lawyers finally left it in the hands of the jury. At close to four o'clock in the afternoon of 30 April, the twelve-man jury retired for deliberation. Rumors spread rampant through the night that jurors had been "purchased like sausages," with some townsfolk freely making bets on how many jurors out of twelve Hearst had safely in his pocket, ranging from five to nine. Those who wagered on nine might have made good on their bets the following morning. By half past eight, news spread through town that the jury had reached a verdict. A large multitude at once set in motion toward the court house and listened "with breathless interest" as the jury foreman, A. O. Wilcox, announced, "We the jurors impaneled in this case find for the defendant." Nine jurors sided with the Hermes Company, while only three voted for Raymond and Ely.[89] Nine was enough, and the court ordered that Raymond and Ely "take nothing by reason of said action" and that they pay $4,987.24, the costs of Hermes's defense.[90]

The case, however, did not end there. Raymond and Ely's lawyers were at court by ten o'clock the following morning filing motion for a new trial. By the end of June, Judge Mortimer Fuller granted that motion. He ordered that the previous verdict be "set aside and vacated" on three grounds: "insufficiency of the evidence to justify the verdict," the verdict contradicted the law, and "irregularities in the proceedings of the defendant and of the jury" that prevented Raymond and Ely "from having a fair trial."[91] Like the earlier court case, interest in Fuller's decision ran high; Hermes and Raymond and Ely officials had planted men in the courtroom who were ready to signal news of the verdict to outside runners. Unbeknownst to each other, both sides had arranged for their signalers to wave a red flag from a court window as a sign of victory. After Fuller found in favor of Raymond and Ely, its representative lifted his banner. Upon seeing the red flag, a Hermes man, thinking it symbolized victory for his company, mounted his horse and rushed to the telegraph office to send the "glad tidings" to company officials at San Francisco. By the time he learned the truth he was already at a saloon preparing to celebrate with a bottle of champagne.[92]

Rather than endure another protracted trial, however, Raymond and Ely brought an unceremonious end to the courtroom drama. They settled out of court, purchasing Hearst's interest in the Hermes mine for an undisclosed "high figure." Hearst later recalled it this way: "Got in with some men who had a set of Pioche mines, sunk a shaft, struck a bed of ore, had a big lawsuit over it, got out of that making two hundred and fifty thousand."[93]

Far from the intimate winter tales of the Paiutes or the spiritual nature of Mormon record keeping, Pioche's creation story found itself jostled about in a courtroom already packed with judge, jury, lawyers, and mobs of spectators. The story emerged from the witness stand as public spectacle, under direct and cross-examination, with powerful lawyers disputing its meaning and even its validity. The founding at Pioche also teaches an important lesson about the economic power structure that came to dominate the region. Absentee capital embodied in men such as F. L. A. Pioche and George Hearst rested firmly on top. Local miners came next, followed by the Mormons, who were relegated to the periphery of the mining economy. The Southern Paiutes ended at the bottom. Even though initially they controlled the silver at what would become Pioche, their bows and arrows proved ineffective against the flood tide of American "progress" that crashed in upon them.

Clearly Mormons, miners, and Southern Paiutes dug their dirt with symbolism that made life meaningful for the peoples of each group. Beyond their founding rituals, however, their three worldviews were enmeshed in a much broader force outside their control. Nationalism as religion dictated progress and destiny, notions much more akin to mining and its promised wealth than they were to either Zion or Paiute sacred space. By 1870, the Nevada/Utah/Arizona border shifted to accommodate one worldview while simultaneously diminishing, spiritually as well as geographically, the other two.

3 Power, Place, and Prejudice

In March 1865, Thomas C. W. Sale, a Southern Paiute Indian agent turned prospector, set in motion a series of events that would forever redefine Mormon, mining, and Paiute space. Sale induced an "old Indian" to lead him to an outcropping of ore at what would soon become the Pahranagat Mining District. The agent quickly became convinced that he had found the much-rumored Silver Mountain for which so many had searched in vain. News of the find spread rapidly and generated intense excitement.[1] Early reports in national mining journals called the mines "richer than any yet discovered" and predicted that in less than a year, "this district will roll out silver bricks in quantities sufficient to shame the Comstock in her palmiest days." One miner called the district "the richest I have ever seen," and another wrote that "there are no more promising mines to be found in Nevada."[2]

The early assumption was that the Pahranagat District *was* in Nevada, but no one really knew. With Pahranagat's promising discoveries of silver at stake, Nevada's politicians and the U.S. Congress could not leave it to chance. They put in motion a series of events that further entangled the crash of meanings already competing for control of Paiute space. While work at the Meadow Valley District came to a virtual standstill, it was the Pahranagat District, from 1866 to 1869, that captured not only local attention but eastern notoriety and capital.

Intervention from Washington, D.C., in the relatively obscure affairs playing out on the southern rim of the Great Basin clearly illustrates important lessons about the relationship of power to the making of space and place. As the historian James P. Ronda contends, "[P]ower is always in motion, sweeping from place to place with restless energy. And as power shifts, it transforms places. The terrain, the very shape of the earth changes."[3] By 1866, the power for making space in southwestern Utah Territory shifted far afield from local Mormon, miner, or Paiute control to the halls of Congress. A hierarchy of power emerged that privileged Nevada's mining frontier over Mormons and Paiutes and that built borders to enforce its prejudices.

Eastern politicians held the power to remap the frontier. They did so, quarrying the ground with symbolism that privileged mining land as somehow more American than either Mormon or Paiute land while simultaneously lumping Mormon and Paiute people together as un-American. In that process, government officials planted a portion of America's national identity into the dirt of the western frontier. The story told here highlights the federal government's construction of political and geographic borders designed to protect that identity, the relationships of power embodied in those borders, and the biases that those borders came to represent.

Typical of Gilded Age politics, greed, power, and conflicts of interest loom large in several episodes of this story. A variety of government officials—Congressman James M. Ashley, Nevada governor Henry Goode Blasdel, Utah territorial governor Charles Durkee, and the Indian agents Thomas C. W. Sale and Captain Reuben N. Fenton—used their public roles for personal gain. The actions of these men seem to echo the sentiments of New York's Tammany Hall politician, George Washington Plunkett, when he said, "'I seen my opportunities and I took 'em.'"[4]

The Mormon and mining part of the border story begins in the 1850s, wherein a growing sectional crisis estranged the nation, North against South, over the explosive topic of the expansion of slavery. That crucible gave birth to the modern Republican party, which ran its first presidential candidate, John C. Fremont, in 1856. The Republican party that year adopted as a plank in its platform the notion that it was "both the right and the imperative duty of Congress to prohibit in the Territories those twin relics of barbarism—Polygamy, and Slavery."[5] The Mormon practice of plural marriage, officially announced in 1852, became a national political issue, on par for at least some in Congress with slavery. Before the Civil War, southern delegates to Congress were able to block attempts at antipolygamy legislation, arguing that if lawmakers could outlaw plural marriage in the territories, slavery would be next. With the election of Abraham Lincoln to the presidency in 1860, however, the

South began to secede from the Union, leaving Republicans in control of Congress. In 1862, Lincoln signed into law the Morrill Act, making polygamy a crime.[6]

Over the next thirty years, Congress passed a string of increasingly stringent antipolygamy bills. During the first session of the Forty-seventh Congress, federal lawmakers entertained twenty-three bills and constitutional amendments aimed at eradicating plural marriage. Of those, the Edmunds Act (1882) made it into law. It not only tightened the noose on polygamy but went so far as to dismantle the election machinery in Utah Territory, replacing it with the Utah Commission. That body consisted of five appointed officials who established an oath that required potential voters to swear to their nonpolygamous status. Before the Supreme Court struck it down, the oath effectively barred an estimated twelve thousand Utahns from the polls. Even more damaging to the Mormon cause, the Edmunds-Tucker Act became law in 1887. Besides its several provisions aimed at facilitating polygamous convictions, it disfranchised Utah women; vested judicial, law-enforcement, and militia powers in federal appointees; stripped control of schools from Mormon hands; and began to dismantle the LDS Church piece by piece. The act represented the height of congressional anti-Mormon legislation. In 1890, as federal officials initiated efforts to confiscate Mormon temples, Wilford Woodruff, then president of the Church, announced a decision to abandon polygamy.[7]

Thus, the Mormon Question, as it came to be called, not only involved ending what was deemed the un-American practice of plural marriage but also halting the Mormon hierarchy's control of Utah Territory. While the solution to both problems largely defined Utah's political history for the last half of the nineteenth century, it also played a role in shaping the western United States.[8] Utah remained a territory from 1850 to 1896, while most of its neighbors were admitted into the union of states. In that process Congress persistently whittled away Utah's territorial land, carving off chunks for other territories and states whose peoples better fit prevailing notions of Americanness.[9] As a territory, Utah suffered from unequal power relations with its neighbors and was at the mercy of Congress in matters of boundary changes. Only Congress held the power to change boundaries between territories, while joint action of Congress and the states involved could move boundaries between territories and states. Residents of the affected territory, however, had no real power in the remapping. The geographer D. W. Meinig contends that this system was designed to respond to local interests in a "quest toward the American ideal of local control over their own affairs."[10] If

Paiute and Mormon interests were considered, however, then in the case of the 1866 Utah/Nevada/Arizona boundary shift that ideal was largely ignored. Outside influence heavily favored Nevada's mining frontier.

The formation of Nevada Territory out of the western third of Utah Territory marked the beginnings of this shift. The momentum stayed with Nevada for several years as its silver-crazed miners pushed east, transforming more and more of Brigham Young's Zion into what he considered outposts of Gomorrah. While Mormons clamored unsuccessfully for Utah statehood throughout the last half of the nineteenth century, miners did the same, successfully, for Nevada. Both groups, as the historian Gordon Morris Bakken sees it, hoped to use statehood as "a device to escape an onerous system of government." The Mormons held seven constitutional conventions, drafting documents designed to gain them statehood and thereby rid Utah of oppressive territorial officials and congressional antipolygamy legislation. Nevada's separation from Utah and subsequent enlargement at Utah's expense, ironically, was to accomplish similar goals, but for Nevadans, the onerous system of government was that of the Mormons.[11] That Nevada's effort was successful while Utah's failed is testament to the power of mining in America's development and the power of prejudice in shaping some of its western borders.

Mormons first settled in the Carson Valley of present-day western Nevada in the spring of 1850, establishing a supply station to capitalize upon the gold-rush traffic then passing through. In 1857, however, Brigham Young called all outlying settlements back to the center of Zion, as the Saints prepared for an invasion of federal troops in what came to be called the Utah War. The non-Mormon, or gentile, population in the Carson Valley region had always chafed under the Saints' theocratic rule and quickly seized upon the retreat to petition Congress to create a new territory. The effort, however, bumped into the slave issue, with southern congressmen adamantly opposed to creating a new, potentially free-soil territory in the West. Nonetheless, in the summer of 1859, with the discovery of the Comstock Lode, the movement toward separating Nevada from Utah gained ground. The Comstock Lode, in essence, "created a new society in the sage brush desert," with a population by 1860 that approached seven thousand, many of whom joined the growing clamor for self-rule.[12]

A few Nevada petitions, filled with exaggerations, reached Congress, begging for separation from Utah and relief from its attendant Mormon outrages. The arguments centered upon what the miners deemed the un-American nature of the Utah theocracy and generally included charges of a Mormon-Indian conspiracy against true American citizens. One such appeal described Mormons of Utah Territory as a "bound" and "controlled" population under "the despotic will of one man" and further alleged that the gentile residents of Carson Valley feared for their lives. Apparently, emigrants passing through to California did too, "and thousands in this great valley have found an untimely grave." The Mormons, the petition charged, had connived with the Indians, "encouraging the savage to his work of death."[13] Another entreaty, this time a Carson Valley grand-jury report, resorted to similar embellishment. It described politics in Utah Territory as abusive and oppressive to the gentiles and contended that the Mormon population controlled all the power and could easily "perpetuate by force and fraud their present Theocratic Tyrany." The Mormons, it continued, "commit daily outrages upon the persons and liberty of American citizens," a long list of which included trampling the law, deriding federal judges, violating the Constitution, prostituting their own females, "disfranchising and murdering individuals, merely for being American citizens," and "with systematic barbarity" inciting "the Indian savages to attack and murder large bodies of unprotected people." While the grand jury left the solution to such offenses in the hands of the "wiser counsels of the paternal Government," it could not help but appeal to Manifest Destiny and offer a bit of prodding: "Our wealth is not only rapidly increasing with the cultivation of our fields, the increase of our herds, and the development of the mines, but it is reasonable to predict that within the next twelve months we will have a population of American citizens sufficient to justify our admission forthwith in the sisterhood of States, and thus complete the chain of civilization, religion, and liberty that now reaches from the shores of the Pacific and Atlantic, and endeavors to bind the continent in one unbroken line."[14]

Additional pleas for separation ensued, but it was not until the South seceded from the Union, taking its senators and representatives with it, that the major barrier to congressional action disappeared. As the historian David Alan Johnson described it, in 1861, "[T]he Republican-dominated Congress, cognizant of the importance of the Comstock Lode treasure in the impending conflict with the South, quickly affirmed" the bill establishing the Territory of Nevada.[15] In so doing, Congress assigned new meaning to the western third of Brigham Young's diminishing desert Zion, linking it to "the chain of civilization" that would continue to bypass Utah for several decades.

Only one year later, as the frenzied mining frontier pushed eastward, Congress extended Nevada's boundary one degree of longitude farther into Utah, thereby converting an additional eighteen thousand square miles of Zion into mining space.[16] Two years later, with Lincoln's reelection at stake, it became politically expedient for national Republicans to add votes to their cause, making Nevada's 1864 constitutional convention "a product of plans hatched in Washington, D.C." At that convention, constitution writing for many delegates became "wartime service," requiring them to create a state that would provide electoral support for Lincoln. With that in mind, and the hope of revitalizing the territory's sagging mining economy, Nevada voters endorsed statehood by a margin of nearly 90 percent.[17] "Born on the eve of battle," Hubert Howe Bancroft rhapsodized, Nevada "took no time for infancy or childhood, but poured out the precious contents of her subterranean treasury with a free hand to the help of the nation, from the very hour of her birth."[18]

That Nevada had a subterranean treasury that could aid a nation at war clearly helped its admission process. When additional treasures were found farther east at Pahranagat, potentially in Utah, Nevada's politicians shouted for its inclusion. It seems that Congress and Nevada's leaders had planned for such an event. They built into the Nevada constitution a provision granting Congress the power to add at will one degree of longitude to Nevada's eastern border.[19] Utah remained powerless to resist. In 1866, Nevada grabbed another chunk of Zion, this time including a section of Paiute ground. Paiute claims to the land were not even considered in the debate that ensued, but Mormon claims were. Congress shortly dismissed them in the name of nationalism, progress, destiny, and money.

The rush to Pahranagat was actually a spillover from the Meadow Valley excitement of 1864. When Indian hostilities largely halted activity there, Orsemus H. Irish, Utah Superintendent of Indian Affairs, sent a subagent, Thomas C. W. Sale, to investigate. In March 1865, Sale set out to meet with Southern Paiutes in southwestern Utah, northwestern Arizona, and southeastern Nevada. Beyond meeting with the various Paiute bands, Sale had other ideas. He took with him a group of restless miners who had been staying at Panaca due to the Indian troubles. Included in the group were three of Stephen Sherwood's friends, Samuel S. Shutt, William McCluskey, and David Sanderson. John H. Ely, a future partner in the Raymond and Ely mine, also went along, as did a local Mormon, Ira Hatch, employed as an Indian interpreter.[20]

As the group visited local Indians, they showed specimens of ore. One Indian apparently told them that "he knew where there was plenty more of the same kind" and led them to the Pahranagat silver.[21] The men did not hesitate to organize a mining district, with Sale elected as recorder, and then smother the region with claims.[22] Perhaps Sale did as much as anyone to spread word of the find, which was no doubt aided by his belief that he had found the famed Silver Mountain for which so many had searched in vain. In a letter to Irish, Sale repeated the legend associated with the mountain and its ill-fated discoverers, the 1849 Lewis Manly party. The Manly group, headed for the California gold fields, took the southern route from Salt Lake City, through Utah Territory, along the Old Spanish Trail, and then west to California. Despite objections from his guide, Manly opted for a supposed short cut, leaving the Spanish Trail in southern Utah and heading west through the treacherous terrain of the southern Nevada desert. Unknowingly he led his group into some of America's driest and most barren expanses, including Death Valley— which the party named. Despite horrific hardships, Manly's group did reach California, losing only one life. According to legend, one member of the company, while passing through the Nevada desert, discovered "exceedingly rich mines of silver" and carried a specimen on to California, which proved nearly pure. Since that time, Sale went on to explain, many expeditions had searched for the source of the silver, but none proved successful—until Sale and his party came along. "'Silver Mountain' is found at last," Sale boasted; or, if not, at least "something worthy of attention is discovered."[23]

It was exciting news, which Irish then passed on to his superiors in Washington, D.C. Before long a local and national effort was under way to ensure that the power to control "Silver Mountain" fell into the right hands. By early 1866, four small mining camps had sprung to life at Pahranagat: Logan City, Crescent City, Silver Canon, and Hiko, with at least one resident petitioning Nevada governor Henry Goode Blasdel for a county government.[24] Sprawling Nye County then encompassed the entire southeastern corner of Nevada. Its county seat at Ione lay nearly 250 miles away, by way of a poor wagon road. A new county government, closer and more attuned to the needs of the district, seemed logical. In response, the Nevada Assembly on 7 February 1866 passed a bill authorizing the creation of Lincoln County to govern the new mining district and bring it under Nevada control.[25]

The Nevada State Senate, however, was not as easily persuaded. Senator F. M. Proctor of Nye County protested the action, stating that the area "'is almost entirely uninhabitable, and the settlements intended to be included in said county, as well as the place designated as the county seat, are in the Territory of Utah.'"[26] Proctor was not the only person who doubted the location of the mines. In late 1865, two miners reported that "the Pahranagat District is believed to be in Washington county, Utah." Another miner, a few months later, wrote that the "exact locality" of the mines was still in question, but he believed that they were in the "extreme southeast portion of the State of Nevada."[27] Even as late as May 1866, at the same time that Congress settled the question with a boundary shift, Dr. O. H. Conger visited the region and made a series of scientific observations. He concluded that the center of the district was "a little more than thirty-one miles within the boundaries of Utah Territory by longitude, and also, about the same by latitude from the Arizona line."[28] Conger's measurements notwithstanding, Hiko, the district's easternmost town, actually fell ten miles *within* the borders of Nevada.[29]

The Nevada state legislature, however, could not be bothered to investigate; it charged ahead. Dismissing Proctor's objections, the bill authorizing the creation of Lincoln County passed the senate and shortly won Blasdel's approval. Three hundred persons from the newborn county still needed to sign a petition for the government to go into effect. Governor Blasdel, "a mining man at heart," decided to collect the signatures himself. Though a rather unusual chore for a governor, rumors of riches to be had at Pahranagat captivated him, prompting a legendary desert crossing with the new El Dorado as the prize.[30]

Not to be left out, the state mineralogist and three members of the Nevada legislature joined the governor's entourage. Rather than sticking to the longer but well-worn Pony Express route, which then cut through the center of Nevada, Blasdel opted for a more direct though hazardous journey from Carson City to Pahranagat. This decision would take the governor's party through the desolate southern Nevada desert, then know as "Death Barren"—a choice that would take its toll. With rations severely reduced, Blasdel and a companion rode ahead to Pahranagat, dispatching a relief wagon loaded with supplies to rescue the rest of the party. The well-laden wagon proved a welcome sight to the stranded survivors. One of their party had died in search of water. The rest, exhausted and hungry, had survived on lizards.[31]

Ironically, after such an arduous trek, the governor could not find three hundred men in the district to sign the petition. He was forced to return to Carson City empty-handed, this time by way of Austin on the standard route. Although privately disappointed in Pahranagat, Blasdel did his part to promote its potential.[32] One national mining journal reported Blasdel's boast that the Pahranagat District "beats everything he ever heard or read of" and predicted that "within the year, there will be there the largest mining company on the Pacific coast." Blasdel even expressed regret "that he is a Governor," telling the miners at Pahranagat of his "determination to be with them as soon as his term expires."[33] In the meantime, Blasdel and his legislative companions returned to Carson City and in the 1867 legislative session created Lincoln County anew, this time eliminating the requirement for local petition altogether.[34] Events in Washington, D.C., had settled the boundary issue, at least on paper, by that point anyway. Congress placed Pahranagat deeper within Nevada's grasp, but the boundary change had a larger effect than that. Nevada's mining frontier, in the same border change, reached farther east to embrace, in what would prove an uncomfortable hug, the future site of Pioche, a string of Mormon ranching outposts, and a significant chunk of Paiute space.

In the meantime, Utah's territorial governor, Charles Durkee, demonstrated his interest in Pahranagat not in any official capacity but solely for personal gain. Durkee's indifference about Mormon settlements in southwestern Utah demonstrates a basic lesson regarding power and its gravity in determining who defines space and place. The power rested with Nevada and ultimately with its sympathizers in Congress. Utah's appointed governor showed little interest in defending the boundary concerns of his Mormon constituents. In the same light, Thomas Sale showed equal disregard for the Southern Paiutes he was appointed to protect. Both men put personal wealth over public stewardship, thereby ensuring that mining interests would ultimately win the right to redefine Paiute and Mormon space.

In 1865, President Andrew Johnson appointed Durkee, a former senator from Wisconsin, as governor of Utah Territory.[35] Shortly after his arrival at Salt Lake City, a brass band and "large number of persons" turned out to greet him. William H. Hooper, Utah's territorial delegate to Congress, introduced the new governor to the people of Utah, giving him a "hearty welcome" and leading the crowd in "three cheers for Gov. Durkee." In the speechifying that followed, one of Durkee's traveling companions from Wisconsin stood to extol the new governor's virtues, promising the Utah crowd that Durkee "seeks no personal end or motive, but the sole object and aim of his administration will be to develop the resources of this Territory, and to assist the people in their onward march."[36]

In his annual message to the territorial legislature that year, Durkee perhaps betrayed his friend's promise when he specified what at least some of those resources were: "Within the past year, numerous mines of coal, lead, and precious metals, have been discovered in various parts of the Territory." He suggested that "many of these mines are of surpassing richness and that their discovery has but just commenced." Durkee then

urged the legislators that "any measures you may be able to adopt to promote the development of our mineral resources, will be most beneficial
to our people."[37] While Durkee never mentioned Pahranagat by name, it
is likely, judging by his later actions, that news of the newfound silver
was dancing through his head when he specified mines of "surpassing
richness."

Less than four months later, Durkee made the first of at least two
visits to Pahranagat in 1866. His initial tour occurred sometime in April,
with Durkee touting "the supposed wealth of our southern mines" as
he passed through Mormon settlements on his way south, giving the
impression to at least one Mormon that "he was going to Pahranagat on
a mining excursion."[38] Durkee apparently liked what he found at Pahranagat. While there, he "made an offer of $8,000 for five hundred feet
of the 'Green Monster' claim" and almost immediately began making
plans to return to the district for an extended stay.[39] By the time of his
second visit, however, Congress had settled the question of the district's
location, placing it within Nevada.

Pahranagat was removed from Durkee's jurisdiction, and to go there
again would require a leave of absence from the governorship. This did
not stop Durkee. "It has been my purpose to spend two or three months
the coming summer at Pah Ranagat," he wrote President Johnson, "for
the benefit of my health, being somewhat afflicted with rheumatism."
Because Congress had recently annexed "one degree of longitude, of the
Territory of Utah to the State of Nevada," he told Johnson, "Pah Ranagat
will be transferred to Nevada. I therefore solicit your permission to carry
out my design."[40] Durkee's health was indeed failing, but his motives for
the trip were clearly for more than his physical well-being. After spending three months at the mines, he returned to his post at Salt Lake City,
where he proudly exhibited "two shining silver lumps," one of which
weighed forty ounces and contained about four ounces of gold. He also
reported his prospects for the district, suggesting that "the Pahranagat
country, be it in southwestern Utah or southeastern Nevada, as the case
may be, is one of the very richest mining areas in the West."[41]

Durkee personally took interest in the mines, but as governor he did
not seem overly concerned about the encroaching Nevada border, nor
about its impact upon Mormon settlers. He told the territorial legislature that, although the Pahranagat mines were annexed to Nevada, they
"will yet, by their contiguity to our settlements and avenues of travel,
be, to a great extent, equally dependant upon us for supplies as those
within our borders."[42] Regardless, it seems clear that Durkee's personal
interests were not at stake no matter where the border came to rest. He

played no role in defending Utah's boundaries, only hoping to profit from Pahranagat's potential wealth.

Utah held little or no power in the struggle to make place and define space. It suffered doubly from its territorial status: its appointed governor was an outsider who had little in common with the people he was charged to serve, and as a territory its political boundaries were susceptible to encroachments from more powerful neighboring states and the whims of Congress.

Governors Blasdel and Durkee were not the only politicians to visit southern Nevada and Utah in the mid 1860s. A much more influential man with power to move meaning by drawing lines also passed through. James M. Ashley of Toledo, Ohio, chairman of the U.S. House Committee on Territories and a member of its Mining Committee, made a trip to the West during the summer of 1865. He arrived in Salt Lake City on 4 July and spoke to a crowd assembled to celebrate Independence Day. As he stated it, his trip was a fact-finding venture so that he could know and understand the wants of the peoples of the western territories.[43]

Ashley had a message to deliver to the Saints as well. During his stay, he met with Brigham Young and other Mormon leaders. At one visit with George A. Smith, counselor to Young, Ashley candidly explained the "religious feeling" in the United States that was intensifying against the Saints. "The religious element now ruled the country," Ashley noted. "[T]he clergy had it their own way and they were determined that the laws of the United States should be enforced in Utah, and that it would be terrible." He went on to suggest that it would be for Utah like it was for the South when Sherman marched through: Sherman's army "ravished every woman that was within 25 miles on each side of his center and then burned their houses," Ashley explained, and that is what the clergy intended to do in Utah. He further indicated that he could no longer politically afford to use his influence on Utah's behalf. He claimed that after drafting a recent bill for Utah statehood, the clergy in his home district "were down on him," and he nearly lost his seat in the last election as a result.[44]

Ashley stayed for over a week in Salt Lake City and then planned to visit Montana, Idaho, Nevada, Oregon, Washington, and California before returning east.[45] On his return trip he traveled via what he called "the southern route," apparently passing through at least some of the area soon to be transferred to Nevada. By virtue of his visit, Ashley claimed to "understand the wants of the people of that country" and became convinced that they and their land better belonged to Nevada. He used his power in Washington to ensure that such a transfer took place.[46]

One of Nevada's senators, William M. Stewart, introduced a bill in 1866 that provided for the boundary shift, moving it one degree farther east, from the thirty-eighth to the thirty-seventh meridian of longitude west from Washington (see figure 2).[47] It was an eighteen-thousand-square-mile chunk of earth that potentially contained the Pahranagat silver strikes. For good measure, the bill also included a portion of northwestern Arizona Territory, running the new boundary down the middle of the Colorado River. This would give Nevada control of Callville (Call's Landing), a Mormon port town at the head of the river's navigable waters, thereby ensuring that the Pahranagat mines would have a close transportation route for obtaining supplies and shipping its riches to market. Three wagon loads of ore from Pahranagat had already passed through Callville on their way to either New York or San Francisco.[48]

Hype promised that the Pahrahagat mines were some of the richest in the West, and hype helped to move a border. The myth of western mineral abundance, not the silver itself, motivated the move. In May 1866, when

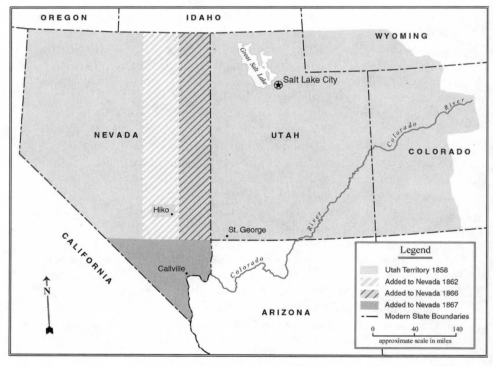

Figure 2. *1866–67 Utah/Nevada/Arizona Boundary Change.*

Congress took action, Pahranagat was still an unproven district, with some reports suggesting that all the excitement was unfounded.[49] Regardless, the mere promise of silver hidden in a small spot of ground, possibly in Utah Territory, was enough to lift a three-hundred-mile-long border and toss it fifty miles east. The proposed transfer quickly won Senate approval and then went before the House, where it also won easy favor, but not before a lively debate offered a peek into congressional attitudes about who possessed the power to assign land its cultural meaning.[50]

As chairman of the committee on territories, James Ashley took guardianship of the bill and steered it through the House. His work on the mining committee proved useful. Before bringing the boundary change to a vote, Ashley attached an amendment guaranteeing that currently held mining claims in the transfer area would be protected when jurisdiction passed from Arizona and Utah to Nevada. In the debate that ensued, Utah's and Arizona's territorial delegates to Congress spoke in opposition to the "dismemberment" of their lands. William H. Hooper, representing Utah, argued not only against the transfer of land itself but against the principle he believed it established. Congress was traveling a new road with this legislation, Hooper surmised, unprecedented in the history of the country: "On the simple action of a committee thousands of square miles are taken from one Territory and attached to another without . . . consulting the people who are to be transferred, [thereby] . . . reducing these people . . . to the condition of serfs."

Hooper then made an appeal to American ideals of loyalty, progress, Manifest Destiny, and the agrarian dream in a discourse that attempted to paint the Mormon people as "the pioneers" of the West and their settlement there as beneficial to national development. According to Hooper, Mormons broke "a path from the Missouri river to the center of this continent," taking with them "the germ of everything now in that country" and doing so "without any expense to the Government." The Mormon people built grist mills, saw mills, cotton factories, and "opened up one hundred and fifty thousand acres of arable land." Their agricultural success alone, Hooper concluded, was ample proof that Mormons were a people "who have done as much as any other to sustain the Government."

Delegate John N. Goodwin, representing Arizona, made his appeals based upon geography and popular consent. He contended that the northwest corner of Arizona Territory better fit geographically with Arizona than Nevada. Beyond that, the bill, in Goodwin's mind, would force former Arizona residents "to take upon themselves the burden of a State government without their consent. I would be perfectly willing that this bill should pass," Goodwin conceded, "if the people of that portion of Arizona can be permitted to vote on this question and decide it by a majority." Otherwise, he feared, as did Hooper, that Congress was establishing "a new precedent in legislation" that oppressed the rights of the people.

Those in favor of the bill addressed Hooper and Goodwin's arguments with discourses that talked past the idea of consent to center upon the notion that land is cultural, implying that those who use their ground in ways deemed to best serve the national interest will hold sway. One representative, for example, claimed to "have a friend living upon this portion of the Territory proposed to be set off" and suggested that if it were put to a vote, and "to common sense, and to the laws of nature," the people would choose Nevada. He concluded, "I hope we will by all means give Nevada a slice"; it is, after all, "well governed and is now yielding a very large revenue to the Government."

Delos Ashley, a congressman from Nevada, was most explicit on this point: "The reason why we want this territory for Nevada is that our people from Nevada have discovered mines in that degree of latitude, and we are occupying the country now." "The people of Nevada are a mining people," Ashley insisted, "while the people of Utah are an agricultural people." Regardless, he only knew of "but one Mormon living in that degree of latitude" anyway, and "the Mormons have always been averse to mining." He further assured Congress "that our people who discover and work mines there do not wish to be under the control of the government of Utah; and I tell you that it is for the benefit of the United States that they should not be." Ashley then made an appeal to Congress's pocketbook. He explained that Nevada's population of nearly fifty thousand people paid taxes of almost three hundred thousand dollars, while Utah's larger population paid only forty-one thousand dollars in taxes. "Let members judge," Ashley coaxed, "which is the most benefit to the United States."

Money talks, and to a Congress attempting to deal with huge Civil War debts while simultaneously trying to finance railroad construction as well as reconstruction efforts in the South, it speaks loudly. The bill passed over the objections of Hooper and Goodwin, neither of whom were voting members of Congress. As territorial representatives, their only power lay in the ability to persuade. Actual power to make decisions resided elsewhere, in congressmen largely unfamiliar with and unaware of the needs of the peoples of the territories. The 1866 boundary shift privileged a state over two territories, mining over agriculture, and money (or, more precisely, the illusion of money) over the axiom of popular consent. Significant power rested in the ground, and more importantly it rested with whatever group mined that ground with symbolism that Congress deemed to be in the nation's best interest.

Paradoxically, in making such a determination Congress betrayed America's long-standing agrarian ideals. Thomas Jefferson had done as much as any man to ingrain those ideals into the American psyche. He envisioned a nation of yeoman farmers spread across North America, each one kept virtuous through his labor in the soil. Tilling the earth, as Jefferson saw it, was the basic and natural occupation of man, and through its influence man would become more democratic, fair-minded, and socially aware. "Those who labor in the earth," Jefferson believed, "are the chosen people of God."[51] Industrialization, however, would bring corruption, social stratification, and an abrogation of broader community responsibility, evils Jefferson hoped America could avoid. Brigham Young held similar views and in many ways established his western Zion as an embodiment of the agrarian dream.[52] Congress anchored that dream in the American West in 1862 when it passed the Homestead Act, a law designed to turn the region into 160–acre parcels of agrarianism.[53] Thus, in the House debate over the Utah/Nevada/Arizona border shift, representatives double-crossed themselves.

Ironically, the Pahranagat District never lived up to even the tamest of claims. By 1868, the mining commissioner Rossiter W. Raymond reported that investors had poured nearly one million dollars into the district, while extracting only about twenty thousand dollars worth of bullion. Even Governor Durkee's Green Monster lode quickly played out, as did most of the other strikes, leaving Raymond to lament that developments in the district "have been conducted with such conspicuous absence of skill and common sense, that they may be said to have produced hardly any results whatever." The following year, Raymond noted that miners had largely abandoned Pahranagat, moving on to the next rush and its attendant lure of riches, this time farther east at White Pine.[54] Although Pahranagat proved nearly worthless in terms of the silver extracted there, for a brief moment it captured national attention and mustered enough power to reshape the political boundaries of the American West. That power not only redefined Nevada, Arizona, and Utah but attempted to remake the Paiute world as well.

———————

Just as Utah and Arizona Territories suffered from unequal power relations with Nevada's expanding mining frontier, the Southern Paiutes found themselves in a protracted struggle against forces more powerful than they. The Paiutes, however, were given even less say than Utah's and Arizona's congressional delegates and no meaningful role in the boundary changes that profoundly reordered their cosmos. Power rested well beyond the center of Paiute space in the hands of Washington politicians and government Indian agents. As with Governor Durkee, the agents appointed to oversee Paiute affairs acted more often out of self-interest than virtue, leaving the Paiutes to fend for themselves in a foreign system that branded them as "savages" and had little regard for Paiute ways. Unlike Utah and Arizona, the Paiutes suffered an additional layer of discrimination. Mormon settlers not only acquiesced but sometimes aided in redrawing Paiute boundaries, ironically at the same time that they were suffering losses in their own border battle with Nevada.

Mormons and Paiutes nonetheless found themselves targets of policy decisions made in distant counsels with little regard for local input. At the same time that Republicans in Congress attempted to solve the Mormon Question, for example, they also struggled to remedy the longer-standing Indian Problem. After the Civil War, the solution to that "problem," Congress concluded, lay in the reservation system—removing Indians from traditional lands where they interfered with Anglo-American colonization and concentrating them on reservations where supervised Americanization could proceed. Rather than one vast Indian Territory for all the tribes, by the 1860s the government had adopted a multireservation system. Government officials selected sites, generally spots undesirable to Anglo-American settlers, throughout the West in relative proximity to traditional Indian hunting and gathering spots and either attempted to entice the Indians to the reservation with promises of money and supplies or violently herded them there.[55]

The 1860s saw other important changes in federal Indian policy that would come to bear upon the Paiutes. In 1865, congressional leaders appointed a joint committee, headed by Senator James R. Doolittle of Wisconsin, to investigate Indian conditions and recommend a definitive policy. The Doolittle Committee concluded that western tribes should no longer be allowed a free, roving existence. Indians would have to give up nomadic life, be concentrated on reservations, and there learn to "walk the white man's road." The Doolittle report did chasten federal officials for unnecessary use of force in handling Indian affairs up to that point and recommended a "Peace Policy" in pursuing concentration on reservations. In this vein, President Ulysses S. Grant began using clergy and prominent laymen to serve as Indian agents, believing that such men could use Christianity as a means to civilize the Indians. While the War Department continued to advocate a Force Policy, recommending

"Americanization at the point of a bayonet," Grant's Peace Policy none-theless saved the Southern Paiutes from the horrors of a violent roundup like the Navajos endured during their Long March to Bosque Redondo in 1863–64.[56]

The other major change in federal Indian policy, however, was not so good to the Paiutes or to Native Americans in general; one historian even called it "revolutionary" for its impact upon Indian power. Through the 1860s, government Indian agents had negotiated treaties with Native American leaders, ascribing to their tribes sovereign status and thereby giving the Indians a voice—albeit a muted and often ignored voice—in the treaties that affected them. By 1871, Congress decided to silence that voice altogether. It passed an act that ended the treaty process and thereafter subjected all Indians to the laws of Congress and the rulings of the president.[57] From then on, power to make place and fix boundaries resided thousands of miles from the center of the Paiute universe in the hands of government bureaucrats, none of whom had likely ever heard of Tabuts, Shinangwav, or Ocean Grandmother, and all of whom had little regard for the worldview they embodied.

In the meantime, however, Moroni, the Paiute that the Mormons William Hamblin and William Pulsipher had befriended, perhaps quickly came to realize the true price of the silver his people once guarded. The dizzying influx of miners and Mormons into Paiute space led some Pai-utes to attempt violently to preserve power. Those attempts, like domi-noes falling down, led to a protracted reservation process for the Paiutes. Congress eventually cut Paiute land into meaningless squares described in longitudinal degrees measured from Washington, D.C.

While Mormons had been missionizing among the Paiutes since 1854, the government had largely ignored them until 1864. Federal inter-vention that year grew directly out of the contest for silver playing out at the future site of Pioche. Paiute land had instantly become valuable in Anglo-American eyes; consequently, a portion of Paiute space was transformed into land that miners would soon argue fit nicely within the broader American notion of Manifest Destiny.

Miners first appealed for government intervention against the Paiutes in August 1864, after Paiute raids had forced them to retreat from the Meadow Valley silver. Stephen Sherwood, Jacob N. Vandermark, William Hamblin, and eighteen other miners, in a petition to Orsemus H. Irish, the Utah Indian superintendent, requested that a "Special Agency" be established among the Paiutes. "A proper person," they said, should be appointed "to superintend the Indians and give them some assistance as a sort of compensation, for their supposed losses." "So many miners

are coming in now," the petition read, "that the Indians are getting uneasy and alarmed lest the game and grass seed on which they have been
principally obliged to depend for subsistance [sic] will be destroyed, and
are already threatening to drive away the settlers and miners." As added
persuasion, the petition then made an appeal to national progress: The
growth of the Meadow Valley Mining District "is not only a matter deeply
interesting to individual enterprise, but must be so to the Government,
and country at large." Utah's territorial governor, James D. Doty, and
secretary, Amos Reed, encouraged Irish along those same lines, advising
him that "the present development of the mineral wealth of that section"
makes an agency in the southwestern portion of the territory "a matter
of necessity."[58]

Irish agreed. Within weeks he wrote to William P. Dole, U.S. commissioner of Indian affairs in Washington, D.C., describing the mountains in
southwestern Utah as "rich in mineral resources" and noting that "our
hardy and adventurous pioneers are fast claiming and as rapidly as possible developing them." To protect such noble Americans in their quest
for wealth, Irish recommended removing the Paiutes to the Uintah Valley Reservation in northeastern Utah. President Abraham Lincoln had
created the Uintah Reservation in 1861 as a settlement site for the Ute
Indians, traditional enemies of the Paiutes. Despite the obvious absur-
dity of such a policy and the Paiutes' repeated insistence that they would
not live with the Utes, the plan would persist among government agents
for the next nine years. Irish did tell Dole that it would "require a great
deal of talking to get the Indians' consent and then a great deal of labor
to collect and settle them." He nonetheless urged their removal.[59]

This plan of action moved forward quickly. Irish appointed Thomas
C. W. Sale to head the Paiute removal. Sale arrived at his new post by the
middle of November 1864 and then spent considerable time "talking"
with various Paiute bands at Panaca, Clover Valley, St. George, and Santa
Clara. At the last place he met with Tut-se-gav-its, an influential Paiute
and an ordained "elder" in the Mormon priesthood whom local Mormons
had appointed "head chief." Sale felt satisfied with this interview, writing
that Tut-se-gav-its "at once fell into my plans and promised his cooperation." Tut-se-gav-its sent runners to other bands, informing them that
Sale wanted to meet with all Paiutes at Meadow Valley, near Panaca, in
mid December. By 14 December, around fifty-five Paiutes had gathered;
Sale killed two small steers "and commenced to feed as hungry a set of
mortals as it was ever my fortune to meet." Two Mormons, Ira Hatch
and Andrew Gibbons, served as interpreters, helping Sale to negotiate
with the Paiute headmen. To Sale the exchange proved profitable. By

the end of the day, the Paiutes told him that "they were my friends and that all the Indians were my friends and would go with me to any place I wanted to go and take care of me and do as I want them to do." They even gave Sale "a high sounding Indian name" meaning "the Indian[']s friend" and concluded the day with "a very solemn dance."[60]

These good feelings did not last long. The Paiutes who gathered at Meadow Valley were likely influenced as much by the beef that Sale fed them as by any overarching desire for friendship. In his travels among the Paiutes, Sale found them "destitute," "very poor—without blankets or indeed any clothing except robes made of Rabbits Skins which reach no lower than the hips & breech clouts." Occasionally he found a Paiute with "a very poor gun," but most were armed only with bows and arrows. He found that they owned no horses or other domestic animals and noted that they "live principally on roots, Pine nuts, small game, reptiles, and insects." In light of such impoverished circumstances, and the Paiutes' perception that the government had ignored them in comparison to other tribes, Sale recommended that they be given "actual presents rather than promises."[61]

Sale followed this course of action for the few months that he worked among the Paiutes, and it was no doubt his gifts that earned him the title "Indian's friend." When he left the area to report at Salt Lake City, for example, the Paiutes again became hostile, prompting the miners to petition anew for government intervention. The miners now complained that after Sale's departure, the Indians "have been seven fold worse than ever," stealing livestock and harassing work at the mines. "The danger of Indian troubles has already been a great drawback to our mining operations," they griped, "which must now necessarily be indefinitely suspended."[62]

Clearly, mining interests heavily influenced the nature of Indian affairs in southwestern Utah. The Mormons, however, also benefitted from Sale's course of action in the security it provided to their settlement efforts in the south. William Hamblin, for example, although originally sent to southern Utah as an Indian missionary, signed the first petition asking for government intervention against the Paiutes. The second petition included signatures of several Mormons at Panaca, and Erastus Snow explicitly endorsed Sale's efforts among the Paiutes. According to Sale, after meeting with Snow at St. George, the Mormon leader gave "assurances of his hearty approval" and drafted a letter that sanctioned Sale's activities and served as a passport of sorts as he traveled among the Mormons. Snow assured Sale that his efforts were "an enterprise in which they [the Mormons] are all directly interested."[63]

While Sale's labors among the Paiutes aimed initially at providing them "a beef animal occasionally" so that "they can be kept quiet," the ultimate goal was to concentrate them on a reservation, preferably the Uintah Reservation.[64] After meeting with the Paiutes on several occasions, however, Sale soon appreciated the folly of moving them to Uintah. "I have endeavored to induce them to leave their present country and go to Uintah Valley and live on that Reservation," he wrote, "but they do not consent." "They say they are afraid of the Utahs," Sale explained; "the Utahs have long been in the habit of stealing the women and children of these Indians and either selling them to the Spaniards or to other tribes." Sale did suggest that the Paiutes "are willing to get together at some place in their own country," but he advised that it would be "impossible to get their consent to place them with the Utahs." His recommendation was that the Paiutes "be taken under the protection of the Government, and if possible brought together and instructed in agriculture."[65]

By that time, Irish had changed his mind too. He warned Dole in May 1865, "I am satisfied that these Pai-Utes cannot be induced to live with the Utahs, except by the use of force," and noted that Governor Doty, Brigham Young, and others familiar with the Paiutes all concurred. As a result, Irish concluded, "[I]t will be necessary to make provision for them upon some other Reservation, located in the neighborhood of four hundred miles south of Uintah Valley."[66]

Irish and Sale's recommendations notwithstanding, Washington officials had other ideas. In September they sent "goods" to Irish to serve as treaty bait for the Paiutes, hoping to entice them into negotiations that were aimed at radically redrawing their boundaries to the Uintah Valley. In accordance with these designs, Irish met with six Paiute chiefs on 18 September at Pinto Creek in Southern Utah. In the bargaining that followed, the Paiutes agreed to "surrender and relinquish" to the United States all of their lands. The six chiefs further acquiesced "to remove to and settle upon the Uintah Indian Reservation within one year." In exchange for these promises, the Paiutes were to be included in the thousands of dollars' worth of annuities Irish had earlier negotiated with the Ute Indians. In addition, Tut-se-gav-its as head chief was guaranteed a house at Uintah, surrounded by five acres of plowed and fenced land and one hundred dollars a year for the next twenty years. As further inducement, Irish threw in "two yoke of oxen, two yokes and two chains, one wagon, one plow, ten hoes, six axes, two shovels, two spades, four scythes and swaths, one saddle and bridle and one set of harness."[67]

The Anglo-Americans who witnessed this treaty signing must have realized what a terribly small reward the Paiutes were promised in exchange for such wonderfully valuable land. Thomas C. W. Sale looked on, but by this time he was serving as recorder for the Pahranagat Mining District. S. P. McCurdy, U.S. district judge for the region, also witnessed the event, as did Dr. O. H. Conger, both of whom had stake in the Pahranagat silver. Their presence at the signing alone suggests a mining connection to the attempted Paiute removal.[68]

As for the Paiutes, it is not clear what prompted such a radical shift in their thinking from the messages they had conveyed to Sale only months earlier. It seems likely, however, that the goods Irish brought with him provided enough immediate appeal to the destitute Paiutes that they marked Irish's paper with X's and then claimed their supplies, never intending to move to Uintah. As early as the turn of the nineteenth century, as contact with Euro-American traders increased along what would become the Old Spanish Trail, many Paiutes had made similar difficult choices. As a means of simple survival, some Paiutes traded their own children for needed food, supplies, and clothing to Spaniards, then Mexicans, and later Mormons. With the influx of Mormons and miners by 1865, the Paiutes' means of subsistence had suffered drastically, so that a heavy cloud of hunger and concern for the survival of their people must have hung over the Pinto Creek bargaining. The chiefs likely chose fixed annuities over potential starvation.[69] Still, the six chiefs did not represent the nearly three thousand Paiutes spread throughout the region, especially the more hostile Pahranagit and Matisabit bands.[70] Regardless, Congress never ratified the treaty, and the Paiutes did not move to Uintah. It would be eight more years before the first of several Paiute reservations came into being, and then executive order, not treaty negotiations, marked the event. The Paiutes, by that time, had lost even the power to acquiesce with an X.

The years immediately following the Pinto Creek Treaty were not kind to the Paiutes. Promised supplies and annuities never arrived, and the government failed to assign an agent to the tribe for four years. Out of desperation, some of the more militant Paiute bands joined with the Utes to raid and plunder the Mormon and mining frontier in what came to be called the Black Hawk War. In 1869, as the southern border region between Utah and Nevada settled down, Captain Reuben N. Fenton, an army officer and newly appointed agent for the Paiutes, arrived at his post. His report almost echoed Sale's four years earlier, describing the Paiutes as "a very destitute tribe, more so than any Indians I have ever seen." By that time, the Paiutes were reduced to relationships of dependency: "[T]he great portion of them, say four-fifths, live by pilfering grain, melons, and occasionally horses and cattle from the whites. . . .

Starvation compels them to steal." The Paiutes that Fenton met were well aware of the government's broken promises and complained "bitterly that their Great Father at Washington has totally neglected them." In such a state, Fenton found the Paiutes "willing and anxious to be placed on a reservation, and there engage in farming." Accordingly, he began the next round of reservation talk among government officials; this time Fenton recommended that a reservation be set aside for the Paiutes on the Upper Muddy River.

A year later, however, nothing had changed, except perhaps that the mining bug had bitten Fenton, just like it did Sale five years earlier. By 1870, Fenton had moved his agency headquarters from the Mormon town of St. Thomas, among the Moapa Paiutes, to Pioche, rather far removed from the majority of his Indian charges but at the heart of the new mining town then bursting with life. It seems that Fenton found mining more interesting than Paiutes, leaving his replacement to complain that Fenton had "shamefully neglected" the Paiutes and was a man "profuse in promises" that he did not keep. Fenton also bilked the government and the Paiutes out of their gratuities, prompting the sheriff to lock him in jail. Tragically, little would change for the Paiutes over the next several decades in the way of Indian agents. More often than not, the men given power over Paiute lives wielded it in shameful ways.[71]

The mining frontier, too, proved a powerful force. When George W. Ingalls took over the Paiute agency in 1872, its headquarters remained at Pioche; but mining's influence over Indian affairs was stronger even than the agency's location at a mining camp. The same potential for wealth that had repositioned the Utah/Nevada/Arizona border also displaced the Paiutes. Ingalls, from his post at Pioche, recommended, like each agent before him, a reservation for the Paiutes, suggesting, like Fenton, the Muddy Valley. By that time Mormon settlers had abandoned their Muddy Valley farms in the wake of the boundary survey enclosing them in Nevada.[72] In Ingalls's mind, it was a perfect spot to teach the Indians farming, because the Mormons had built there a "good system of irrigating ditches" costing over seventy-five thousand dollars but available to the government "without consideration."[73]

Ingalls gave the usual Americanization mantra as a reason for such a move: it would help the Indians give up "their savage, wandering life, and give their attention to agricultural and mechanical pursuits, and adopting a civilized mode of living, and securing the benefits of an education." From Ingalls's vantage point in time and space, however, there was an important bonus in the Paiute expulsion: the "rapid development of the Arizona and Nevada silver mines."[74]

In the language of Indian-agent doublespeak, with its attendant incongruity, Ingalls recommend that a Muddy River reservation be set aside as an agricultural spot for Paiutes. In essence, the ground along the Muddy would become the means of removing both an obstacle to Paiute civilization and an obstruction to silver mining. Ironically, the proposed reservation largely encompassed abandoned Mormon farms and ditches, part of the soil that six years earlier Congress had deemed best suited for "a mining people." Even more ironic, it was land that in Ingalls's eyes held agricultural potential and therefore civilizing power. He failed to realize, however, that Paiute peoples had been growing squash, melons, and corn from that same ground long before Anglo-Americans came along to contest its meaning.[75] The Mormon agricultural frontier, then, retreated in the wake of Nevada's advancing mining frontier but was quickly reinvented as a civilizing spot on the Indian frontier where the Paiutes could learn to farm.

Such inconsistency notwithstanding, Washington officials seemed eager to act upon Ingalls's ideas. President Ulysses S. Grant, on 12 March 1873, issued an executive order setting aside some 3,900 square miles of traditional Paiute lands as a reservation for all Paiutes inhabiting southern California, Nevada, Utah, and northern Arizona (see figure 3). It was a remarkable coup for the Paiutes to get such a large tract of land, and the following year, when Ingalls recommended expanding its boundaries to add timber and additional farming lands, Grant again complied, pushing the boundary farther north, east, and west. That, however, was as big as the new Paiute world—measured now in longitude and latitude—would get. The mining frontier would not long stand for such a vast chunk of potential wealth to be locked up in Paiute hands.[76]

The Pioche newspaper objected to the reservation, calling it an "outrage." Initially, the argument took up the cause of the handful of farmers along the Muddy who had taken over the farms left abandoned in the wake of the Mormon retreat. Those farmers now found themselves unwittingly encompassed by the newly created reservation, with the federal government offering thirty-two thousand dollars to buy them out. The *Pioche Record* complained about giving over "the best farming lands of Southeastern Nevada to the Piutes." It was land that in Paiute hands, the newspaper frothed, had no more value than "any jack-rabbit range in the State."[77] A protracted battle ensued between the farmers and Washington over the federal government's offering price for the land.

Daniel Bonelli, the only Mormon farmer to stay on his Muddy Valley land when the rest of the Saints moved back to Utah, found himself in the middle of this skirmish. He wrote at least three letters to the U.S.

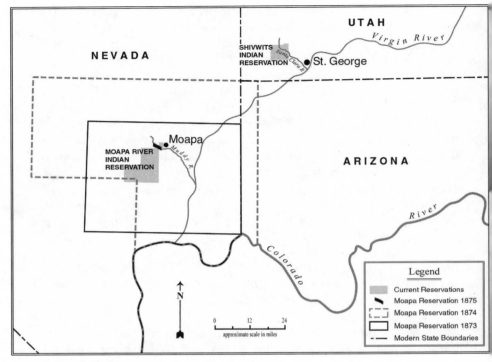

Figure 3. Moapa and Shivwits Reservations.

commissioner of Indian affairs, agitating for twice the government's assessed value for his land. The wife of one farmer, Mrs. Isaac Jennings, even traveled to Washington, D.C., to lobby Congress against appropriating money to buy off the farmers. It was not enough money, she said, to compensate them for their lands. Apparently she influenced Nevada's senators and representatives so that, by the end of 1874, Congress had refused to appropriate the thirty-two thousand dollars, leaving the reservation in a contested state. The white farmers controlled the best lands and water rights, while the four hundred Indians were left with almost nothing.[78]

The fight over farmlands, however, created a facade that obscured the real issue preventing congressional funding. The owners of the ten land claims in dispute, except Jennings, had agreed to the government's price by 1874, but Congress still failed to fund the buyout.[79] By early 1875, the Paiutes' new agent, A. J. Barnes, had resigned himself to the fact that the appropriation would likely never happen and laid the blame at the feet of Nevada politicians. He lamented that "no Indian agencies of the United States have suffered more, and struggled harder, for an existence than the two in Nevada." The enemies of the reservations, he wrote, occupy "high positions of trust" and through their opposition have "kept the Indians nearly necked [*sic*], and on the point of Starvation." With tears in his eyes he had recently witnessed Paiutes in his charge eagerly eat the flesh and entrails "of a poor horse or mule" that had died "from poverty or disease." In light of such destitute conditions, Barnes bitterly complained that as yet he had been given no funds to disperse. He offered to abandon efforts regarding the settlers' claims if Congress would only grant "an appropriation, solely for the purpose of aiding the Indians."[80]

It was not the settlers' claims, however, that were at the heart of the matter. The "people of Nevada are a mining people," representative Delos Ashley had insisted during the boundary debate years earlier, and it was mining interests, not farming, that would end in the reservation's reduction to a fraction of its original size. According to Daniel Bonelli, the "great objection of the Representatives and Senators of the West" to funding the reservation was not the farmers' land claims at all. "This Reservation aims to embrace a vast area of desert territory," Bonelli explained, "full of metalliferous ranges of undeveloped but great prospective value which should be left free for development."[81] Bonelli's solution was to "reduce the dimensions of the Reservation by excluding all its metalliferous territory," which he called "the pivot point of objection."[82] Before long, others were chanting the same theme. The reservation doctor argued that Nevada's influential men opposed the reservation because of the "great amount of mettaliferous [*sic*] territory" it included and suggested changing the boundaries to exclude it.[83] A. J. Barnes came to the same conclusion: he agreed to set aside any potential mineral wealth then included in the reservation if it would help win funding. Despite such admissions of those at the reservation, in February 1875 the Nevada state legislature petitioned Congress requesting that the president rescind the executive order that had created the Moapa Reservation in 1873. The primary reason for this request was that "said land embraces nearly one-half of the agricultural land" of Lincoln County.[84]

Congress proved receptive. On 3 March 1875, it reduced the original 3,900–square-mile reservation to a mere one thousand acres, stipulating that the new location "not include the claim of any settler or miner."[85] Barnes surveyed and selected the abandoned Mormon town of West Point on the Muddy, which fit those requirements. Power once again infused the western myth of metalliferous abundance. As with the Utah/Nevada/Arizona border shift, it was not proven mineral wealth that nearly reduced the Paiute world to spatial oblivion but rather the mere hope for such riches. In the words of Bonelli, the land had "great prospective value," and that was enough.[86]

Neither Mormons nor Paiutes used their lands in ways deemed valuable to American development, at least when juxtaposed with Nevada's advancing mining frontier. Faced with the Mormon Question and the Indian Problem, Congress found ways to privilege mining interests over Mormon and Paiute concerns. Biases permeated the West's shifting frontier, the borders of which cut new meaning into the desert soil and attempted to separate and reorder three worlds already tightly intertwined. More strikingly, however, federal officials unmasked the ugliness of those biases in two attempted, even more radical reorderings that failed.

The first of those attempts took place in early 1869 when Representative James Ashley proposed changing, yet again, Utah's borders. This time Ashley's remapping was not in response to silver strikes but was crafted specifically to make "the best disposition which can be made of the Mormon question." Ashley proposed to redraw the West, and in so doing to draw the Mormon Zion into oblivion (see figure 4). His bill reduced the size of Utah Territory to a mere twenty-two thousand square miles, while it divided the excess land—and more importantly, the Mormon population—among its surrounding state and territories. Ashley's purpose was, first, to dilute the Mormon vote by absorbing Mormon peoples into Utah's neighboring populations. Then, when those bordering entities had sufficient gentile populations to swallow the main body of Mormons living at Salt Lake City, to finish the job by drawing Utah out of existence. Ashley admitted that he drew the bill originally "to blot out the Territory" from the start, but his fellow committeemen suggested waiting so that the populations of the adjacent territories and state would not be "overborne by the consolidated vote of that [Mormon] oligarchy." The bill, Ashley told his fellow congressmen, would serve to give "the Mormon community notice that no State government will ever be organized there by our consent"; it would also ensure that "the control of affairs there shall be given to the 'Gentile' population."[87]

While it is difficult to know Ashley's motivation for such a punitive measure, Brigham Young's counselor, George A. Smith, suggested it was repayment for Ashley not being furnished with female companionship during his 1865 visit to Utah. Smith believed that Ashley's bill was "severe penalty . . . to inflict upon a whole community because Alderman Sheets a strict Presbyterian failed to furnish the chairman of the com-

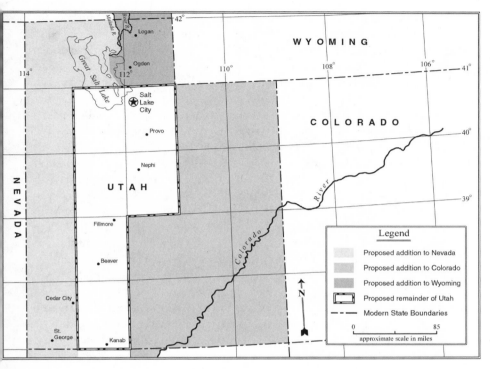

Figure 4. 1869 Proposed Utah Boundary.

mittee on territories a woman to sleep with while he was visiting . . .
Salt Lake City."[88] Others suggested that a quest for wealth and power
lay behind Ashley's plan. Ashley's bill was designed not only to eradicate
Utah but to enlarge the states of Nevada, Minnesota, and Nebraska and
the territories of Colorado, Montana, and Wyoming. Add to that the fact
that Ashley proposed his bill after losing his reelection campaign in 1868
and it made him "a lame duck congressman looking for a political post."[89]
The *Baltimore Gazette* argued that Ashley "expects to be appointed by
the new [Grant] Administration Governor of Montana. . . . The whole
programme is already arranged by which he is to become a millionaire
and a United States Senator."[90] Whether prearranged or not, upon the
expiration of Ashley's term in the House, Grant did appoint him governor
of Montana Territory. He held the post for only a year, however, when
for unknown reasons Grant removed him from office.[91]

Meanwhile, Ashley attempted to railroad his bill through the House
without giving Delegate Hooper, then ill, a chance to respond. Cooler

heads prevailed, however. Hooper spoke a month later, calling the bill "despotic" and suggesting that a map of the proposed changes looked as though a "legislative earthquake" had prevailed upon it. Hooper ascribed the whole proposal to prejudice designed "to build up artificial boundaries" and to confine the Mormons "within a Chinese wall of territorial limits." "Were the question of Mormonism not involved, or some other [question] appealing equally to special prejudice," Hooper challenged, "I do not hesitate to say that a map thus disfigured with mutilations would not for a moment be contemplated with favor."[92]

It is difficult to know how favorably the bill was actually viewed; it died without coming to a vote. Even still, there seems to be some truth in Hooper's words. "Special prejudice" does wield considerable power in the hearts of some individuals, enough to mutilate a map, not only in an attempt to solve the Mormon Question but as a solution to the Indian Problem as well. For the Southern Paiutes, a federal attempt to blot them from the map of their homeland came in 1873, but it was nothing new. The Pinto Creek Treaty had essentially attempted the same thing. Despite its failure and the creation of a Paiute reservation along the Muddy River, federal officials liked the idea of a tidy Paiute removal and resurrected the plan to remap the Paiutes onto the Uintah Reservation. Even though John Wesley Powell and George W. Ingalls, special commissioners to the Paiutes, recommended that the Paiutes "be taken to the Muddy" as a gathering spot, the commissioner of Indian affairs, Edward P. Smith, felt otherwise. He instructed Powell and Ingalls to induce "some of the chiefs and principal men of the Pai-Ute tribe" to visit the Uintah Reservation and encourage them "to make their homes at that place."[93]

Removing the Paiutes would solve the conflict with the white settlers over federal compensation for their land at Moapa; and Powell and Ingalls likely encouraged Smith toward this plan when they favorably reported on the resources at Uintah. They detailed, for example, "an abundance of good soil, plenty of water, and convenient timber," concluding that "there is no finer valley than the Uintah in the territory of the United States west of the hundredth meridian" and suggesting that "there is room enough for all the Indians of Utah."[94]

Whatever the reason, Smith pushed for the Paiute removal. When Powell and Ingalls set out to promote such a plan among the Paiutes, however, the response was predictable. Similar to Hooper's impassioned speech in defense of Zion's threatened border, two Paiute chiefs, Taú-gu and Mo-ak-Shin-au-av, spoke on behalf of their people. They told Powell and Ingalls that the idea of going to Uintah "had been repelled by all the people, and there was no voice raised in favor of their going." Just as

Paiutes had explained to Sale years earlier, the two chiefs emphasized that "the Utes of Uintah had been their enemies from time immemorial; had stolen their women and children; had killed their grandfathers, their fathers, their brothers and sons, and, worse than all, were profoundly skilled in sorcery, and that under no consideration would the Pai-Utes live with them." Powell and Ingalls apparently got the message. Without using force, they concluded, it would be impossible to induce the Paiutes to join the Utes. The "Peace Policy" prevailed, and for the next twenty years the Muddy Valley Reservation became the sole focus of the government's attempts to remap the Paiutes.[95]

The actual and proposed borders that aimed to separate miners, Mormons, and Paiutes were stacked thick with meaning and clouded with prejudice. Mormons and Paiutes fell outside of prevailing notions of what it meant to be an American. The frontier helped define those notions, especially as power brokers muscled borders to shore up American ideals and absorb differences. Ashley's attempted dismemberment of Utah Territory, for example, had at its heart the assimilation of the Other embodied in Mormonism into prevailing notions of Americanness. It was an effort to civilize the Mormons, strikingly similar to the civilization rhetoric built into the borders of Indian reservations across the American West. In fact, for some the line between the two groups grew very thin, a point made abundantly clear in one of Nevada's petitions desiring to separate from Utah in the late 1850s. It called the Mormon people a "dangerous and growing *tribe*" and suggested that "the most effective way of ending our Mormon difficulties" would be to subject "the Mormon population . . . to our Indian policy."[96]

For others, solving the Mormon Question would not take such drastic measures. The mining frontier, as an agent of civilization, could do the job by itself. One miner, for example, at the height of the Pahranagat excitement characterized the Mormon towns in southwestern Utah as "not such sticklers for the 'priesthood' or polygamy." He predicted that the day would come when southern Utah Mormons would "protest against the trickeries of these fattening hierarchs at Salt Lake, and swarm from Brigham's bee hive, never to return." That miner looked forward to the time "when the gentile elements of civilization, and those mighty agencies of enterprise, the furnace and the quartz mill, shall develope [*sic*] south-western Utah." "Who knows what changes may occur there," he queried optimistically.[97] Government agents expressed similar optimism for the Paiutes and imbued the borders of their new reservation with comparable power to civilize. Powell and Ingalls wrote regarding the original Muddy Valley Reservation, "[T]he circumstances are very favorable to the project of making farmers of the Pai-Utes, . . . and converting them from vicious, dangerous savages to civilized people."[98]

The chasm separating Mormons and Paiutes from the broader American scene, however, likely had less to do with prevailing perceptions of savagery, polygamy, and theocracy than it did with the two groups' relative lack of interest in the acquisitiveness permeating Gilded Age America. More than anything, it was gold seeking, individualism, materialism, capitalism, progress, and development that were pitted against the Mormon Question and the Indian Problem. Perhaps it was George Wheeler, the government surveyor sent to determine officially where the Utah/Nevada/Arizona border actually landed, who said it best. After immersing himself in the culture of the border region for some time, he was taken with its potential wealth, much as Governors Blasdel and Durkee and Indian agents Sale and Fenton had been before him. Wheeler concluded that the ores of the region "are assuming quite a respectable status among mining schemes, and the future will open to them a history unknown to the past. Good results may be looked for," Wheeler predicted, "and what the Indians have called 'bullets,' and the Mormons 'lead,' will prove, under the hand of true American industry, to contain large amounts of that power that rules the prosperity of peoples—money."[99]

When the dust on the southern rim of the Great Basin finally settled, after new lines cut fresh meaning in old dirt, a hierarchy of power emerged, with post–Civil War nationalism and its attendant notions of Americanness resting firmly on top. Nevada's mining frontier fit nicely within those ideals and shared in its power, while Mormon polygamy and theocracy found themselves outside prevailing biases of what it meant to be an American. The region's long-term inhabitants, the Southern Paiutes, fared even worse: they lay at the bottom of the power structure, discriminated against in national policy and in local practice.

In the end, Sale's famed Silver Mountain proved relatively worthless in terms of the silver extracted there but immensely powerful in terms of its attempt to Americanize Mormons and Southern Paiutes through the remapping of their worlds. Patricia Nelson Limerick called it conquest through "the drawing of lines on a map."[100] The remarkable nature of this story, however, is that the new lines on the Paiute and Mormon maps conquered no one. To be sure, the Paiutes suffered the most, and a portion of the Mormon Zion withdrew in retreat, but dismissing the story as "conquest" obscures its true relevance—the protracted cultural negotiations that persisted long after the cartographer's ink had dried.

4 *"Listen Not to a Stranger"*

The federal government's attempts to draw lines of separation notwithstanding, the new political borders proved little more than strokes on official maps. Mormons, miners, and Southern Paiutes continued to mix with each other, their paths intersecting in time and space, but against a geographic backdrop of their own making. Even though Mormons and Paiutes were given no meaningful voice in border politics, they assumed spirited roles in shaping the western frontier. They were not merely victims of oppressive state power but aggressive wielders of power themselves. They actively guarded their differing worldviews but at the same time modified them to fashion new universes for themselves, miners included.

Mormons, miners, and Paiutes carved a unique intercultural space where they met to labor, trade, proselyte, fight, kill, and die. The rules of engagement shifted rapidly and varied with nearly every contact, but generally cultural borders designed to keep outside tendencies in check shaped the interchanges. Over time, these three disparate communities spent tremendous energy attempting to defend their differing notions of geographic, economic, political, and spiritual space.

Beginning with the Paiutes, the next three chapters seek to understand the subtleties of those defenses, how each group viewed the others, and the inconsistency that characterized the interaction. As the historian Richard White observes, once westerners left the boundaries of their communities, they "entered a different social and moral universe, and they acted differently toward those they met there. They rarely applied to outsiders the relatively generous standards of mutuality that applied within the community."[1] Mormons, miners, and Paiutes were no different. Occasionally episodes of intercultural respect punctuated their dealings, but distrust frequently held sway. The exchanges between the three groups not only teach fundamental lessons about the ability of people to coexist amid diversity but also highlight shifting relationships of power on a local level. They further illustrate the difficulty that these three communities had at being good neighbors, especially to peoples with drastically different values.

The Paiute portion of the story is one of desperation and survival. Confronted with a rapidly changing world, the Paiutes defended their space with a variety of strategies, including plunder, accommodation, and withdrawal. Over time they remained remarkably resilient, although increasingly marginalized. They refused to bow to governmental pressure designed to move them onto a single reservation but instead clung with rugged determination to their god-given ground. Nevertheless, by the early twentieth century they found themselves placed upon a sprinkling of reserves scattered across their traditional homeland.

Long the victims of Spanish, New Mexican, and Ute slave traders, "the Southern Paiutes were a harassed people leading disrupted lives when they first met Anglo-Americans." Hoping to create a buffer against long-standing enemies, the Paiutes actually invited Mormons to settle in their area in the 1850s. Not only would the Mormons provide a barrier to slave raiders, they would also offer access to technology and knowledge that had long been used against the Paiutes.[2] This strategy worked for a time, but the 1860s brought a flood tide of Mormons and miners into Paiute lands, forcing the Paiutes to find new ways to adapt. Over the next forty years they searched for solutions to the new stresses that Anglo settlement created. Mormons and miners occupied Paiute traditional springs and garden plots, they killed Paiute game animals, and their cattle depleted the tribe's seed resources.

The Paiutes were only loosely organized as a tribe and presented no unified front against the Anglo incursion. The basics of Paiute daily life took place within small family bands, with the band leader serving as moral guide and director of hunting and gathering activities. Some headmen enjoyed more influence than others, but by the 1860s a chief's prestige was primarily a function of his ability to forge ties to the Anglo power structure. Mormon authorities, for example, regarded Tut-se-gav-its, the leader of the Santa Clara band, as "head chief" among the Paiutes, a role he filled until his death in 1871. After that, government agents viewed

Taú-gu as chief of the Paiute "alliance." He was leader of the Cedar band and the same man whom Mormons called Coal Creek John.[3] Other Paiute headmen included Chief Beaverats of the Beaver band; "Old Kanarra" near Parowan; Tsoog in the upper Virgin River Valley; Amos near Virgin City; Moqueak, a Shivwits leader whose band ranged between St. George and the Colorado River; Ná-guts in the vicinity of Toquerville; Tó-shoap, or To-ish-obe, along the Muddy River; An-ti-av in the Paranagat Valley; Thomas, chief of a band on the Beaver Dam Wash; Moroni, whose band ranged between Shoal Creek and Clover Valley; Chuarruumpeak, head-man of the Kaibab band; and Tem-piute Bill, leader of a renegade band of Shoshones and Paiutes west of Pahranagat.[4]

These chiefs were by no means dictatorial rulers. Adult community councils generally made governing decisions, which the chiefs were ex-pected to carry out. A chief did serve as spokesperson for his community, especially in dealing with other tribes or outsiders, but mostly he func-tioned as a father figure to the band. Each morning began with a chief's speech wherein he instructed band members on the day's activities and exhorted them "to live in harmony with each other."[5]

Paiutes shared a broad-based concern for tribal members. Despite being scattered across a vast region and politically detached from each other, the bands were tightly connected through marriage and kinship. Paiutes spoke of distant relatives in language similar to that used to de-scribe brothers and sisters. The various bands formed an extensive safety net of community concern, especially as Anglo settlement depleted the Paiute population. Bands combined or welcomed new members into what proved an open and fluid system.[6]

Religion was an important part of Paiute daily life and included a spiritual awareness of the world in which they lived. Paiutes viewed the sun as a visible manifestation of the One Who Made the Earth. Many Paiutes prayed to the sun daily and cast cornmeal or ashes from their fire toward it, "asking it to take away any evil dreams they had had during the night and to make their day a good one."[7] Such rituals must have taken on new significance as Paiutes sought to deal with the bewildering changes bearing down upon them. The Paiutes' worldview guided their actions as they adapted to an altered universe that now included Anglo-American settlers. Their strong sense of community required vigilance on the part of each band member to protect the group and its ground from potential harm. Paiutes were taught to trust each other and to be wary of outsiders. Tribal elders reinforced this principle with a wintertime campfire tale:

One day, Chu-ar-ru-und-pu-run-kunt, a stranger known as "he who

digs the roots of the yucca," went about his work. While doing so he noticed a buck and a doe nearby. He quickly hid himself and fashioned a
whistle so that he could imitate the cry of a young fawn. As he began to
blow, the buck and doe immediately responded. When they came near,
however, Chu-ar-ru-und-pu-run-kunt killed and ate them.

Following his feast, Chu-ar-ru-und-pu-run-kunt looked about and
noticed two fawns. He approached them, pretending to be their friend.
"There are some bad people around here," he said. "They have killed
your father and mother. Go with me. I will show you where to hide."
He took them to a nearby pit and left them there.

Three days later, Chu-ar-ru-und-pu-run-kunt returned to eat the
fawns. When he arrived, however, he was dissatisfied with their scrawny
appearance. He instructed them to graze on nearby grass and then return
each day to hide at the pit, in case the wicked people reappeared. After
several months the fawns became "fine fat deer"; they grew wiser, too.
They said to each other, "Who knows but this man may have killed our
parents, and maybe he will come back and kill us?" They decided to seek
advice from To-go-av, their grandfather the rattlesnake.

Upon hearing their tale, To-go-av scolded, "My children, you were
very foolish in believing the words of Chu-ar-ru-und-pu-run-kunt; he is
a great deceiver. When you are in trouble listen not to a stranger but go
to your friends for advice." To-go-av then took the deer to Mar-ka-gunt
Kai-vwai-i, a plateau east of the headwaters of the Sevier River, where
they would have plenty of grass to eat, water to drink, and aspen groves
for shade.

To-go-av returned to his home to find an angry Chu-ar-ru-und-pu-
run-kunt waiting there. He had gone to the pit but found it empty and
followed the deers' tracks to To-go-av's abode. "Where are the deer I had
in my pit?" he demanded. "You have stolen them and eaten them." To-
go-av denied the accusation, only stating that the deer had come to him
for advice, and he had taken them to a region where they would be safe.
To-go-av then told him, "Now I know that you are a liar and a bad man.
You shall die!" And To-go-av slew him.

As John Wesley Powell attested, the Paiutes used this tale as a
touchstone designed to reinforce community standards "for not believing strangers."[8] The tale further implies that outsiders were deceptive,
greedy, and self-centered and should not be trusted. Perhaps such lessons
influenced at least some of the Paiutes as they sought ways to defend
their space against encroaching Mormons and miners.

Overall, it is difficult to discern a marked difference between the way
the Paiutes viewed their Mormon and mining neighbors. On occasion,

however, slight contrasts surface, suggesting that the Paiutes shrewdly dealt with the two groups based upon prevailing circumstances and in ways that best served their interest. The Paiutes differentiated between Mormons and Americans in speech, calling the former Mormonee and the latter Merikac or Mericats, a distinction some Mormons may have cultivated for selfish reasons. The historian Sondra Jones contends that Great Basin tribes in general "sized up a stranger by asking, 'Is this man a Mormon, or an American?' and drew strong lines of demarcation between the two in favor of the Mormons."[9] The Paiutes nonetheless developed relationships with members of both groups to further their own purposes.

Such was the case in January 1866, when a Mormon, Ira Hatch, worked as an Indian interpreter for a group of prospectors. As the party traveled to the Pahranagat region to investigate conditions there, Hatch met with several Paiute acquaintances. One Paiute seemed particularly pleased to see Hatch and took the opportunity to unfold his "secret feelings" to his Mormon friend. The Paiute, well aware of the Mormon stance against prospecting, told Hatch that he was not interested in the gold that the mountains contained. He shrewdly pressed his advantage with Hatch and seemed "sure he would get blankets and shirts" as a reward for his announced aversion to mineral wealth and "would be telling it to his friends."[10]

Other Paiutes hoped to use Hatch as a mediator with the Americans. Asherump told Hatch of miners recently killing an Indian and reported that other "Americans" whipped three Paiutes so severely that their "blood ran to the ground." Asherump asked Hatch to "intercede with the Americans" on behalf of the Paitues or, he warned, "there would be trouble." As the trip continued, Hatch met additional Indians, some of whom he claimed could "see there was a vast difference between Mormons and Gentiles. The Gentiles were always talking about mines and about squaws." Hatch, in contrast, spoke to them of "their forefathers and the Book of Mormon" and taught them "that the day was near at hand when we should know the Lord."[11]

Several Paiute chiefs further cultivated relationships with Mormon leaders and appealed directly to Erastus Snow or other local men of influence when problems arose. In 1865, when rumors reached To-ish-obe that "Snow and some of his men were going to the Muddy and poison the water and kill off all the Indians," To-ish-obe sought Snow for an explanation. He approached the Mormon leader in an "angry and excited manner," but after listening to Snow deny the charges and explain away the rumors, he became "mild and subdued." He left feeling satisfied with the interview.[12] Tut-se-gav-its perhaps fostered the strongest relationship with Mormons. As an ordained elder in the LDS priesthood, he occasionally accompanied the Indian missionary Jacob Hamblin on preaching tours to other tribes and frequently used his communication network to inform settlers of potential raids. When he died in 1871, the Saints remembered him as "a man of peace, and a wise counselor to his people."[13]

Certainly the Paiutes had more in common with the Mormon world-view than that of the miners. Paiutes and Mormons shared long-term visions of their relationship with the land, while the miners only wanted its wealth. The Mormon permanence, however, proved a lasting bane, and the Paiutes allied themselves with the miners on occasion. In 1866, a gathering of about three hundred Muddy Valley Paiutes told a group of miners passing through of their anger toward the Saints. They declared that "they were not hostile to the 'Americats,' but to the Mormons. That the Mormons had stolen stock and laid it on them."[14]

Such examples notwithstanding, the Paiutes generally acted independently of Mormons and miners. In the 1860s and early 1870s, Paiutes aggressively defended their space. Stock raiding proved the most discernible tactic that they employed. They stood to lose the most from the contest for space that came to redefine their existence and reacted forcefully.[15] Mormons and miners were invading their world and drastically altering their way of life. To compensate, some Paiutes incorporated Anglo cattle into their diet and economy. Their motivation was likely multifaceted. Paiutes killed and ate some of the cattle, but the large number of animals that they stole likely served a purpose beyond that. Some Paiutes may have attempted to replicate the type of power that they had earlier witnessed among Utes. Waccara, an influential Ute leader from the early 1840s to 1855, created an extensive raiding and trading network from the Great Plains to California. Waccara's activities took him through the heart of Southern Paiute territory, where the Paiutes observed his vast wealth and became victims of his trade in slaves. As the 1860s brought a crush of Mormons and miners into Paiute lands, some Paiutes may have recalled Waccara's success and tried to duplicate it through cattle raids of their own. Black Hawk, an Ute leader in the 1860s, also conducted extensive raids throughout the Great Basin. His example likely emboldened the Paiutes and perhaps provided them distribution channels for the stolen cattle.[16]

Nevada's mining towns offered markets for the cattle and may have even prompted the raids in the first place. In 1871, a Paiute named Jackson informed Mormons that two Indians, Shavehead and his brother, were to blame for a recent round of cattle raids on the Clara range. According to Jackson, the two raiders were not acting independently. Captain Reuben N. Fenton, the former Paiute Indian agent, and a Mr. Patterson were ultimately responsible. The two men apparently operated a corrupt brokerage service designed to capitalize upon the demand for beef at Nevada's mining camps. Fenton and Patterson paid Paiutes for stolen livestock, which they then funneled into the lucrative cattle markets at Belmont, White Pine, and Pioche. For the Paiutes who participated, the trade offered an avenue to power within an otherwise restricted Anglo market economy.[17]

The Paiute plundering in southern Utah and Nevada has generally been linked with similar raids throughout Utah territory during the Black Hawk War (1865–72). That conflict represents the largest Indian uprising in Utah history, as Black Hawk's Utes raided towns, stole cattle, and killed settlers. According to John Alton Peterson, the war's foremost historian, throughout the course of the conflict at least seventy whites were killed and perhaps twice as many Native Americans.[18]

It is difficult to determine the full extent of Black Hawk's influence over the Southern Paiutes, however. Peterson contends that it was significant and notes that "Black Hawk's runners clearly encouraged Indians [along the Muddy River] to make raids of their own." He also believes that Black Hawk instigated similar activity elsewhere throughout southwestern Utah and southeastern Nevada. In 1866, a miner from Pahranagat put it this way: "Blackhawk . . . is more of a warrior than has been credited. He has succeeded in uniting with his own band a number from all the different Indian tribes of the southern part of the Territory."[19] Nevertheless, Paiute raids predated the Black Hawk War and continued even after the Ute hostility had largely subsided. While Black Hawk may have urged the Paiutes on, they were not merely pawns in the broader conflict but combatants in their own struggle.

Even before 9 April 1865, the day the Black Hawk War officially erupted, Paiutes in the Meadow Valley vicinity were aggressively defending their space. In that process they wielded significant power, enough to slow the advance of Nevada's mining frontier and force a portion of Zion into retreat. Paiutes harassed Mormons at Clover Valley, Panaca, and Eagle Valley almost from the time of settlement in 1864. They also badgered the miners attempting to extract silver at the Meadow Valley district. The Indian superintendent Orsemus H. Irish observed that the Paiutes "witness the establishment and rapid development of mining interests with apprehension and jealousy." He noted that "they threaten to stop all prospecting, and have done so in some portions of the Territory."[20]

The settling of Meadow Valley and the influx of prospectors attracted a number of Paiutes, who quickly became "exacting in their demands" of the whites. Sometimes the Paiutes intimidated women and children while the men were away, shot arrows at miners, and killed cattle. No wonder that by the end of 1864, the Cotton Mission secretary, James Bleak, characterized the region's Indian–white relations as "strained."[21]

Occasionally the tension of that relationship snapped and turned bloody. In August 1864, a large band of Paiutes raided several tiny Mormon outposts and drove off "considerable stock and tried to kill several of the men." During that interchange the Mormons took three Indian prisoners who then dared an escape attempt. In the ensuing confusion the Mormon guards killed them. Needless to say, this greatly enraged other Paiutes and set the frontier settlers on edge. Erastus Snow instructed the Saints to adopt defensive measures and even suggested abandonment as a possible solution.[22] About half the Mormon families at Panaca left for safer locales, but tenacious Mother Lee refused. The Lees and a few others stayed and were soon joined by miners seeking refuge from Indian raids.[23] The Paiutes had, in essence, reclaimed their silver and would for the next five years maintain at least nominal control of Meadow Valley and surrounding locales.

Despite the Mormon rumblings of withdrawal, it was two more years before Brigham Young would officially dictate an abandonment policy. In the meantime, hostile Paiutes continued raiding Mormon frontier settlements and mining camps. Work at the Pahranagat mines came to a virtual standstill for nearly seven months as a warring band of Paiutes harassed the miners and stole their livestock. In July 1865, the Indian agent Sale met with Ti-pi-ute (perhaps Tem-piute Bill), the leader of several militant Paiutes, along with other chiefs from the region. One miner reported that the meeting "ended in a friendly manner, the chiefs assuring us that we can work the mines without molestation and that our stock can safely grass in the valley."[24] By the end of July, however, only nine men remained at the mines. The Indians "mustered in such numbers, and in so threatening a manner, that the camp was again deserted, the prospectors returning to the Mormon settlements." By October, emboldened by an increase in numbers, the miners went back to Pahranagat and stayed.[25]

Even still, the Paiutes continued to harass them. The constant risk compelled the miners to guard their animals day and night. In early 1866, a prospector, W. T. Nichols, threatened that as soon as the Pahranagat men could raise "a strong party," they would pursue the Indians and "clean them out." The Paiutes, nonetheless, maintained the advantage;

they knew the land and were skilled in making quick raids and then disappearing into the desert. One prospector named Platts learned this lesson the hard way. On a trip from Austin to Pahranagat, a band of Indians attacked and shot him twice with arrows. He survived the wounds and struggled into Pahranagat where he recovered, but the attackers were never found.[26] The miners thereafter deemed the road from Austin to Pahranagat unsafe for travel, "unless in sufficient numbers." In June 1866, the miners did retaliate. An angry group of five men from the region scouted "after some hostile Indians" who had recently stolen stock. The party found a band of "twelve bucks, eight squaws, and children" and attacked. They killed the Indian men, except for one escapee, and "accidentally" murdered one woman and child.[27]

The Mormons, too, felt the effects of the Paiute anger. In early 1865, the Paiutes harassed settlers at Clover and Meadow Valleys, stealing and killing livestock. When they raided Clover Valley for cattle in April, a posse of Mormons pursued. The search party found a band of about twenty Paiutes and disarmed them and burned their camp. Unintimidated, four days later Paiutes stole seven more animals from Clover Valley, despite the "night and day vigilance of the settlers." In total, the Paiutes rustled some seventy-five head of cattle that winter and spring from Clover Valley alone.[28]

Farther south along the Muddy River, the Paiutes continued their marauding. In February 1866, one Paiute raid earned about sixty animals. It was a well-planned and -executed assault that included a makeshift bridge to aid in crossing the Muddy, as well as a string of strategically buried water containers to facilitate a quick escape across the desert. Two Mormon posses searched in vain for the Paiutes and the stolen cattle.[29]

Whether officially linked with Black Hawk or not, the Mormons viewed the string of cattle raids in the mid to late 1860s within the broader context of that war. In response, Brigham Young, in May 1866, sent orders to Erastus Snow and other southern leaders instructing them to fort up: "To save the lives and property of people in your counties from the marauding and blood-thirsty bands which surround you, there must be thorough and energetic measures of protection taken immediately. ... Small settlements should be abandoned, and the people who have formed them should, without loss of time, repair to places that can be easily defended."[30] Over the next two years, Mormons built forts and banded together for safety. Young's abandonment policy led to the closure of dozens of settlements and hundreds of ranches throughout Utah, southern Idaho, and eastern Nevada. In the Cotton Mission alone the Mormons vacated settlements at Gunlock, Grafton, Duncan's Retreat,

Dalton, Mountain Dell, Shunesburg, Northop, Springdale, Clover Valley, Long Valley, Eagle Valley, Beaver Dams, Simonsville, Mountain Meadows, and St. Joseph.[31] Miners, too, fled to the Mormon forts for protection. Thus, from 1864 to 1868, Paiute aggression dramatically affected Mormons and miners alike. For a time, it proved a viable avenue to power for the Paiutes, giving them an edge over the invading Anglo-Americans.[32]

However, even as some Paiutes attempted to preserve their world through confrontation with whites, others adopted different strategies. Several bands of conciliatory Indians pursued a peaceful approach, which emphasized adapting to their new neighbors rather than resisting them. In 1865, for example, "friendly Indians" informed miners at Pahranagat that "some Muddy Indians were on the way to the mine to kill them and take their live stock." On other occasions Paiutes similarly aided Mormon settlers.[33] Tut-se-gav-its in particular used Indian runners and a vast intelligence network to not only keep his band informed of potential raids, even by neighboring Navajos, but to pass such knowledge onto Mormon leaders as well.[34] This lack of a unified strategy undermined the strength of the Paiute insurgency, especially as friendly Paiutes assisted the whites in killing some of the defiant leaders. Ironically, both avenues along these divergent paths fell well within the Paiute worldview. It seems that Paiute headmen from either group, although opting for opposing tactics, sought to make sense of the changes disrupting their lives within the context of centuries-old spiritual space.

Bush-head and Moroni perhaps best encapsulate this dichotomy and underscore its effects on the Paiutes. Bush-head personified Paiute antagonism. The historian Juanita Brooks called him a "menace" and "chief among the troublemakers" on the southwestern Mormon frontier. She blamed him for inciting other Indians to anger and for the "malicious attitudes" some of the Paiutes espoused.[35] Bush-head, in fact, masterminded Okus's assault on the Kentucky miner George Rogers in 1866. He reportedly prodded Okus into the deed when he told Okus that "he couldn't be a brave till he killed a white man."[36] Bush-head was thereby not only defending Paiute geographic space but its spiritual space as well. He incorporated Rogers as prey into the Paiute cosmology. Paiute rites of passage for adolescent boys centered on the hunt, generally in quest of rabbits, deer, antelope, or mountain sheep. In this case, however, the quarry became the next available Anglo invader.[37]

For Okus it clearly was a hunt. Like any good stalker, he waited patiently for five days before his game happened along. Rogers became a means to power for Okus within his own culture; the murder not only yielded its booty but also earned Okus status and manhood among his peers. He returned from his quest riding Rogers's horse, wearing his clothing, carrying his money, and bragging of the deed.[38]

Other Paiutes such as Moroni chose a conciliatory philosophy toward whites, emphasizing a different aspect of their worldview. These Paiutes defended their spiritual ground with what the religious historians David Chidester and Edward T. Linenthal call the "politics of exclusion"—"an integral part of the making of sacred space." For these Piautes it became essential to the "sanctity of the inside" to reinforce "boundaries that kept certain persons outside the sacred place"—even if it meant killing members of their own tribe to do so.[39]

The Paiute system of justice involved a strong sense of community values and emphasized expected behavior. In a chief's morning speech, he might exhort camp members to be friends or counsel them to be unified, and frequently he would cite "the actions of the ancients to give point to what he may say." In addition, elder members of the tribe "constantly inculcated habits of obedience in the younger." To the Paiutes, obedience was deemed "a great virtue," and an effective band leader commanded respect from his followers.[40]

Those who violated community standards were punished according to the nature of the crime. Sometimes members of the band harangued an accused person about his or her wrongdoings. Paiutes captured one woman who had run away from her husband and brought her back to her clan: "Each man in the band, one after another, walked up to her and, giving her a lecture on the enormity of her crime, struck her with a ramrod once." In other cases, Paiute custom allowed a person who had been wronged, or a relative, to seek retribution from the offender. With grave offenses such as murder, a person seeking equity could beat the accused with clubs or stones, burn his hair, or kill him.[41]

Moroni extended these aspects of Paiute law to include offenses against the invading Anglo-Americans. After capturing Bush-head near Clover Valley, the posse invited Moroni's band to witness Bush-head's execution. Moroni and his people accepted the offer and even participated in the event. Before the hanging, Moroni "preached to Bush-head in relation to his evil course" and informed the Mormons and miners that he considered the judgment just. Following Moroni's speech, Mormons, miners, and Paiutes looked on as Bush-head was hanged.[42] It was a moment wherein the three worldviews converged. Moroni signaled his willingness to mesh Paiute law with his de facto acceptance of white power.

Other Paiutes reacted similarly. In 1866, following some of the cattle raids along the Muddy River, Thomas and To-ish-obe informed the Mormons that their bands opposed the stealing but were unable to prevent it. Thomas S. Smith, leader of the Muddy Saints, lectured the Paiutes on the gravity of the crimes and their effect upon the settlers. Shortly thereafter, Thomas, To-ish-obe, and another chief held a counsel and agreed upon a survival strategy designed to save the main body of Paiutes. The three leaders concluded that the men who had instigated the recent forays were "outlaws" and determined that they should be punished. As a result, some Paiutes helped capture Co-quap, a leader among the pillagers, whom the Mormons then shot.[43] Thus, in the face of white power, some Paiutes used "the politics of exclusion" to eradicate a few aggressive Indians. In doing so they sacrificed individual Paiutes in an effort to preserve the entire tribe.

In June 1866, seven Paiute chiefs and sixty-four of their men held a council with Erastus Snow that solidified a conciliatory approach as the accepted policy toward the Mormons.[44] This did not put an end to Paiute hostility but clearly marked a turning point. The executions of Okus, Co-quap, and Bush-head, combined with the Mormons' and miners' retaliatory raids, had apparently been effective.

Even still, occasional confrontations between Paiutes and whites occurred over the next few years. In 1868, as Mormons began to move from their forts to reoccupy old lands and settle new towns, fresh troubles arose. When the Saints attempted to claim land along the upper Muddy River at West Point, the Paiutes held them in check. A band of angry Indians with blackened faces and armed with bows and arrows demanded that the Mormons pay for the land. An Indian interpreter, Andrew Gibbons, attempted to smooth over the troubles, but the settlers' rifles were apparently more effective than talk in keeping the confrontation from turning bloody. Once reports of the impasse reached Erastus Snow, he ordered a retreat. Informants told Snow that the Muddy Indians had about twenty acres of wheat planted near the new town and that the Mormon livestock "running at large" would likely damage those crops. This would no doubt create "difficulties" between "the brethren and the natives," which Snow believed were best to avoid. He ordered the temporary dispossession of West Point. Paiutes also intimidated Mormons at Junction City, a new port town on the Colorado, helping force its abandonment.[45]

By 1869, Paiutes had developed an equal distrust of miners, which led the Shivwits band to murder. When Oramel and Seneca Howland and William Dunn, three of the explorer John Wesley Powell's men, became frightened by the treacherous nature of their Colorado River expedition, they determined to hike out of the river gorge and walk to safety. In course of their pursuit they came upon a Shivwits band of Paiutes whose members supplied them with food and pointed the way to the Mormon settlements. Shortly after the white men left, however, an Indian from the east side of the Colorado River arrived at the Shivwits camp with disturbing news. The informant told the Shivwits "about a number of miners having killed a squaw in a drunken brawl" and concluded that Powell's men were the perpetrators. The visitor insisted that "no person had ever come down the canyon; that was impossible"; the three whites had lied about being explorers and were merely "trying to hide their guilt." His speech agitated the Shivwits "into a great rage." In response, band members followed Powell's men, surrounded them in an ambush, and "filled them full of arrows." Tem-piute Bill's band similarly attacked lone prospectors west of Pahranagat as late as 1875.[46]

By the early 1870s, however, it seems that Paiute aggression had largely given way to other means of relieving the stressful conditions confronting the tribe.[47] At times the Paiutes used the gentiles and Mormons to their advantage. When Powell and his party toured the area in 1871–72, they disbursed "blankets, shirts, cotton cloth, drill, a few pieces of blue flannel, butcher knives, and some hoes, axes and shovels" to members of the Shivwits, Santa Clara, and Kaibab bands. Following this distribution, one Paiute leader, Old Moqueop, gave a speech to his people, urging them "that they must be good 'wano' Indians or the Americans would make them no more presents."[48] At least some of the Paiutes must have followed this advice. By 1875, the Indian agent A. J. Barnes complained that the Indians in his charge "have for so long a time been in the habit of receiving blankets, clothing, &c., from the Government . . . that they believe the Government is bound to provide for them under any and all circumstances."[49]

Other Paiutes used different methods to obtain material goods. On three days in March 1875, 166 members of the Shivwits band entered the Mormon waters of baptism. Church leaders also ritually blessed an additional twenty-six Shivwits children who were not deemed old enough for baptism according to Mormon custom.[50] Perhaps influencing these events, Taú-gu, or as the Mormons called him, Coal Creek John, had recently been baptized and ordained an elder in the LDS priesthood. He thereby gained acceptance into Mormon circles. John preached at a St. George conference, and Brigham Young himself signed a letter of introduction for him. The letter certified John's standing in the Church and instructed Mormon leaders that "Coal Creek John is authorized to preach the Gospel of Jesus Christ to his people of the Lamanites and to baptize and lay hands on them in the Name of Jesus, and to teach and encourage them in every good word and work." It also asked southern

Utah "Bishops and leading men and all Saints to encourage him in the faithful performance of his duties."[51]

Brigham Young apparently perceived a movement afoot among the Paiutes that was bigger than Coal Creek John's baptism. In response he sent a circular letter throughout the region instructing local leaders to aid the Paiutes in adopting "more of the customs and usages of civilized life, by devoting themselves to farming and other labors." Young told the Saints to furnish the Paiutes with "land and implements and patient considerate instruction where needed; and use them in such . . . labors . . . as may be advantageous to them and to you." He further admonished his followers to "act as missionaries to bring about the time when [the Indians] may be called a white and delightsome people."[52]

The mass baptisms at St. George took place only one month following the circulation of Young's letter. One Mormon account attributed the event to "the result of some supernatural influence" working among the Paiutes.[53] The Indian agent A. J. Barnes, a Baptist, saw it differently. To him the ritual was performed "with all the pomp, ceremony, and display calculated to make an impression on the Indian." He described the scene this way: "The Mormon bishop in the center, up to his waist in water; hundreds of dusky forms all around him, while a vast concourse of saints looked approvingly on." More upsetting to Barnes than the actual event, however, was its sequel. "Every Indian who participated in this farce," he complained, "thinks he is a better Mormon to-day than Brigham Young himself, and that the ceremony alluded to has clothed him with a sort of armor against any responsibility which he may incur for such trifling matters as horse stealing, or other petty thefts. If he be caught in an overt act, he proudly exclaims, 'Me good Mormon Indian; me heap wash.'"[54]

The baptized Paiutes, as Barnes saw it, were not truly committed to a changed path but rather used their new faith as a shield. Other Indian agents described similar mass baptisms elsewhere in Utah in 1875 and claimed that Mormon invitations were general throughout the territory. One agent alleged that the Mormons made many promises to induce the Indians to be baptized and called it a "corruption akin to the spirit actuating the famed Mountain Meadow massacre."[55]

Although the Indians' motivation is difficult to ascertain, for the Shivwits it may have been as simple as food, blankets, and labor opportunities. Following the largest day of baptisms at St. George, the local Saints collected "food to sustain [the Paiutes] for the time they remained." The first Sunday after the baptisms, a "goodly number of Indians" attended church services and listened to Erastus Snow advise the Saints "to give employment to as many of those natives as can be got to work." Zaidee Walker, a Mormon boy of twelve at the time of the baptisms, much later recalled that the Shivwits returned to St. George on another occasion again asking for baptism—with its accompanying food and clothing.[56]

Regardless of the benefits, some Paiutes avoided Mormonism altogether. In 1878 a Paiute nicknamed "Buck" visited Pioche after spending time at St. George. He reported that the Mormons in that neighborhood had been telling the Indians to "get baptized," "that God come by' me by and kill all the Indians." As a result of such preaching, Buck declared, "'heap Indians swim.'" As for Buck, he told the Mormon Bishop, "'You gib me six white sequaws, me heap swim; you no gib me six white sequaws, me no swim.'" The Pioche newspaper concluded that "as Buck wasn't baptized we presume the Bishop wanted all the white 'sequaws' for himself."[57]

Other Paiutes found additional ways to negotiate the new complexity of their ever-changing cosmos. Many Paiutes sold their labor at mining camps and Mormon towns, which became the predominate mode of Paiute interaction with whites from the 1870s into the twentieth century. Their neighbors employed them at menial tasks for wages at a rate one-third to one-half of those paid non-Indians. Nonetheless, those Paiutes who found work among the Mormons and miners demonstrated a willingness to adapt, which no doubt helped preserve their lives and may have offered a more stable existence than otherwise available. For the Southern Paiutes, wage labor "was a radically new way of living." Even still, the anthropologist Martha C. Knack contends that "it shared many characteristics with the Native economy that enabled compatibility with continued hunting and gathering." The Paiutes could therefore absorb wage labor into "a mixed system," which allowed them to utilize a "diversity of economic resources." They blended traditional foraging with reservation farming, cattle herding, and wage labor to create a new economy that reflected the stark truths of their altered environment.[58]

Even though those truths were often harsh for the Paiutes, they responded with remarkable flexibility in ways that served their best interest. As Knack claims, "[W]age work *was* the rational choice, and Paiutes made it." That choice altered the Paiute economy as well as the Anglo-American one. Early on, Mormons and miners found it difficult to live without Indian labor. "Within ten years of initial settlement," Knack asserts, "many whites were expressing dependence on Southern Paiute labor."[59] Such was the case at Pioche, when the piñon harvest of 1875 occupied the Paiutes away from town. The newspaper advised its readers who had been employing Indians to "do your own work for a month or two."[60] During another piñon harvest, the *Record* lamented: "Yes, an Indian is a rare thing in Pioche, and . . . is greatly missed by many of our residents. Those who wish his services cutting wood and doing chores miss him, and the poor house wife, having dislocated her back bone bending over the washtub, wearied and tired at night, heaves a heavy sigh and wishes the nasty squaws would return." "The usefulness of the Indian," the newspaper concluded, "will hereafter be appreciated."[61]

The type of work that the Paiutes performed varied widely. For women it included harvesting crops, washing clothes, and cleaning, while the men cut wood, built roads, tended cattle, and cultivated fields.[62] At Pahranagat, a few Indians worked as mail carriers, bridging the communication gap between that remote camp and the Nevada interior.[63] Paiutes at Eagle Valley did "considerable chores for the settlers, and farm[ed] a little on their own account."[64] Likewise, a group of Paiutes lived with a Mormon rancher, James Holt, where they farmed and worked on his ranch.[65] A family of "friendly Indians" headed by Brush-head worked for the ranchers at Hebron, "watching on the frontiers" of their herds and serving as guards. Hebronites generally paid the Indians in beef or other non-cash items, which, in John Pulsipher's mind, helped the band "live much better than the wild Indians."[66] Three Paiutes took jobs with Lyman Lafayette Woods of Clover Valley, where they helped him haul lumber and mining timber to Pioche. A few skilled Paiutes also broke horses for Mormons at Panaca.[67]

This employment offered Paiutes opportunities to bridge cultural gaps and defend Indian ways. An incident at Pioche perhaps best illustrates this point: On 24 March 1873, a Shoshone Indian known as Captain Andy entered a house on Lacour Street. He emerged dragging Jennie, a Shoshone woman, who was "screaming at the top of her voice." A passerby, seeing the trouble, interfered, knocking Captain Andy over with "three stunning blows." Freed from Andy's grasp, Jennie ran in desperation back toward the house, with Andy, only temporarily detained, lunging after her. By this time, a crowd, "many of whom were Indians," had gathered to watch the fracas. A story quickly circulated among the white onlookers that "Captain Andy wanted to get the squaw out to kill her for infidelity, according to the Shoshone and Piute custom." Officer McKee arrived shortly and attempted to arrest Andy, who outran the officer and fled from town. McKee pursued on horseback, and following an exchange of gunfire, returned to Pioche with Andy in tow. Once securely in jail, public opinion mounted against Andy. Most townspeople became convinced that his "object in trying to get the woman beyond the city limits was to murder her."

The *Pioche Record*, however, dug a little deeper. In a rare moment of intercultural insight, the newspaper "succeeded in getting the Indians' side of the question, which presents it in an entirely different light." Bill Robinson, a half-Paiute, half-Shoshone Indian, claimed that Jennie was mother to a newborn infant, whom she had left back at her wickiup a few miles northwest of the city. The baby, at the time of the incident, was "suffering for that nutriment which the mother only could give." Robinson further explained that "Captain Andy was exercising his authority as sub-chief to make her go and relieve her child." Jennie had never been accused of infidelity, and her life was not in danger. Robinson posited that she might have been whipped for leaving her infant to famish, but she would not have been killed. After hearing this version, the newspaper declared itself "glad" that McKee had spared Captain Andy's life. Andy spent two nights in jail, after which McKee let him go, "there being no complaint entered against him."[68]

This and other reports from Pioche suggest that there was a significant Shoshone and Paiute presence in the town. By 1880 each tribe had established camps about a mile outside of town where twenty to thirty families resided.[69] Although the *Pioche Record* frequently described these Indians as "vagrants" and "red vagabonds," it seems that some of them earned wages as well as respect at the mining camp.[70] In the case of Bill Robinson, he was able to use his influence to smooth over a potentially volatile affair and likely saved Captain Andy's life.

By no means does this imply that the Paiutes enjoyed relationships of equality with either the Mormons or miners. Even though at Pioche and Pahranagat it was Paiutes who first showed whites the silver, the Paiutes later only worked at the mining towns in subordinate roles. Likewise, despite a long history as agriculturalists, the Paiutes worked on Mormon farms, not the reverse. The Indian agent Barnes in 1875 best described the cruel truths facing the Paiutes: "Their lands have been taken from them by the whites save a few small patches and there being no game, and unable to raise enough food by farming, they have frequently been compelled to beg and steal." The mining camps offered some hope, Barnes noted, but not enough: "Quite a large number have always found work among the mining settlers and are greatly needed by the whites for laborers, but the *larger portion* can never find any legitimate means of a living." The destitution of some of the Indians had grown so extreme, Barnes sympathized, that "their women are often induced to prostitute themselves to the lusts of a certain class of men, in order to secure means to support themselves and families."[71]

For Barnes, the solution was to induce the Paiutes to the Moapa Reservation, where he hoped to build a better world for them. In 1875, however, Barnes was appointed Indian agent over the entire Nevada agency and transferred to its headquarters at Pyramid Lake. Following his departure, Moapa suffered from neglect and corruption, and the Paiutes largely fended for themselves. In 1880, when James E. Spencer took over the Nevada agency, he traveled to Moapa to investigate conditions there. His report chronicled a "painful history" of failure: He found the buildings "dilapidated," the farm implements "worn out or long ago fallen to pieces," and the reservation "entirely deserted by the Indians." The Paiutes had "scattered over the surrounding country for 200 miles around, eking out a precarious existence by working, begging, root-digging, and insect-eating—a life not of their choice." "Wisely or unwisely," he wrote, "not one Indian has resided on the reservation to be demoralized by the sad spectacle thus presented of the white man's waning civilization."[72]

With the Moapa Reservation offering no inducement to stay, the Paiutes entered what the anthropologist Ronald L. Holt calls "the bitter years." From the mid 1870s to the early twentieth century, they withdrew farther and farther into the desert, occasionally attaching themselves to white settlements, while their population dwindled from disease and poverty.[73] In most cases, they were trapped as laborers in an Anglo-American economy, or worse still forced to beg or steal to survive. As Holt sees it, by the early 1900s the Paiutes had lost their autonomy and had declined into "a tiny, powerless minority."[74]

The last two decades of the nineteenth century were bitter for the Paiutes, but dismissing the bands as powerless hides a remarkable portion of their story. Largely left to their own devices, the Paiutes engaged in subtle defenses of their space, each band clinging with tenacity to its traditional domain. It was a strategy that the Paiutes had formulated as early as the 1860s in response to governmental pressure to go to reservations, and one that they perfected over the ensuing decades. The Paiutes employed everyday forms of resistance, the most effective of which was simply staying on their land. Their sheer survival is testament to their determination and ample proof of an unyielding devotion to the ground at the center of their world.

As early as 1865, when Sale first discussed removal to a reservation, the Paiutes held tightly to their space.[75] Even though some Paiutes readily acquiesced in the reservation system—a move that the anthropologist Robert C. Euler suggests reflected "the stress conditions" under which they operated—they still insisted that its implementation be on *their* terms. They argued not only against removal to Uintah but against a single reservation for the various bands. They informed Powell and Ingalls that "each small tribe" desired to "have a reservation somewhere within the limits of its own territory." Some Paiutes were willing, in other words, to accept reservation life as a means of obtaining "a more secure land base," but only if it meant staying on their homelands.[76]

Other Paiutes opposed reservations altogether. In 1874, Taú-gu (Coal Creek John) traveled to Pioche and explained his band's position. His people found the Muddy Reservation an "irksome" restraint and had no desire to live there. Instead, they wanted to stay on their land, "around the springs of Southern Utah and Nevada—where they could cultivate their little patches of corn and vegetables and get along as best they could." John concluded that the Paiutes could "manage better for themselves if they were let alone."[77]

Powell and Ingalls dismissed such proposals as "manifestly impracticable," as did other agents after them. The government demanded that its relationship with the Paiutes be channeled through the reservation system.[78] The Nevada superintendent twice proposed moving the Southern Paiutes to the Walker River or Pyramid Lake Reservations and combining them with the Northern Paiutes at one of those sites. Nothing ever came of those suggestions, however.[79] Meanwhile, the Paiutes struggled to maintain a grip on their ground. In late 1880, John Wesley Powell received a letter from Jacob Hamblin, his former guide and interpreter among the Paiutes. Hamblin wrote on behalf of the Kaibab Paiutes in the hope of securing assistance for their "'very destitute circumstances.'" "'Fertile places are now being occupied by the white population,'" he explained, "'thus cutting off all their means of subsistence except game, which you are aware is quite limited.'" Hamblin requested that Powell send "'some surplus merchandise for the immediate relief of their utter destitution.'" Powell's response, however, was clearly drafted to shore up the reservation system. It would be "'impossible to do anything for the Indians in that region'" unless they reported at either the Uintah or Muddy Valley Reservations. "'Indians who do not report at Agencies are not assisted,'" Powell flatly declared.[80]

For the Paiutes, the Uintah Reservation was simply not acceptable, and given the state of affairs at Moapa, neither was that agency. The Kaibab group, therefore, stayed on its land, as did the other Paiute bands. Over time, their perseverence won out; they forged their own economic ties with local whites independent of government oversight. In 1887, when an inspector arrived at Moapa, he found it nearly deserted. He reported that the Paiutes were scattered over "'the surrounding country for 200 miles in all directions from the Reserve, *making their own living,* some among the Mormon farmers others in the Mines.'"[81]

By the turn of the century the Paiute link to the white economy grew
so strong that when the federal government finally established reservations for the Paiutes, some whites even resisted.[82] In 1907, Washington
officials sent Frank Churchill to northern Arizona to buy land for the
Kaibab Paiutes, and he learned this for himself. He related that "as soon
as it was noised about that my errand was to confer with Indians, I was
waited upon by a number of the principal people of Kanab, who objected
strenuously to the Indians being removed from their vicinity, as . . . they
relied upon both the men & women as laborers."[83] Other whites, however, supported the creation of reservations, especially as shifts in the
economy dried up the need for Paiute workers.[84]

Still, the Paiutes dredged new channels of power for themselves.
As the government created their reservations, it no longer attempted
to relocate the various bands in one place. Paiute endurance earned for
them what Powell and Ingalls had originally deemed "manifestly impracticable." The government established for nearly "each small tribe" a
"reservation somewhere within the limits of its own territory" (Shivwits,
1891; Kaibab, 1907; Chemehuevi, 1907; San Juan, 1907; Las Vegas, 1911;
Indian Peaks, 1915; Koosharem, 1928; Kanosh, 1929).[85] It was something
that the Paiutes had negotiated for in 1873 but only gained piecemeal
after the turn of the century. Through accommodation, flexibility, withdrawal, and everyday resistance, the Chemehuevi, Shivwits, Moapa, Las
Vegas, Koosharem, Kanosh, Kaibab, Indian Peaks, Cedar City, and San
Juan bands survived the press of forces bearing down upon them and
stayed on their lands.

When considered within the broader context of nineteenth-century
Indian removal, the Paiute experience is unique. Single reserves and
violent roundups characterized the larger story, but the Paiutes avoided
such a fate. By the turn of the twentieth century the Paiute world had
changed drastically, but even as reservations came to dot their ground,
Paiutes still defined its cultural borders for themselves. Economically,
many Paiutes continued to earn their own way, largely out of sheer necessity. The new reservations were small and the land marginal at best.
In fact, "[A]t no time did more than one-half of the Southern Paiute
population live on reservations, and it was not until the 1930s that the
majority was even enrolled."[86]

Perhaps Simon's experience is representative of how at least some Paiutes managed. Simon grew up near Hebron in the 1860s and 1870s, where
he cultivated a lasting friendship with Dudley Henry Leavitt, a Mormon
boy his age. Decades later, sometime after the turn of the century, Simon
found his old friend "Hen," then living at Bunkerville in southeastern

Nevada. Juanita Brooks, Leavitt's young daughter, recalled the occasion as her father came home and found Simon waiting there: "They came together with a real impact. They did not shake hands; they gave each other a genuine hug." At dinner the friends reminisced about old times. Leavitt told his family, "'I've eat at Simon's house lots-a times. He was my best friend. We used to herd cows together. We would rastle and run and chase chipmunks and lizards. We never quarreled.'" He explained that "'at Hebron there were more Indians than white men. I played with other Indian children, but Simon was special. He stuck up for me, and I stuck up for him.'" As the two men enjoyed the evening together Simon shared the purpose for his visit. He wanted to borrow Leavitt's rifle: "'I go up to top of mountain purty soon. High up. By Noon Peak. Maybe see mountain sheep up there. You know, big sheep with crooked horn.'" Leavitt unhesitatingly lent Simon his gun, along with a box of bullets, and the Paiute walked out of town.

Nearly a month later, Simon again appeared at the Leavitt house, this time proudly to report on a successful hunt. He returned Leavitt's gun and box of bullets, with only three missing, and left a gunnysack filled with roasted pine nuts in gratitude.[87] Clearly, Simon found his own solution to what were likely difficult circumstances. He drew upon resources that incorporated aspects of old Paiute ways as well as acknowledged that the Paiute world had changed.

In negotiating the complex cultural world that redefined their space, Paiutes relied upon various aspects of their cosmology. Long ago, To-go-av admonished two fawns, "When you are in trouble listen not to a stranger but go to your friends for advice." Such counsel was important to the Paiutes for more than its guidance regarding outsiders; it also reflects the prominence that the Paiute worldview played in defending their soil. The Paiutes acted within a spiritually based framework. "Homeland" is a profound concept to native peoples: "It encompasses their personal and cultural identities, their histories, and their religions,"[88] "the ultimate relatedness of all life on earth."[89]

The attempts of government officials to redefine Paiute space clearly failed to take this into account. For most of the nineteenth century, the Moapa Reservation proved useless to the Paiutes. They therefore reinvented their economic space, incorporating their new neighbors into a mixed system. While that system fixed the Paiutes at the lowest rung of the white economic ladder, it opened fresh ways to supplement a subsistence economy. More importantly, it allowed Paiutes to stay on their homelands. In Bill Robinson's case, the economic interaction carried additional benefits, as it offered opportunity to defend Indian ways. For the Paiutes as a whole, it also proved valuable in gaining white allies who grew dependent upon Indian labor.

Most notably, the Paiutes acted out their story on a stage of their own making. Perhaps Orsemus H. Irish said it best in 1865. In recommending that a permanent agency be established for the Paiutes, he deftly noted that it should be done "without reference to Territorial lines which the Indians do not regard."[90] The Paiutes proved him right. They were much more than passive bystanders as Mormons, miners, and government officials attempted to reshape their world. They actively defended their space, while simultaneously modifying it to include the outsiders who had come to live among them. As To-go-av instructed, they largely relied upon each other for strength. Some killed the strangers, while others befriended them, but most simply found ways to survive in spite of them. In each case the Paiutes acted as independent agents in the new intercultural space that settled in at the southern rim of the Great Basin. Along with their Mormon and mining neighbors, they fashioned a world-between-worlds where their lives intersected, quite apart from political or reservation boundaries.

5 "To Hold in Check
Outside Influences"

The Mormon apostle Erastus Snow toured the fringe settlements of the Cotton Mission in southwestern Utah and southeastern
Nevada in July 1869. His trip took him to Hebron, Clover Valley, Panaca,
Eagle Valley, and Spring Valley, a string of ranching outposts that, in the
words of Snow, formed a "frontier line" close to the mines of soon-to-be
Pioche. Snow recorded his assessment of the region in a letter to Brigham Young, noting that "notwithstanding their proximity to the mines
and a periodical influx of adventurers, the people, generally, with a few
exceptions seem to be striving to live their religion." Nonetheless, Snow
perceived that these folk of the fringe were vulnerable and advised that
they "need the watch care of a . . . thorough and efficient man." That
man, Snow clarified, should be someone who had "a little knowledge of
law as well as gospel" and more importantly, someone who possessed
"practical sense and wisdom to hold in check outside influences."[1]

Although it is not clear that Snow ever found his man, the policy he
dictated—"to hold in check outside influences"—came to characterize
the nature of Mormon settlement on its southwestern edge. The five
villages that formed that "frontier line" spent much of their nineteenth-
century existence posturing defensively, not only against miners at Pioche
but also against the Southern Paiutes. The tale that follows explores the
complexity of the Mormon defense, first against the miners and then
against the Paiutes. It also seeks to understand the nature of the Saints'

involvement in the intercultural space that they, along with the miners and Paiutes, helped to build.

More than the Paiutes, the Mormons were directly affected by the political lines that limited Zion's borders. They spent considerable energy attempting to safeguard their geographic and communal space against the perceived threat of mining. Over time, Mormon defensive tactics, like those of the Paiutes, were plagued with inconsistencies and evolved to meet the changing circumstances of frontier life. The Saints, nonetheless, were committed to their cause; it was more a spiritual contest than a geographic, economic, or political one for them, with eternal implications. When miners moved in, it was easy for frontier Mormons to cast the contest as a struggle between the kingdom of God and that of the devil.

Brigham Young defined his kingdom largely in relationship to gentiles. At a counsel meeting in July 1847, four days after his arrival in the Salt Lake Valley, Young articulated a policy that he would spend the rest of his life encouraging his flock to follow: "'We do not intend to have any trade or commerce with the gentile world, for so long as we buy of them we are in a degree dependent upon them. The Kingdom of God cannot rise independent of the gentile nations until we produce, manufacture, and make every article of use, convenience, or necessity among our own people.'" He further expressed his determination to "'cut every thread'" connecting the Saints to the gentiles and vowed to "'live free and independent, untrammeled by any of their detestable customs and practices.'"[2]

In essence, Young erected a rhetorical wall around his western Zion that divided space between Mormon and gentile, the sacred and the "detestable" profane. Historians have primarily focused upon the Mormon capital as the site where outside influences eroded Zion's communitarian space, thereby dragging Utah into mainstream American political, economic, and social worlds by the end of the nineteenth century. Even Mormon leaders perceived a corrosive force at work in Salt Lake City. In 1865, Heber C. Kimball, first counselor to Brigham Young, declared to a Centerville, Utah, congregation: "I admit that the people are better in the country towns than in Great Salt Lake City, for the froth and scum of hell seem to concentrate there, and those who live in the City have to come in contact with it; and with persons who mingle with robbers, and liars, and thieves, and with whores and whore-masters, etc."[3] Even though Salt Lake City bore the brunt of the gentile impact, the contest over Zion's soul also engulfed Utah's southwestern frontier. In fact, due to the physical separation of gentile and Mormon towns, southern Utah leaders could more clearly draw lines meant to divorce the good from the evil.

Mormons attempted to defend those lines on a variety of levels. Initially the battle raged geopolitical, as frontier Saints jostled with miners over land and resources in the wake of silver discoveries and the shifting Utah/Nevada/Arizona border. After 1870, however, Pioche burst to life and rapidly assumed regional economic importance. Thereafter the contest over land for the Mormons devolved into an effort to resolve conflicting temporal and spiritual concerns. The Saints struggled to define the terms of their contact with Pioche; many of the faithful, including Brigham Young, cuddled with it economically while declaring themselves spiritually repulsed. It was a problem that southern Utah Mormons learned to live with but never fully resolved.

On the geopolitical front, the Saints sought to outmaneuver the gentiles and claim the best land for Zion. Mormon concern over its southwestern fringe directly correlated with the attention that miners showed the region. The number of Nevada settlements quadrupled during the 1860s, as the lure of gold and silver, the horrors of the Civil War, and the construction of the transcontinental railroad combined to increase the flow of people into the Far West.[4] In June 1864, when a portion of that flow spilled into the Meadow Valley District, Erastus Snow expressed anxiety over the Saints' ability to occupy the land and its resources for Zion. Snow himself had filed on the silver at Meadow Valley and then directed the founding of Panaca. He instructed settlers there to lay claim to the "principle lead" in the vicinity and exhorted them to "build up a clean thriving respectable town first, and then, if they mined, let it be secondary consideration in their feelings and works."[5]

Even still, Snow felt "satisfied that it is the intention of General Connor and other gentiles to settle there, and not only claim the mines of silver in that vicinity, but also the farming lands, water privileges, etc. in those and surrounding valleys." In light of such a threat, Snow "deemed it wise to strengthen those settlements and to send a man there to preside." He selected John Nebeker, then living at Toquerville, for that purpose, along with "about twenty-five individuals that were comparatively foot loose in the Southern settlements." Snow instructed them to "hold claim to the most desirable locations in those upper valleys" but still worried that the Dixie Saints did not have the strength and numbers to "fill up and occupy" the area. He hoped that Young might send settlers from the north to possess the land surrounding the mines.[6]

Mormon attention again turned to the region in 1866, this time in response to the Pahranagat rush. One report from Muddy Valley noted that "the Herd Ground at the Muddy Springs has been staked out by Gentiles," but promised to "reverse this." Ira Hatch similarly disclosed that another valley along the Muddy appeared "to be in danger of being occupied by the Gentiles." He added that the Pahranagat miners were "going in all directions hunting new country and new roads" and had "taken up nearly all the land."[7] Farther north, Mormons at Eagle Valley helped explore and claim the adjacent Spring Valley, "with the view of holding it" until a survey could be made. The Eagle Valley brethren were "alive" to the importance of retaining the valley but felt weak in numbers.[8]

That perceived deficiency was amplified in 1869 when prospectors returned to Meadow Valley and shortly founded Pioche. One Mormon soon grew uneasy, noting that "the Panaca mining district is considerably agitated at the present time; the miners are coming in very fast. They think there will be five thousand men in the mines this summer. Some of them talk of jumping land in the Valley."[9] By the end of 1869, the Cotton Mission secretary James Bleak summed up the Saints' apprehension this way: "This year activity in mining at Pioche has caused numerous companies of miners to look with greed on Meadow Valley. They acted in a very lawless manner, frequently threatening to dispossess the actual settlers, and otherwise deporting themselves in an offensive manner." To make matters worse, the miners not only poured into Pioche but also founded Bullionville, a mill town only a mile outside of Panaca.[10] No wonder Erastus Snow looked with concern upon the region. John Nebeker, the man he had sent to preside there five years earlier, neglected his call. "Occasionally he visited these settlements," Snow complained, "but made no move to locate there, and I released him. Not for the want of ability but because the mission was irksome to him." In consequence, Snow brooded over the area and wondered how best to hold it.[11]

Things grew increasingly complicated when the Utah/Nevada border sliced through the middle of the Mormon outposts. The 1870 government survey finally determined the boundary, severing Panaca, Clover, Eagle, Spring, and Muddy Valley settlements from Utah. As early as 1867, Nevada officials had attempted to collect taxes from the Saints in those towns, payable in only U.S. gold and silver coin. The cash-poor Mormons refused the assessments, at least until they knew for sure that they actually lived in Nevada. In the meantime, they continued to pay taxes, in kind, to Utah.[12] The Lincoln County sheriff in late 1869 attempted to force the issue when he served a summons on the settlers for delinquent taxes. An angry Erastus Snow told the frontier Saints to take their Utah tax receipts to the Lincoln County courthouse, then at Hiko, and to "arm, and defend your property if necessary." A few days later, after pursuing more diplomatic alternatives, Snow mellowed his counsel. He told the Saints to "keep down any violent measure" until the government survey fixed the boundary location. In the meantime, he instigated legal and political action in an effort to protect Zion's border.[13]

The situation again threatened to boil over later that year. According to Mormon accounts, in early August the deputy sheriff from Pioche, accompanied by three men, walked into the Mormon cooperative store at Panaca and demanded a list of the store's goods, "with a view to exact license in behalf of the State of Nevada." When the clerk refused to produce a list, the men from Pioche drew and cocked their guns, read a summons, ordered the clerk and bystanders from the store, and then locked the door. They left one man with the key to stand guard while the other three returned to Pioche. Word of the incident spread quickly at Panaca. Mormon men armed themselves and sent the town constable after the key, which he recovered "without any remonstrance." The summons, nonetheless, demanded that an agent for the store appear before the justice of the peace at Pioche on 11 August. Leaders at Panaca advised the men to "stand their ground, and sue a writ of injunction when opportunity offers."[14]

The tension was no doubt palpable the following month when the Lincoln County assessor, N. H. Carlow, himself an apostate Mormon, made his tax rounds. Nearly every Mormon either refused to give him a list of property or did so under protest.[15] At Panaca, Carlow noted a few responses to his visit: Thomas J. Jones "refuses to give list" and "is bitter"; John N. Lee "refuses to give list" and "attempted violence"; and feisty Mother Lee "refused to give list" and then "ordered assessor out of her house."[16]

For the Mormons, however, taxes were only one aspect of the struggle. They were building God's kingdom, a geographic as well as spiritual task. The frontier for them became a barrier against the outside world, and it required manpower to defend it. Thus, Meltiar Hatch, a local leader at Eagle Valley, sent a representative to Hiko to answer for the Saints on the tax matter but still fretted about holding the land for Zion. "Miners are flocking to Pioche by hundreds and threatening to take and hold, all this country if possible," he worried. "Miners are roving around the country laying claim to the hills and timber in every direction. We are doing all we can, but we feel we are weak handed, we have not men sufficient."[17] No doubt desiring to attract more settlers from the north, another Mormon, J. A. Little, wrote to the *Deseret News* in Salt Lake City extolling Eagle, Meadow, and Spring Valleys' potential: "'These valleys afford excellent facilities for industrious Saints to make homes. There is an abundance of good land unoccupied, with good water, and an unlimited amount of firewood and fencing, a large proportion of meadow land, and an extensive range for stock.'" The valleys, Little promised, contain everything necessary "'to make Saints comfortable and happy.'" The land was not only suited to produce earthly delight, however. For the Mormons, like the Paiutes, it embodied spiritual ground with eternal importance: "'[W]e expect to see these fertile valleys teeming with a dense population,'" Little hoped, "'that will love God and keep His commandments, fitting themselves for association with angels and gods.'"[18]

Those lofty aspirations soon collided with the realities of the frontier. When government surveyors finished their work in December 1870, they rendered further Mormon resistence futile. Each of the fringe settlements except Hebron found itself in Nevada. For the beleaguered settlers along the Muddy, Nevada's oppressive taxes offered an excuse for abandonment.[19] Brigham Young personally visited the Muddy River towns and, after thoroughly examining the region, left dissatisfied. One settler recorded, "[T]here was nothing on the Muddy nor the Colorado that pleased the president," and another quoted Young as saying, "'[I]f the Gentiles wanted that country they were welcome to it.'" Young later counseled the colonizers to decide by vote the fate of their towns. The vast majority chose to withdraw into Utah.[20]

The Mormons surrounding Pioche, however, chose a different option. "No doubt you will find the burden of taxation in Nevada very onerous," Snow advised them. "You will, . . . therefore, feel . . . at liberty to determine for yourselves whether to sell out, as opportunity offers and leave the State or remain." Even still, Snow shrewdly noted an incentive to stay: "[T]he advantages of market afforded by your proximity to the mines would enable you to pay the Nevada taxes much easier than the brethren of the Muddy can do."[21] Some from Panaca and the other western valleys did return to Utah, but the majority persisted. They successfully breached the new cultural divide embodied in the advancing boundary to form small outposts of Zion sprinkled within the newly defined borders of Gomorrah. They survived, for a time at least, enjoying the benefit of Pioche's mining boom. Many worked as traders and freighters and welcomed cash payments into a cash-poor Mormon economy.[22]

With the boundary question settled, Mormon defensive strategy veered from a geographic concern over Zion's land base toward a spiritual anxiety over Zion's soul. Settlers at the outposts seemed to resign themselves to the fact that Pioche was there to stay. Erastus Snow even made peace with the idea. He visited in 1872, met with Raymond and

Ely, and according to Mormon accounts was treated "very kindly."[23]
Nonetheless, Snow returned to St. George and continued to paint the
raucous camp darkly. In essence, southern Utah Mormons worked out
a defense filled with inconsistency. Economically they enthusiastically
embraced Pioche; spiritually, however, they viewed it as a threat to Zion,
the embodiment of a modern-day Babylon.

Brigham Young's mining policy, replete with contradictions of its
own, no doubt lay at the heart of the frontier settlers' stance. Young had
long preached, warned, threatened, and cajoled the Saints to avoid seeking temporal wealth. During the California gold rush he told his followers, "[Y]ou will do better right here than you will by going to the gold
mines." "As for gold and silver, and the rich minerals of the earth," he
added, "there is no other country that equals this; but let them alone;
let others seek them, and we will cultivate the soil."[24] A *Deseret News*
editorial echoed these sentiments. "'The digging of gold is a feverish,
ignoble pursuit,'" it declared. "'We can think of no labor that is not
positively dishonorable, the effects of which are more degrading than
gold digging.'"[25] Mormon scripture emphasizes the same theme. Book
of Mormon prophets blame "riches," such as gold and silver and "all
manner of precious things," for the "great sorrow" that came into the
ancient American church. Its adherents occasionally were "lifted up in
the pride of their eyes, and . . . set their hearts upon riches and upon the
vain things of the world."[26] Such pride generally brought wars, bloodshed,
and calamities upon the Book of Mormon peoples, a lesson that must
have resonated with Young's anti-mining diatribes.

Such evidence notwithstanding, the historian Leonard J. Arrington
contends that Brigham Young and the Latter-day Saints were "never opposed to mining, . . . even to the mining of gold and silver." Young himself
sent several Saints on a clandestine mission to the California gold fields
in the hope of building the Church treasury and sustaining the coinage of
gold. Young additionally organized salt, sulfur, silver, lead, iron, and coal
mining operations as part of his effort to build a self-reliant kingdom.[27]

Despite the Saints' involvement in a variety of extractive ventures,
Young remained an outspoken critic of mining. Broadly speaking, it was
a matter of control, an important distinction in understanding Young's
anti-mining stance. It was not so much the act of mining that Young
disliked as it was the individualism, instability, and social stratification
that the search for wealth tended to breed. The boom-and-bust cycle of
mining also deterred him. He was building a permanent home for his
flock and needed sustainable and reliable resources. As long as mining
operations existed for the benefit of Zion and could be managed on the

cooperative plan, Young approved. Erastus Snow explained the distinction this way: "If the mines must be worked, it is better for the saints to
work them than for others to do it, but we have all the time prayed that
the Lord would shut up the mines. It is better for us to live in peace and
good order, and to raise wheat, corn, potatoes and fruit, than to suffer
the evils of a mining life."[28] Young's nemesis, Patrick Connor, hoped to
use mining as a detriment to Zion, which also required Young to warn
his flock against prospecting.[29]

Thus, after the silver at Meadow Valley slipped from Mormon hands,
it was easy for Young and other leaders to assign Pioche a spot in the
devil's kingdom and begin defending Zion on spiritual grounds. Young
equated kingdom building to sacred toil anyway. "To me all labors are
spiritual," he declared to southern Utah Mormons. "[O]ur labor is one
eternal spiritual work."[30] Defending Zion's borders, therefore, held celestial implications. Once gentiles controlled the southern region's mineral
deposits, Snow and Young began establishing defensive walls around
the Mormon outposts closest to the mines. If they could not possess the
mines for Zion, they felt strongly about avoiding mining and trading
with non-Mormons altogether.

Much like the Anglo-friendly Paiute chiefs who assisted the whites
in eradicating rebellious Indians, Mormon leaders also defended their
communal boundaries with the "politics of exclusion." Young himself
helped establish a pattern. In 1869, the Church president first disfellowshiped and then acquiesced as a council excommunicated William
S. Godbe and E. L. T. Harrison. According to the historian Ronald W.
Walker, "Godbe and Harrison had defied President Young's leadership;
they had questioned the prevailing norms of Zion; and they had rejected
church authority." One facet of their dissent centered on an outspoken
opposition to Young's mining policy. While such protest cost Godbe and
Harrison their memberships, Walker believes that by 1871, it also led
Church leaders to revise their approach toward mining: "The new church
policy signaled a frank recognition that many Mormons were now prospecting for precious metals and that former proscriptions had lost their
force."[31] Perhaps for northern Utah, 1871 did mark a turning point, but
on Zion's southwestern frontier leaders continued to toe a rigid line, at
least until Young's death in 1877.

At Eagle Valley in 1865, Snow told the settlers that "he wished any
man that would go to the Western mines [Pahranagat] as a miner to be cut
off the church."[32] In 1868 local authorities informed Hebronites that trading with non-Mormons would be considered a "matter of Fellowship."
Hebronites were also admonished to "quit sustaining gentile merchants

. . . thereby giving them our trade, our money, influance [*sic*] & the power to cut our throats, to bring armies upon us, to outnumber us in Voting, & electing the wicked to rule over us & break us up & again drive us from our homes."[33] Three years later, at the groundbreaking ceremony for the St. George Temple, Young's counselor George A. Smith prayed God to pour out his wrath upon the enemies of the Saints and to "overrule the discovery of minerals in this land for the good of thy people."[34] Then, in 1872, in contradiction to Snow's advice at the time of the boundary survey, Young himself told southern Utah Mormons, "[T]hose who will stay at home and mind their legitimate labors will be better off, eventually, than those who will go to the mines and work for the gentiles." He went on to prophesy "that those who would persist in running to Pioche and other Gentile cities, and neglect their duties at home, would lose by this course temporally and would ultimately apostasize [*sic*]."[35]

In 1873, Young returned to St. George to reinforce that message at the height of the Pioche bonanza. Annual bullion output had peaked at over five million dollars the previous year and would reach nearly four million dollars in 1873. Population estimates for Pioche run as high as ten thousand people during those boom years, but more realistic guesses place the number at between four and five thousand. Even at that many, Pioche would have been home to more residents than all the Mormon settlements in Washington County combined. Clearly, not only its wealth and population but its reported seventy-two saloons and thirty-two houses of prostitution stood as ominous threats to Mormon values.[36]

Such notions must have weighed heavily upon Young in 1873. Concern over Pioche permeated his messages to Dixie Saints that year. He "deprecated the desire of many to go to the mines and mingle with the wicked—learn to swear-drink-gamble, lie and practice every other wickedness of the world." He lamented that "the desire to make money caused many to forget the object of our mission on the Earth—which is the salvation of the living and the dead. Many were becoming lukewarm," Young warned, "and, unless they repent, will have to be cut off the Church." Similarly, his nephew Joseph W. Young admonished southern Mormons that they "had no right to go to Pioche and trade off our lumber, chickens, eggs and grain," particularly as it put a squeeze on the subsistence nature of Utah's farm economy. Erastus Snow expounded upon the harmful effect of such trading upon the Saints, especially upon their tithing obligations. They were supposed to offer up one-tenth of their increase to the Lord, a duty that the inhabitants "of the Western Valleys, in the vicinity of the mines," had not taken seriously. They were "at the foot of the list" among tithe payers in southern Utah.[37]

Before returning to Salt Lake City in 1873, Young punctuated his preaching with an oath. He stood before a gathering of southern Utah Mormons and called upon "the mechanics, farmers, cotton raisers and others that feel willing to build up Zion and nothing else, to raise their right hands and covenant" to do so. This commitment made, Young then instructed local leaders to "sever those from the Church who will not cease their wickedness."[38] Young, in essence, established the terms for membership in the kingdom. As he put it, "[T]he time had come" for the line to be drawn "between those who are willing to build up Zion and those who are following after Babylon."[39] It was a principle upon which Young refused to relent. In 1877, the year he died, he preached what had become a familiar theme to his Dixie flock, this time also aimed at the new mining town of Silver Reef, about fifteen miles northeast of St. George. At the dedication of the St. George Temple he again urged the Saints to "go to work and let these holes in the ground alone, and let the Gentiles alone, who would destroy us if they had the power." "You will go to hell, lots of you, unless you repent," he announced.[40]

He largely left it to local leaders to translate his rhetoric into action, a task that proved troublesome given the frontier location of their spiritual ground. Their defense largely coincided with Young's notions of economic self-sufficiency and an avoidance of trade with gentiles. Yet the abundance of work available at the mining camps and the allure of cash payments in a near-cashless economy pitted dogma against economic necessity. It forced settlers at the outposts closest to Pioche to enforce the speechifying through disfellowshipment and excommunication.[41]

In August 1868, ecclesiastical leaders at Hebron met to decide the fate of a family that had strayed, quite literally, from the Mormon flock. Erastus Snow presided at the gathering, and under his direction the Hebron congregation decided to "cut off" Lucinda Jane Crow from the Church. Apostle Snow and the Hebron congregation excommunicated her "for leaving her husband & the society of the S[ain]ts & choosing to live with the wicked at a gentile camp." At that same meeting, Benjamin Brown Crow, Lucinda's husband, was also "suspended from fellowship" with the Saints "til he makes satisfaction, for moving his family away from the gathering place & exposing them to be over come in society of the wicked."

Crow had moved his family from Hebron to Meadow Valley and located his new home near a saw mill "erected by outsiders" from Pahranagat. One of the mill hands soon became a frequenter at the Crow home, and in the process employed "soft oily, low whispered words" to seduce Lucinda away "from home and from God." Three months later, no doubt humbled by the loss of his wife and his fellowship in the Church,

Crow returned to Hebron and made public confession. He expressed his sorrow for the course he had taken and declared his determination to be a Saint. Hebronites restored him to fellowship by a unanimous vote. As for Lucinda Jane, it seems her relationship with the "ill-favored gentile" did not last. Less than a year later, she returned to friends in southern Utah "in agony of mind, reaping the rich harvest of sorrow she had sown with her 'manly beauty of a gentile' in the distance."[42]

Other frontier Mormons faced similar threats to their memberships. Hyrum Burgess left Shoal Creek for Pahranagat in 1865 and participated in the founding of a mining district there. In 1868 Church leaders cut him off "for unfaithful conduct."[43] Burgess later returned to Hebron as an excommunicated Mormon; he was allowed to live among the Saints, but in 1874 he was the only resident who did not participate in the town's United Order effort, an attempt at economic communalism.[44]

According to one miner, Burgess was not the only Latter-day Saint to move to Pahranagat: "Quite a number of families from the Mormon settlements have gone in and settled on lands there, and many more contemplate going in, early in the spring. Most of them . . . are apostate mormons; they consider it a fine chance to divest themselves from Brigham's power."[45] Whether fleeing on their own accord or being forced out, mining involvement became a test for some of their commitment to the kingdom. Local leaders excommunicated Richard C. Gibbons at Pinto, a ranch town east of Hebron, in 1869. The accusations against him included "disseminating tracts . . . published by the Josephites," as well as being "active in prospecting with the wicked for precious metals."[46] William Hamblin and Peter Shirts were also "cut off," although the complaints against them were less specific. They were excommunicated on charges of "apostasy," a sweeping and multifaceted indictment.[47] Both men's involvement at Pioche likely factored into the decisions against them. Shirts lost his membership in 1873, the same year he testified at Pioche in the *Raymond and Ely v. Hermes* case, the only Mormon to do so as a witness for Hermes. On the witness stand he described the "peculiar views of the Mormons relative to mining," which caused "some considerable amusement" among the spectators. He also recalled that Brigham Young had given him a "terrible word-whipping" back in 1864 "for leading Gentiles to the Panaca mine."[48]

The irony of such excommunications lies in Snow's and Young's own economic involvement at Pioche. In May 1871, Erastus Snow held a meeting at his home at St. George with some of the leading business and religious leaders of the region. The gathering was designed to establish "the best method to regulate the trade of vegetables, fruit, and grain to

Pioche." Estimates among the assembled brethren suggested that southern Utah Saints could peddle "three tons of vegetables, fruit, and grain
per week" at the mining town. The men also deemed it "important" that
"an agency should be established to direct and control the business." In
accordance, they organized the Dixie Cooperative Produce Company and
selected five agents to coordinate the enterprise. Company leaders then
assigned each southern Utah town a trade quota and a specified day of
the week on which residents could peddle their goods. For Erastus Snow,
Mormon commerce at Pioche was clearly not the issue; who controlled
it was. Snow desired that the trade be conducted in a way that benefitted
all who had a surplus to sell.[49]

For the Dixie Cooperative, however, things did not work out as hoped.
Bishop J. T. Willis of Toquerville chafed under the attempt to channel
Pioche trade through the produce company. His protest killed the cooperative in its infancy. In July, peddlers from Toquerville, a small town
twenty miles east of St. George, violated their quota of one load per week,
assigned to arrive on Tuesdays. Three Toquerville men had taken loads
of fruit to Pioche in the same week and disrupted the established pattern. Agents of the Dixie Produce Company wrote to Bishop Willis and
castigated him for the violation. They even warned Willis that failure to
comply with company regulations was a matter of Church fellowship.

Such a rebuke enraged the bishop. Snow himself, Willis said, refused
to make compliance with the company's regulations a test of fellowship.
More to the point, Willis questioned the very principles of the company
and its harmful effects upon Toquerville's ability to subsist: "You have
an agent in Pioche, and say that our place is entitled to send one load a
week," he seethed. "Why gentlemen, the people here should doff their
hats, for such extended liberality and generosity. One load a week!! Only
think of it." Even more sardonic, Willis continued: "Gentlemen, we
thank you. By your proscription, our hard earnings must rot on the ground
and the people reduced to the utmost state of destitution. Are we living
in the dark ages?" Willis vowed to bring the company's "insolent note"
before Erastus Snow, where it seems that the determined bishop's plea
for free enterprise won. Snow soon abandoned his attempt to control
Mormon trade at Pioche and returned to rhetorical defenses against the
iniquitous camp.[50]

Brigham Young had better luck at the mining town. In June 1871
he made plans to extend a line of the Church-owned Deseret Telegraph
Company to Pioche. He hoped that "when completed it will soon pay
for itself." By October, Mormon workers finished the line, and Young's
wish quickly came true. In 1868, gross receipts in tolls for the company

had totaled a mere $8,400. By 1873, however, the company's receipts had jumped to over seventy-five thousand dollars; the Pioche office alone accounted for almost 45 percent of that total.[51] Pioche residents seemed grateful. When the line opened, some of them telegraphed Young: "We thank you for your enterprise, in placing us in telegraphic communication with the outside world."[52]

On a local level, a similar paradox characterized settlers' relationships with Pioche. Many Mormons freighted and traded at the mining camp, all the while denouncing the evil that it embodied. In 1872, Bishop George H. Crosby of Hebron reported that everything was "prosperous" at his town and emphasized the financial benefit that proximity to Pioche represented: The co-operative store paid a yearly dividend of 30 percent, residents enjoyed "a ready cash market for all their produce," and peddlers received "sufficiently higher" prices at Pioche "to make it profitable to the freighter."[53] Orson Huntsman concurred: "I made several trips to Pioche with lumber, in company with Father Terry and others from our place," he wrote. "Pioche proved to be a great camp, . . . [and] made a good market for lumber and other products or produce, also a great amount of labor. Bullionville was also a place of great note."[54] Over the next several years, Huntsman continued his forays to Pioche and Bullionville. He generally returned home well-pleased with his cash payments, especially after one trip where he sold "one little horse" for fifty dollars in gold.[55] Despite the economic benefit, Huntsman still described Pioche as "a very wicked city," or, "at least," he explained, "there is some very wicked men and women in and around Pioche."[56] Huntsman's father-in-law, Thomas S. Terry, thought the same. After one trip, Terry returned to Hebron and reported "new mines being discovered Very rich—plenty of money—& people awful wicked."[57] At one priesthood meeting, a Brother Jesse gave a similar account when he described "the wickedness in the mining region" west of Hebron. Nonetheless, proximity to the mines was a fact of life at Hebron. As Bishop Crosby told the Hebron men, "[W]e will be the frontier settlement & miners be among us."[58]

Mormons at Panaca and Eagle Valley responded similarly. Despite the Panaca co-op store earning huge profits from its Pioche commerce (in the spring of 1872 it distributed a dividend of more than 100 percent, with sales in excess of a hundred thousand dollars), some residents felt ill at ease among the wicked. One settler at Eagle Valley even suggested that "the State of Nevada was no place for the Saints."[59] Many at Eagle, Spring, and Clover Valleys drifted off throughout the 1880s and 1890s; by the turn of the century, only a handful of Mormons occupied those outposts.[60] At Panaca, those who stayed defended their spiritual ground with what the historians Leonard J. Arrington and Richard Jensen call "moral protectionism." Local leaders preached against horse racing, playing ball, or riding broncos on the Sabbath. They warned the youth against staying out late, playing cards in saloons, public drunkenness, and forming "associations with outsiders."[61]

Hebronites constructed similar walls around their communal space. In 1873, when the Raymond and Ely lawsuit forced many miners out of work, John Pulsipher recorded its impact upon Hebron: The court case "left many bands of thieving individuals prowling hungrily around preying upon our stock, taking property that peaceable people have acquired by minding their own business." Even still, Pulsipher noted, "We general[l]y find plenty to do at home taking care of our families & whatever else the Lord has given us & if we are not in Debt we are happy whether we see much or little money."[62] Two years later, when work at the mines again slowed, Pulsipher used the economic downturn as proof of the division between the kingdom of God and that of the devil: "Business is rather dull, money scarce, not much outside business going on. Clover Valley is being Deserted. . . . [The people there] have depended on hauling lumber or other services of gentiles and [are now] out of employment & are moving back into our territory as poor as when they commenced work for unbelievers. . . . This is about the history of all that have a mission and calling in the K[ingdo]m of God & go to get rich building up the D[evi]l's K[ingdo]m."[63]

At times, defending Hebron's spiritual ground required more than keeping Hebronites away from the mines; it required keeping the miners away from Hebron. In 1872, settlers lost about eight hundred dollars worth of livestock, stolen by "the many thieves from the mining camps." The miners eventually sold the stolen stock, and officers were able to track down two of the bandits through the bills of sale.[64] More damaging to the kingdom, however, was the perceived threat that the stealing of Mormon women presented. At Panaca, priesthood leaders did their best to guard against gentiles who invaded ward dances, whiskey in tow.[65] Hebronites also held dances for town youth, which attracted outsiders. Bishop George Crosby set the standard for that town: He "wished the dances conducted with soberness & not kept to late & not invite any profane rowdies that sometimes come from other places with the Spirit of Liquor which drives away the Spirit of the Lord."[66] To combat such occurrences, Hebron leaders appointed one of the elderly men to preside at the dances and keep outsiders away. In 1877, St. George leaders traveled to Hebron and emphasized this point. John D. T. McAllister, a regional Church head, warned Hebronites "against mixing up with gentiles

& partaking of their spirit for that is a plan of the D[evi]l to lead people astray." He also advised the congregation not to allow gentiles into their dances and gave "good advice" on courtship. He instructed Hebron men to "not be sparking 4 years & then not marry—but marry these girls & not let gentiles have them."[67]

Finally, defending against outside influences also required modification of the home as sacred space, at least for one Hebronite. In 1877, after returning from a trip, Bishop Crosby called the townsmen together for a meeting, primarily because he "wished to hear how everything was getting along, as he had been away for some time." The priesthood brethren reported that a "general good feeling" pervaded the town and that the people had "a desire to try to improve in all good works." One resident, Thomas S. Terry, however, disclosed a challenge that he faced in defending the spiritual space of his home. Terry operated a ranch outside of town on the main road to the mining camps. His place had become a popular stopping spot for the stagecoach and other travelers to and from the mines. Hosting those visitors became a challenge to Terry and his family. He told the bishop that "he was trying to do the best he could under the circumstances; with the outside influence could not always attend to prayer." Terry did make it "a rule to get his family together and attend to prayers whenever [he] could, when those who would make light were not present, but when such parties were around, [he] did not believe in casting pearls before swine." The bishop accepted this report and advised the rest of the men that under the same circumstances they should follow Terry's lead.[68]

On a practical level, then, the frontier struggle between Mormon and gentile involved much more than diatribes from the pulpit about the kingdom of God versus that of the devil. It required defending flocks from thieves, Mormon dances from imbibing ruffians, Mormon women from gentiles, and the Mormon home as prayer space from taunting outsiders.

Although such "moral protectionism" has never waned among Latter-day Saints, on the frontier the rigid defensive stance against mining did become more pliable by the end of the 1870s. Young's death in 1877 marked an easing of restrictions, even in the south. Young's successor, John Taylor, was less committed to communalism and more open to capitalism and business.[69] Mormon economic interaction at Pioche, Bullionville, and newer mining camps continued well past the turn of the century, with little fear that such activity would be made a matter of fellowship. In the 1880s, William Godbe, the excommunicated Mormon who had opposed Young's mining policy, made his temporary headquarters at Bullionville. He bought up 170,000 tons of tailings left by the Raymond and Ely mines and began reprocessing them. For over seven years he worked the tailings and largely kept Bullionville and Pioche alive.[70] During that time, Mormons at Panaca, much like the Paiutes had done, reconciled themselves to their "ungodly" neighbors without nearly the same apprehension that typified earlier interactions. In an 1883 Sunday sermon, Bishop Lee told the Panaca Saints "to follow the Lord's example in their dealings with the 'outsiders,' and if imposed upon, to bear in mind the words, 'Father, forgive them, for they no not what they do.'" Following this speech, a Brother Keele included "neighbors" at Pioche and Bullionville in his closing prayer.[71]

Interaction at Panaca dances in the 1880s perhaps still posed a problem, but the Pioche newspaper suggested "lozenges" to aid in courtship of the Mormon girls. It also noted that "the Bullionville store does a large business alone from the sale of fancy toilet articles, as it takes a bottle of scent to make the average young Bullionite presentable to his Panaca sweetheart." It further warned "all Gentiles" attending Mormon dances "not to press the young ladies too closely to their manly bosoms, for it is against the rules of the Church." Nonetheless, by 1900 the need to protect Mormon women from outsiders had all but vanished. That year, the Young Ladies Mutual Improvement Association at Panaca threw a "grand ball" and extended "a cordial invitation to Piochers to come and join in their amusement." In response, the *Pioche Weekly Record* observed that "a number of our young folks are arranging to go down."[72]

Likewise, when DeLamar burst onto the mining scene in the 1890s, Mormons hardly thought twice about participating. In 1894, prospectors founded a town about forty miles southwest of Pioche and named it DeLamar after a prominent investor.[73] By 1896, reports in the St. George newspaper detailed activity at the mines. One account from DeLamar noted that "most of the men that are working here are from Utah."[74] News from Panaca told that "there is a great deal of freight passing through our little town to DeLamar, Pioche, and other places around us." It also described "some little excitement" over "gold and silver prospects," with no hint of disapproval of Mormon participation in such activities.[75] Another report even bragged that "a new strike has just been made by Spring Valley boys, on the Utah and Nevada line." The writer, a Panaca Mormon, proudly announced that "some of Panaca's sons have a six months lease on a fraction of the main ledge, and expect to pull out with a neat sum."[76] While still guarding their communal space against outside influences, by the turn of the century, frontier Saints had not only made peace with the region's mineral wealth but sought it for themselves.[77]

Mormon interaction with the Paiutes, as with the miners, was filled with contradictions. Such discrepancies reflect a clash between Mormonism's Indian doctrine and the realities of frontier life. Just as the Paiutes pursued mixed policies toward the Mormons and miners, the Mormon stance toward the Paiutes varied in time and space according to changing circumstances and differing personalities.[78] Altruism sometimes tempered selfishness, while on other occasions vengeance overpowered compassion. Mormons fed and fought with the Paiutes; they defended some and murdered others; they played with Paiute children, employed Paiute men, and married Paiute women. One local LDS leader helped create the Shivwits Reservation in an effort to prevent the Paiutes from killing his cattle. The relationship, needless to say, was complicated.

Historians have long viewed Mormon Indian policy as bound by two competing forces: On the one hand, Latter-day Saint doctrine taught that Native Americans were literal descendants of ancient Israel and in need of redemption. On the other hand, the Saints needed Indian land to build Zion. As the historian David J. Whittaker explains, "One view stressed [Native Americans'] religious nature, the other emphasized their savageness. Where one could argue for their perfectability, the other could suggest their destruction."[79] Correlating with this dichotomy, historians have also argued that Church leaders frequently urged kindness toward the Indians, while settlers who actually lived among the natives often resorted to less noble approaches. "The incidence of misbehavior and culpability," Ronald W. Walker suggests, "seemed to grow with each concentric circle radiating from Brigham Young and the Mormon leadership."[80]

Certainly those paradigms fit the Mormon-Paiute experience, but the relationship was more complicated than those models convey. Mixed messages from Church leaders left some settlers confused and contributed to conflicting methods of interaction on the frontier. Mormon Indian policy was not only caught between visions of Indian redemption and the need for Zion land, but also between divergent Indian doctrines. Furthermore, frontier settlements were not always sites of wrongdoing toward Indian peoples. Some communities put Young's humanitarian preaching into action and peacefully coexisted with their Paiute neighbors. All levels of Mormon society were responsible for both good and ill toward the Paiutes.

Brigham Young's oft repeated maxim, "[I]t is cheaper to feed Indians than to fight them," broadly governed his Native American policy, at least after 1852.[81] At the height of the Black Hawk War, he even told

Springville settlers, "'We should now use the Indians kindly, and deal with them so gently that we will win their hearts and affections to us more strongly than before.'" He further admonished the Saints to "'let the Lamanites come back to their homes, where they were born and brought up. This is the land that they and their fathers have walked over and called their own; and they have just as good a right to call it theirs to-day as any people have to call any land their own.'"[82]

On other occasions, however, Young proffered that the land belongs to no man—it is the Lord's, and it is meant for everyone to share.[83] Young reflected in 1853, "When we first entered Utah, we were prepared to meet all the Indians in these mountains, and kill every soul of them if we had been obliged so to do." He told the Saints, "I shall live a long while before I can believe that an Indian is my friend, when it would be to his advantage to be my enemy." Nonetheless, he continued, "We are here in the mountains, with these Lamanites for our neighbors. . . . They are of the House of Israel, and the time has come for the Lord to favor Zion, and redeem Israel." In short, he instructed Mormons to watch, pray, carry weapons of defense, and be ready for the Indians.[84]

Young would not let Native Americans stand in the way of his mission to build Zion. That mission brought the Mormons to Utah in the first place and remained a strong motivating force throughout the nineteenth century. As with his mining policy, Young's principal focus was his divinely appointed commission; he was not overly concerned if that commission produced contradictions in Indian policy. For the most part, Young struggled to ensure that kingdom building was as easy on the Native Americans as possible, but its side effects were beyond his ability to ameliorate. Disease and the loss of land devastated the Great Basin tribes.

Some of his preaching, along with that of other Church leaders, may have added indirectly to the Indians' plight. While the Latter-day Saint ideal of Indian perfectibility prompted a mission in 1854 among the Paiutes, a countervailing doctrine also emerged, equally rooted in Mormon scripture, that suggested that the Indians were beyond redemption. That doctrine centered around the Gadianton robbers, a nefarious band of thieves described in the Book of Mormon.

The Book of Mormon chronicles God's dealings with a branch of Israelites on the American continent from the time of the biblical confounding of the languages to about AD 400. The two principal groups in the story are the Nephites (initially more righteous) and the generally wicked Lamanites. The Nephites eventually forsake their belief in Christ and sink to a level of depravity worse than that of the Lamanites, at which point God permits their extermination at the hands of the Lamanites. According to nineteenth-century LDS beliefs, these Lamanites were the ancestors of the American Indians. The Gadianton robbers were a greed-motivated group of murderers who arose among the Christ-worshiping Nephites around 50 BC. They formed a secret oath-bound society that eventually became so powerful that it challenged the legitimate government.

To prevent detection and annihilation, Gadianton, the leader of the band, removed his followers from the Nephite capital city and fled "into the wilderness."[85] Tempted by power and riches, other Nephite dissenters joined this band almost daily. From their hiding places the robbers infiltrated Nephite cities to "commit murder and plunder." They then retreated "back into the mountains, and into the wilderness and secret places, hiding themselves that they could not be discovered."[86]

As the robbers increased in strength, they threatened the very existence of the Nephites and the righteous Lamanites. As a result, by about AD 18 the God-fearing Nephites abandoned their lands and gathered at the Nephite capital city to withstand the Gadianton siege. The robbers promptly "began to come down and to sally forth from the hills, and out of the mountains, and the wilderness, and their strongholds, and their secret places . . . and began to take possession of all the lands which had been deserted by the Nephites, and the cities which had been left desolate."[87] In this case, the Nephites triumphed and eradicated the robbers, but only after three years of warfare.

About three hundred years later, Gadianton robbers re-formed and resumed the conflict. This time their satanic activities brought a curse upon the land: "And these Gadianton robbers . . . did infest the land, insomuch that the inhabitants thereof began to hide up their treasure in the earth; and they became slippery, because the Lord had cursed the land, that they could not hold them, nor retain them again."[88] Ultimately, "this Gadianton did prove the overthrow, yea, almost the entire destruction of the people of Nephi."[89] To nineteenth-century Mormons, this group of robbers must have represented most things evil, including murder, theft, secret combinations, cursed land, the dispossession of cities, and even potential annihilation.

Over time, the robbers from Mormon scripture grew into a cultural discourse among nineteenth-century Latter-day Saints, especially as Brigham Young and other Church leaders created a Gadianton robber persona that they linked to Native American tribes of the Great Basin.[90] While touring southern settlements in 1851, Brigham Young commented to Saints at Parowan that the local Paiute Indians were "'descendants of the old Gadianton Rob[b]ers who infested these Mountains for more than a thousand years.'"[91] Two years later, on 6 April 1853, Presiding Bishop Edward Hunter stood atop the newly positioned southwest cornerstone of the Salt Lake Temple and demanded: "Do you remember the history of the Gadiantons as told in the Book of Mormon? We are surrounded by their descendants; those loathsome, effeminate specimens of humanity, which we daily see in our midst, are their children; low, degraded, sunken to the lowest depths of human existence. We have our location amid their strong holds; where the ruins of their cities, towns, and fortifications are yet to be seen; they continue unto this day."[92]

In 1860, Young's counselor, Heber C. Kimball, declared from the Old Tabernacle: "We read in the Book of Mormon that the Gadianton robbers came down from the mountains—they robbed, plundered, and in many instances slew the Saints. I can tell you, brethren and sisters, that we have similar characters in these mountains, who are making pretty rapid progress in preparing to destroy this people. This I know to my sorrow."[93] About twenty years later, John Taylor, Brigham Young's successor, officially connected the robbers to southern Utah. "If we had not possessed these narrow valleys and defiles," he announced in the St. George Tabernacle, "they would have been in the possession of bands of Gadianton robbers, who would have preyed upon the people and their property."[94]

Local Saints also understood this concept. A resident of Harmony in Washington County told of a dispute that erupted during one Sunday meeting over "the great and all absorbing question of amalgamation with the natives." A Brother Fream preached upon the principle, telling the brethren that "it is our duty, as Latter-day Saints, to take the Lamanite women to wife and by that means make them our fast friends." Father Groves, another member of the congregation, however, opposed such an idea. He insisted that "these Indians in these mountains are the descendants of the Gadianton robbers, and that the curse of God is upon them, and we had better let them alone." The bishop ended the dispute when he "put a stop to further teaching of the doctrine of amalgamation." He claimed that "he had received no orders to instruct the brethren to take Indian women for wives."[95]

Certainly, tension between these divergent preachings influenced settlers' views of Paiutes. As descendants of Gadianton robbers, Paiutes were to be feared, left alone, and sometimes eliminated. When Muddy Valley Mormons caught ten Paiutes butchering a cow belonging to one of the settlers, they destroyed the Indians' bows and arrows and took the men captive. The Mormons then marched their prisoners ten miles back to town, where they tied the leader of the group to the top of a wagon and whipped him "some fifty lashes." They did the same with the rest of the captives, adjusting the whippings according to the age of each. When the punishment was over, the Paiutes "laid there for hours before they moved." Worse still, when the Muddy Saints executed Co-quap, the leader of a band of rebellious Paiutes, they made sport of it. They took him two miles outside of town and let him loose. The men shot at him as he dodged their bullets, jumping and running. He nearly escaped, but they shot him dead.[96]

In response to additional Paiute aggression, Erastus Snow sent the Mormon militia to Meadow Valley in 1864 to help build a fort and to protect settlers. In August, the Mormons shot three Paiute prisoners who attempted to escape after being captured in a stock raid, and later they killed two other Paiutes.[97] Upon learning of these difficulties, Erastus Snow recommended to Edward Bunker, the ecclesiastical head of the frontier settlements, "the policy of taking no prisoners, but of killing thieves when taken in the act." Snow did "hope," however, "that God will over rule it for the best."[98]

Especially during the Black Hawk War, Mormons resorted to similar harshness toward the Paiutes. The worst atrocity of that war occurred at Circleville in south-central Utah in 1866. Mormons killed sixteen captured men, women, and children, slitting the throats of some. That same year, war hysteria led to other acts of inhumanity toward the Paiutes farther south. When two Mormon ranchers were killed southwest of St. George, enraged LDS militiamen shot eight Paiutes in retaliation.[99]

In general, southern Utah Mormons adopted a militaristic approach to defending Zion during the Black Hawk War. It was a tactic that frontier Saints never employed against threatening Anglo miners, only Paiutes. For the duration of the war, military muster became an integral part of frontier life. At Shoal Creek, an inspection found that residents owned twelve guns, ten pistols, two swords, and about one thousand rounds of ammunition, "all in good order."[100] In 1867, the men organized themselves militarily; those from Shoal Creek Fort combined with the men from Mountain Meadows to form a company. John Pulsipher was elected captain and Thomas Terry adjutant, with four platoons commanded by Dudley Leavitt, Levi H. Calloway, Jacob Truman, and E. L. Westover.[101] In September 1869, the units throughout southern Utah met for general training and drill about three miles east of Harmony. Orson Huntsman recalled, "[T]his was the largest camp that I had seen for some time past. There was a string of wagons for over a mile long encamped side by side. We arrived in camp in time to be inrolled [*sic*], and at eight o'clock the bugle sounded and the whole army was called out on parade under command of Apostle Erastus Snow, brigad[i]er general, and marched all day long on foot, the next day on horse back and the next day we charged on the great train of wagons just as though they were the foe, and the next two or three days we fought one army against the other." "To say the least," Hunstman concluded, "it was a very lively time before we got through."[102]

This heightened sense of military readiness coincided with Native American hostilities during the Black Hawk War. While the Saints had largely pursued avenues of legal recourse against encroaching miners over the boundary shift, they resorted to arms against the threatening Paiutes. In this manner they aligned themselves with fellow Americans, asserting Anglo-American superiority, enforced at times at gunpoint.

Even during the Black Hawk War, however, Brigham Young preached a conciliatory policy toward Native Americans that emphasized their covenant relationship with God. As fallen descendants of ancient Israel, the Paiutes demanded compassion, uplift, and the gospel message. In 1866, Young admonished the Saints to exercise faith toward the hostile Indians and learn the will of the Lord toward them. He urged the Saints to give them presents and "tell them they must stop fighting." "It is better to give them $5000," he concluded, "than have to fight and kill them, for they are of the House of Israel."[103] Just as the Gadianton-robber doctrine might have excused violence toward Native Americans, the Israelite precept prompted some frontier settlers toward benevolence.

The main thrust of Erastus Snow's Indian advice to frontier Saints centered upon defensive measures. In 1864 he instructed that "if it be necessary to assume the offensive and make war upon them [the Paiutes] . . . I consider that Governor Doty, or General Connor with the governor's approval, should attend to that." Snow instead admonished the settlers at Panaca and Eagle Valley to "either concentrate and adopt the measure of defense recommended, or abandon the place with your families and stock." At Shoal Creek, settlers followed this counsel and used "great caution & energy" to keep their families and livestock safe.[104]

Similarly, as tension between Mormons and Paiutes increased during the Black Hawk War, Brigham Young admonished settlers to pursue a policy of "vigilant defense." This included the abandonment of small communities and ranching outposts, as well as maintaining military readiness.[105] More than retaliatory violence, Young's policy characterized the position taken by Mormons at Panaca, Shoal Creek/Hebron, Clover, Eagle, and Spring Valleys during the war.

Snow modified Young's advice to suit local circumstances as well as to fit his own vision of colonization in southern Utah. He traveled to

Shoal Creek in July 1866 and complimented its residents on the "good place" they had selected to build a fort. Snow also praised the outpost dwellers for their wisdom and policy toward the natives, observing that "there has been no complaint of the Indians against the people of Shoal Creek." He then advised them: "I feel that you need a good Ft. & 40 good men filled with the power of god and *well armed*." He announced that he would instruct Clover Valley settlers to vacate their homes and settle at Shoal Creek.[106]

In choosing Clover Valley for abandonment, Snow's main concern centered on Indian relations. Clover Valley had more residents than Shoal Creek and had a longer-established fort, but Snow still selected the latter as a gathering spot.[107] Clover Valley settlers were directly affected by hostile relations with Paiutes, a fact that had shaped the physical layout of their town. When Orson Huntsman arrived there in 1865, he found the settlers "mostly all living in a little fort." They "had built their log houses close together, forming a hollow square, in order to protect themselves from the indians, as they had been hostile."[108] Snow therefore advised Clover Valley residents to relocate to "Shoal Creek and other places where you will be more safe."[109] In that process, Snow implied that he valued friendliness over hostility and in essence rewarded Shoal Creek settlers for their amicability toward the Paiutes.

Those at Shoal Creek continued such a policy even as they abandoned their fort and founded Hebron. During the winter of 1864–65, John Pulsipher noted that "a large number of indians are camping about our settlement & are being hungry as usual." He went on to explain the townspeople's approach to such a situation: "We have to deal out Potatoes Squash, Meat &c. not that they demand it—they are peac[e]able—We pity their suf[f]ering condition—cold winter we[a]ther & no game, scarcely, to be had & 90 Indians together without houses—we gave them the big[g]est part of 2 beef cattle this fall." Such generosity was not easy, however. "It is a heavy tax on us . . . to feed them as much as we have to," Pulsipher explained, "but Bro. Brighams Policy is good: it is cheaper to feed than fight them."[110]

Even during the Black Hawk War, when Saints elsewhere were living in fear of their Native American neighbors, the settlers at Shoal Creek encouraged an Indian family headed by Brush-head, along with some of his friends, to live with them. Pulsipher described the relationship in 1866: "We furnish them some clothing & something to eat, & let them have land, seed &c so they have raised a good crop. They work for us some & we pay something [that] they want so they live well & are a guard to us."[111] Three years later, Brush-head and his family still lived among Hebronites and were incorporated into the Saints' monthly fast-offering distribution. LDS practice dictates that Mormons set aside one day a month as "fast day," wherein they go without food or water for a twenty-four-hour period. The food that they otherwise would have eaten is given to those in need. In February 1869, Pulsipher described that month's distribution: "Today I p[ai]d it to Brushheads Family, our lamanite neighbors. The woman is sick & needy. So we relieved their wants & prayed the lord to relieve her of her sickness. They are good honorable people."[112]

Clearly, Young's maxim—it is cheaper to feed than fight them—shaped the nature of at least some Mormon–Paiute interactions, even on the frontier. Perhaps Young's policy also guided settlers to view their neighbors as "good honorable people." Still, an air of cultural superiority permeated the exchanges and illustrates the rapid degree of alienation some Paiutes experienced from their lands. Pulsipher's words, for example, are telling. He described Hebronites letting Brush-head's family "have land," not the reverse. Mormons believed that the land was theirs to give, despite the Paiutes' longer-standing claim. This irony no doubt escaped the frontier Saints, especially at Hebron, where settlers acted out of a desire to alleviate their Paiute neighbors' suffering, perhaps not fully grasping their own implication in that suffering.[113] Brush-head nonetheless must have benefitted from the relationship. His family's proximity to Hebron provided access to work opportunities, desirable material goods, and an extended community of caregivers in times of need.

Elsewhere on the frontier, Mormons worked out a peaceful coexistence with the Paiutes. During the 1870s and 1880s, the two groups largely shared their space in a variety of ways that placed the Mormons in a paternalistic role, shaped by their desire to civilize the Indians. Jacob Hamblin, Ira Hatch, Dudley Leavitt, and others married Paiute women as an outgrowth of this goal. Few of these interethnic marriages were successful, however, and rarely were the Indian wives or their children accepted as equals in Mormon society.[114] Mormons baptized over 160 Paiutes in 1875 and viewed it as "a sign that the Lord was hastening His purposes."[115] Although such aims largely failed to recognize Paiute cultural autonomy, they nonetheless provided opportunities for Paiutes to gain access to Anglo-American goods and to supplement the increasingly scarce traditional resources.

In 1869 Mormon settlers began reoccupying land abandoned during the Black Hawk War. Lyman Lafayette Woods that year moved to Clover Valley and established a farm. He "adopted a kind and conciliatory attitude" toward the Paiutes and shortly hired three of them to help haul lumber and mining timber to Pioche. On one occasion Woods used this association to intervene in a Paiute matter of justice. When an entourage of Paiute leaders gathered at his ranch to return fourteen stolen horses and to punish the perpetrator, Woods saved the young Indian from being whipped and announced that "this is no way to make friends." His action helped to change the nature of Indian relations at Clover Valley and ensured that settlers there "never again experienced trouble with the Indians."[116]

In addition to work relationships, Mormons and Paiutes frequently interacted in matters of trade. The exchange of goods was not always one-sided, as Paiutes possessed merchandise sometimes desired by Mormons. When Mormon communally produced wooden-bottomed shoes did not suit the Hebronite Orson Huntsman, he turned to the Paiutes for a solution.[117] He went to Moroni's camp and struck a bargain with the chief. Huntsman gave Moroni "a pan full of potatoes and a little flour" in exchange for Moroni making him "a good pair of Moccasins." Huntsman wore his new footwear to church the following Sunday, where "the Bishop and others had to acknowledge that the moccasins took the shine off of the old wooden shoes, both for comfort and hansome." As Huntsman recalled, his trade spelled "the end of the wooden shoe here."[118] Other Mormons frequently traded with Paiutes for pine nuts. As John Lewis Pulsipher fondly remembered: "I learned to look forward with considerable anticipation to the approach of pine nut season and the coming of our Indian friends to gather them and trade with us."[119]

By the 1880s, it seems that the Paiutes had become a part of what the historian Ronald W. Walker calls "the warp and woof" of frontier Mormonism.[120] The Mormons by then greatly outnumbered the Paiutes, and the tension of the settlement period had eased. The Mormons clearly emerged more powerful than the Paiutes and could therefore dictate the terms of interaction. Mormons freely intermingled with Paiutes during the last two decades of the century with little fear of the Paiutes as a harmful "outside influence." Dudley Henry Leavitt and John Lewis Pulsipher recalled youthful adventures at Hebron with their Paiute "playmates," "roaming over the hills" with their bows and arrows.[121] The Mormons had successfully resisted the Paiutes' geographic threat to Zion and were therefore more at ease with such intimate interactions.

There is, however, one notable exception that led to a new Paiute reservation. When in the early 1890s Paiutes economically threatened Anthony W. Ivins, a prominent rancher and leading southern Utah Mormon, he instigated a Paiute removal. In 1890, Ivins and other investors purchased the Mohave Land and Cattle Company, which ran its herd on the Shivwits Plateau, a vast section of country south of St. George at the west end of the Grand Canyon. Remnants of the Shivwits band had retreated to this same land in the wake of the Anglo-American advance. In their destitute condition, these Shivwits occasionally hunted Ivins's cattle for food. Ivins soon concluded that "ranching could not be success-fully carried on, while the Shevwits remained on the land." He appealed to the Bureau of Indian Affairs for aid and suggested to bureau officials that land be purchased on the Santa Clara River so that the Shivwits could be "moved in from the mountains to a place where they could be civilized." Congress approved this action, and the Department of the Interior appointed Ivins a "Special Disbursing Agent" to secure land for the Shivwits.[122]

However, government officials informed Ivins that the land was only to serve as a temporary collecting spot for the Shivwits. Federal policy, shaped by the General Allotment Act of 1887, opposed establishing res-ervations. As one official explained to Ivins, "'[T]he present policy of the Government is to gradually break up the Indian reservation system, allot the lands in severalty, extinguish the Indian title, destroy tribal relations, deal with the Indians in their individual capacity, and absorb them into the national life as American citizens.'"[123] At Shivwits, however, allot-ment never occurred, and the government formally established it as a reservation in 1903.[124] Ivins served as agent to the Paiutes for two years, during which time he purchased and fenced land, bought teams, wagons, and agricultural implements, and established a school. His aim, like that of the government, was to civilize the Paiutes through agriculture. As was typical, however, the land base proved too small to sustain the Shivwits, and they largely continued to fend for themselves as seasonal laborers on Mormon farms. In this case, Ivins's self-interest dovetailed nicely with government policy to further marginalize the Paiutes.[125]

The Shivwits Reservation notwithstanding, through the turn of the century the Mormons continued to interact with Paiutes in relationships of their own making. Mormons employed Paiutes, played and worked with them, and even raced ponies against them.[126] As with the miners, by the turn of the century frontier Mormons came to view their Paiute neighbors with considerably less apprehension than that which had char-acterized earlier interactions.

———————

While both miners and Paiutes threatened Zion's geographic space, Mormons responded differently to those threats. During the boundary-tax dispute, Erastus Snow advised frontier settlers to "arm and defend" themselves, but quickly recanted. When the boundary survey placed several fringe communities within Nevada, those on the Muddy River withdrew back into Utah. Those closest to Pioche, however, stayed and capitalized upon the freighting and trading opportunities available at the mining town.

With the boundary issue settled, Mormons turned to verbal defenses against Pioche. The rhetoric did translate into the politics of exclusion on occasion, with several frontier settlers losing their membership in the kingdom over what were judged to be too intimate embraces with Babylon. Beyond that, moral protectionism generally characterized Mormon defenses against miners. Ecclesiastical leaders warned against gentiles at dances and the threat of losing Mormon girls to the outsiders. As the century wore on, however, especially after Young's death, frontier Saints settled into an acceptance of their mining neighbors, although never an acceptance of their ways. Bishop Lee of Panaca encouraged tolerance toward miners, and the Saints even prayed for their neighbors at Pioche and Bullionville. By the turn of the century, Mormons worked and prospected at DeLamar and other locales without the same threat to membership that had earlier accompanied such activities.

A similar transformation took place within Mormon policy toward the Paiutes. During the initial stages of frontier settlement, Mormon–Indian relations were tense and then grew worse during the Black Hawk War. Throughout central and southern Utah, Mormons retaliated violently against Paiutes, and a general war hysteria led to the murder of several Indians. On the frontier, however, the settlers generally adopted Young's vigilance policy. They abandoned small outposts and huddled together for safety, largely remaining on the defensive. Military drill and organization accompanied these efforts, a practice only briefly hinted at by Snow in regard to encroaching miners but put into full effect against raiding Paiutes. Clearly, the Mormons recognized their position on the hierarchical ladder of Americanism. A military clash with miners would bring undesirable repercussions that could further threaten Zion's already suspect spot on the national stage. Military actions against the Paiutes, however, would fall in line with the government's own practice, thereby placing the Mormons on par with other Anglo-Americans.

Following the Black Hawk War, the pendulum of Mormon–Paiute interaction swung the other way. Frontier Saints, especially those at Hebron, established intimate relations with their Paiute neighbors, much more than ever existed with the miners at Pioche and Bullionville. Although a tension between conflicting preachings likely confused some Saints and might have been used to justify either murdering or marrying

Paiutes, Mormons never resorted to the same type of rhetorical defenses against Paiutes that they employed to keep the mining frontier at bay. While one Latter-day Saint did argue against marrying the Paiutes, another encouraged the practice as a method of redemption, and at least a few frontier Mormons took Paiute wives. Intermarriage with miners, however, was never encouraged.[127] Mormon interaction with miners almost always took place at the mining camps, and usually for economic purposes. Early on, when the miners came to Mormon dances, the Saints attempted to keep them away. In contrast, the Paiutes posed less of a threat to Mormon communitarian space. Mormons at Hebron invited Brush-head's family to live among them; Hebronites ate with the Paiutes, traded with them, played with them, employed them, and gave their religious offerings to them. John Pulsipher even called Brush-head's family "good honorable people," an appellation he never applied to the miners at Pioche.

Frontier Mormons, in essence, seemed more threatened by miners than Paiutes in what boiled down to a matter of power—who possessed it and who did not. The Mormons saw themselves as culturally superior to the Paiutes and adopted a paternalistic role, designed, as Anthony W. Ivins put it, to "civilize" them. By 1890, Ivins, at least, deemed that such civilizing could best take place on a reservation, particularly away from his cattle. Even that removal, however, did not end Mormon interaction with the Paiutes outside of reservation boundaries. The miners at Pioche, in contrast, represented more of a challenge to Mormonism's nineteenth-century errand to build Zion. Anglo-American outsiders, not Indians, had driven the Saints to the Great Basin, and by 1864 other outsiders were pushing against Zion's back door. For the Mormons, the battle with the miners was over Zion's soul, whereas the challenge with the Paiutes centered on saving fallen souls. By 1900, the Mormons had negotiated an intercultural space for themselves somewhere between the Paiutes and the miners.

6 "The Out-Post of Civilization"

The "booming of anvil guns," the "firing of bombs," and other "demonstrations of joy" announced the Fourth of July festivities at Pioche in 1873. The swelling "throng" of people who gathered that day offered "forcible evidence" that "Pioche was determined not to be behind any of her neighbors in the display of patriotism on Independence Day." The Pioche Brass Band led a long procession of people through the streets in what the newspaper deemed "an imposing pageant." Little Lizzie Ward was chosen as the "Goddess of Liberty" and was "handsomely and appropriately attired so as to represent the Red, White and Blue." Mexican War veterans, county officers, public school children, mining company representatives, and citizens on foot, in carriages, and on horseback joined the procession. One notable entry, the "Ship of State," carried thirty-seven "misses," each representing a different state in the Union. Another crowd pleaser was the "magnificent American flag" borne by William Funk, a member of the city's engine and hose company. Funk's "brawny arms" held the banner aloft "to the gaze and admiration of the multitude." The stars and stripes were "trimmed with heavy gold bullion," and a silver shield adorned the flag's rosewood staff.

As attention turned toward the festivities of Independence Day, however, the Pioche newspaper reminded its readers that the town's "stalwart miners" did not rest. They continued to wield the hammer and pick "untiringly." The powerful engines at the mines "never ceased to beat," their "steady pulsations" night and day unearthed rich ores, providing "substantial evidences" of the town's "prosperity." The unstated message was clear: the mines at Pioche were yielding the bullion that would continue to trim American progress with gold and silver. From the moment of the nation's founding, the newspaper proclaimed, "success, prosperity and victory have been the constant companions of the banners of the Great Republic." Pioche residents saw themselves as a part of what one local poet termed the nation's "growing greatness."[1]

At Pioche, nationalism *was* religion. "All personal and political feelings will be hushed for to-day," the *Daily Record* announced, "and all who revere the sacred memories of the past will join heartily and with patriotic zeal in the celebration of the Fourth." While Mormons and Paiutes held worldviews that put them at odds with prevailing American values of progress and acquisitiveness, the miners at Pioche embodied them. In the Independence Day parade at Pioche there was no ship of state for the Territory of Utah, and the Paiutes were not represented either. As miners at Pioche defended their space against neighboring Mormons and Paiutes, they did so largely out of a desire to transmit a "priceless heritage" to "posterity." In 1874, Judge D. Corson, the town's Fourth of July "Orator of the Day," admonished: "Mothers, teach your children in their infancy the duties they owe to their country. . . . Fathers, teach your sons that 'eternal vigilance is the price of liberty.'" "As citizens of the State and nation," he proclaimed, "we must guard our institutions with jealous care against both foreign and domestic foes; guard them against secret as well as open enemies."[2]

While the Mormons struggled to defend Zion, and the Paiutes to protect their sacred space, the miners at Pioche guarded prevailing American values. Instead of the Mormon Zion or the Paiute center, Pioche was national space, and its connection was to progress, wealth, and destiny. The laissez-faire capitalism that permeated Gilded Age America played out at Pioche in a boom-bust cycle more exaggerated than that of the American economy from the 1870s to the 1890s. As a right of citizenship, Piochers were only there for the wealth, anyway. They were chasing the American Dream, the fulfillment of which many believed lay buried in a godforsaken corner of the West. One distant observer praised the "enterprising Piochers" for the magnitude of their business operations and extent of their trade. In his mind, Pioche proved that the nation's vast plains, rugged mountains, and deep ravines proffered "no barrier to American enterprise." To the young and restless of the East who "can scarcely save a dime," he advised, "'Go west, young man; go west,' even unto Pioche."[3] In the late 1870s, as the town's mines played out and its population dwindled, Pioche still saw itself as "the out-post of civilization" in southeastern Nevada.[4] From such a vantage point, the miners judged Paiute folkways and Mormon polygamy and theocracy and found them un-American and uncivilized.

––––––––––

Ironically, as the historian Laurie F. Maffly-Kipp suggests of California's gold rush society, the mining community at Pioche "was not in itself a stable alternative to eastern culture but was instead a community founded on the values of mobility and rapid change."[5] Like mining societies across the West, Pioche was filled with rootless single men (in 1870, the sex ratio—the number of males for each hundred females—was 1,248).[6] Pushed by the desire to escape the ravages of the Civil War and pulled by the western lure of wealth, America's 1860s migration brought thousands of fortune seekers west. The historian Dean L. May contends that such a context created in these migrants "a people perhaps more prone to be individualistic" and "less obligated to the broader society."[7] To make sense of such a self-reliant world, the miners at Pioche located themselves "within larger frameworks of meaning, frameworks whose horizons stretched well beyond the chaotic boundaries of El Dorado."[8]

At Pioche, "abstract nationalism" became a binding force through which the miners "acquired a sense of self-identity and personal direction."[9] For the native-born miners, the town's diverse population in 1870—48 percent of whom were foreign-born—must have heightened the need for a broadly based unity. No wonder that the Fourth of July parade at Pioche honored Mexican War veterans, but not those from the Civil War. There was no need for the divisiveness of that conflict to sour the festivities. The Mexican War represented Manifest Destiny at its pinnacle and provided a national triumph that the miners could rally behind. On a daily basis, perhaps Mormons and Paiutes filled a similar void, albeit in a negative way. As guardians of American progress it was easy for the miners to turn a suspect eye toward culturally distinct others, especially Mormons and Paiutes, whose values mocked the miners' quest for wealth.

The irony of the Pioche slant on the Mormons and Paiutes was the town's own incivility and lawlessness, especially from 1870–76. Those boom years were replete with incidents of wife beating, chicken stealing, dog poisoning, shooting, chloroforming, robbery, lawsuits, indecent exposure, jail break, fist fighting, drunkenness, and suicide.[10] One report characterized the town this way: "Pioche is overrun with as desperate a class of scoundrels as probably ever afflicted any mining town on this coast, and the law is virtually a dead letter. Murders and attempted murders are almost of daily occurrence, and the six-shooter and bowie-knife are the only arguments used in settling the most trifling difficulties."[11]

It was not only violence, however, that distinguished the town. Pioche residents seem to have had a general disregard for the physical condition of their camp. Its hillside location caused considerable difficulty during spring runoff. "The streets are running with streams of muddy water," the newspaper complained in March 1874, "and the mud is becoming a serious impediment to travel by vehicle, on horseback or on foot."[12] When mud was not a problem, "garbage and filth" was. At various times the *Daily Record* criticized a "reeking mass" of rubbish, "decaying refuse," and "offensive and decaying matters" polluting town avenues. One article described Main Street as "demoralized by packing cases, old boots, rags, discarded clothing, old wrapping paper and litter of every discription." Occasionally merchants tackled the problem, but the newspaper still suggested scavenger birds as a solution: "Here, as we have no sewerage system nor cleansing natural stream, [the raven's] services are especially desirable."[13]

There was no town government at Pioche to provide a community infrastructure. The town became the seat of Lincoln County in 1871 and thereafter relied upon county commissioners to oversee community affairs. County officials were frequently corrupt and self-serving, however. Throughout the nineteenth century, commissioners struggled to finance the county government in the wake of a graft scandal involving the construction of the courthouse at Pioche. The fraud cost tax payers hundreds of thousands of dollars and earned the building the nickname "the million-dollar courthouse."[14]

The true leaders of Pioche were the capitalists who owned the mines and mills and provided employment to its restless population. William Raymond and John Ely enjoyed success as operators of the Raymond and Ely mines, which produced 60 percent of the town's ore during the boom years. The Meadow Valley Mining Company accounted for another 30 percent of the metals extracted. Both companies, operated out of offices at Pioche and San Francisco, were traded on the San Francisco stock market, and were largely funded by California businessmen. Besides the two French financiers F. L. A. Pioche and Louis Lacour, a long list of San Francisco's "best-known capitalists" invested in the Meadow Valley Company, including Isaac Friedlander, Lloyd Tevis, Darius Mills, and William Ralston. The company also benefitted from the expertise of Alexis Janin, a prominent mining engineer and graduate of the Royal Academy of Mining in Freiberg, Saxony, then the "world's most prestigious mining school." Janin established the mill procedures used to extract silver from the rock mined at Pioche.[15]

By the mid 1870s, however, the Raymond and Ely and the Meadow Valley Companies hit water in their shafts and soon fell on hard times. Around the same time, prospectors discovered silver in sandstone at what would come to be called Silver Reef, a new mining camp over one hundred miles southeast of Pioche in Utah. Many Pioche miners, merchants, and mill owners simply moved to the new bonanza town—buildings and all—in what some called the "Pioche stampede." By the spring of 1878, one former Piocher described Silver Reef as "flourishing" and estimated that over one thousand inhabitants resided there. He believed that "fully eight hundred of them are from Pioche and vicinity. Many of the old Piochers established here are doing well," he continued, "among whom are John Cassidy, Jacobs & Sultan and Peter Harrison." He went on to describe Harrison's large and commodious building, which served as a grocery store, furniture store, and "first-class lodging house." Other former residents of Pioche had moved saloons, hardware stores, and other businesses to Silver Reef and were all benefitting from the boom.[16]

As Silver Reef rose, Pioche fell. By the early 1880s, Raymond and Ely mortgaged their company to a San Francisco bank. Meanwhile, Joseph Eisenmann, a local merchant, and W. E. Griffin, a Pioche banker, bought the Meadow Valley property. In the mid 1880s, William S. Godbe, the excommunicated Mormon and critic of Brigham Young's mining policy, purchased the Meadow Valley mines and also secured title to the former Raymond and Ely ores. Godbe then organized the Pioche Consolidated Mining Company, capitalized at five million dollars. It was a move that marked a shift from San Francisco to Salt Lake City as the center of finance for mining at Pioche. For a time, Godbe breathed new life into Pioche and Bullionville, but in the wake of the nationwide depression of 1893, he too lost his fortune and soon ended operations.[17]

For its capitalists, Pioche was only a temporary way station on the road to wealth anyway. Franklin Buck, a merchant, rancher, and investor of mines at Pioche, explained it this way: "All our mining companies are incorporated in California; have their headquarters in San Francisco. Our people are constantly flitting back and forth. From Pioche to San Francisco is four days. When people make enough money here they go there to live and spend it and send their children there to school."[18] Pioche's mine laborers likewise developed little sense of place. When one worker, Andy Williams, received word that his brother had died and left him seventy-five thousand dollars and a "fine farm" in Ohio, he wasted little time getting "jolly drunk" and heading east. The newspaper hoped that "he will not forget his old stomping ground" but nonetheless predicted that "many of the poor miners in camp" would regularly check at the post office "in the hope that some wealthy relative has kindly remembered them in their wills."[19]

Clearly, the miners at Pioche were focused more upon themselves than they were upon long-term community building. Franklin Buck described the prevailing attitude in a letter to his sister: "You are right in thinking that we live here just as we please. If we want a hot whisky toddy we have it. If we cho[o]se to lay abed late, we do so. We come and go and nobody wonders. . . . We are free from all fashions and conventionalities of Society, so called with you. I like this."[20] Individualism and the quest for wealth reigned supreme at Pioche, and the tenacious prospector was valued above all. In 1875, as the town's silver extraction began to slow, the *Record* ran an article championing the persistent search for new locations. Even though many efforts failed, the newspaper still encouraged that "one success often proves abundantly able to remunerate all former mishaps. . . . We say honor to the brave and hardy prospector, for it is those energetic, fearless men that discovered the metallic riches of Nevada and proved it to be the treasure-house of the world."[21]

In such light, the miners' defense of their space against Mormons had at its roots the starkly contrasting treasures—earthly versus heavenly—that the two groups sought. Early on, the miners viewed their Mormon neighbors with distrust and scorn. The historian James W. Hulse, a native of Pioche, characterized the town as "overwhelmingly anti-Mormon" and noted that "there was occasional tension between the miner and Mormon communities in the early years."[22] That tension was not unique to Pioche but was rather reflective of a broader American antagonism. As the historian David Brion Davis contends, in the nineteenth century many non-Mormons saw the Latter-day Saints as "undermining political and economic freedom in the West," actions that shined in the face of America's "glorious heritage" and stood in the way of its "noble destiny." Like Americans elsewhere, the miners at Pioche turned their Mormon neighbors into an inverted image of themselves. As such, the frontier Saints challenged dominant American values embodied in "Jacksonian democracy and the cult of the common man." To outsiders there was no individualism in Mormonism, but rather the Saints were "deluded by a false sense of loyalty and moral obligation." Zion was the antithesis of free society, and it worked "to overthrow divine principles of law and justice."[23]

Brigham Young's outspoken policy against mining stood as an affront to the value system at Pioche and placed the Saints outside of prevailing

American norms. Miners and government officials were clearly aware of the Mormon policy, which became a fundamental barrier between the two cultures. Stephen Sherwood, a founder of the Meadow Valley mining district, described feeling "unsafe" as a prospector because he believed that "the Mormons were opposed to opening mines."[24] The mining commissioner Rossiter W. Raymond claimed that "few" Mormons were willing to work as miners, and the government surveyor George Wheeler noted that "the Policy of the Mormons has been to discourage mining." General Patrick Edward Connor alleged that "miners and mining are denounced by the Mormon leaders" and claimed that while stationed at Fort Douglas he found it necessary to furnish "escorts of my troops to prospectors and miners to protect them from violence."[25]

For at least some, therefore, the problem was not simply that Mormons opposed mining but that they violently sought to stop it, a notion that carried over to the frontier. In 1866, when the miner George Rogers was found dead, fellow prospectors at Pahranagat quickly concluded that he "was murdered by the Mormons." As the miners saw it, the Saints of southern Utah were already "celebrated" for their "deeds of blood." The miners were determined to "protect themselves against the Mormons" and vowed that "there would be hell to pay in a short time."[26] Although that particular incident proved an Indian murder, the Mormon reputation among miners as conspiratorial killers persisted.

The Mountain Meadows Massacre, although already over a decade old by the time Pioche sprang to life, still colored the gentile perception of Mormons in southwestern Utah. The massacre occurred in 1857, a year in which war hysteria permeated Utah society. Brigham Young had declared martial law, and the Mormons braced for an invasion of federal troops in what came to be called the Utah War. Within that context, zealous southern Utah Mormons reacted beyond the bounds of reason to murder all but the youngest members of the Baker-Fancher party, a California-bound immigrant group from Arkansas. Aided by Southern Paiutes, Mormons from Cedar City, Parowan, and other southern Utah towns slaughtered as many as 120 men, women, and children at Mountain Meadows, a popular camping spot on the Old Spanish Trail. The Mormon participants then took an oath of silence to conceal their roles in the tragedy, laying blame at the feet of the Paiutes. The federal government successfully prosecuted only one Latter-day Saint, John D. Lee, for the crime. In 1877, officials took Lee back to the site of the massacre, where a firing squad executed him.[27]

The massacre and its subsequent cover-up offered plenty of opportunity for miners at Pioche to view their Mormon neighbors with a jaundiced eye. Blood from the slaughter soaked deeply into the southern Utah soil, but never deep enough to disappear altogether. Pioche developed its own connection to the massacre, which miners used to re-stain Mormonism with grisly proof of murder and conspiracy.

In 1871, Philip Klingensmith, bishop at Cedar City at the time of the massacre, became the first participant to break his oath of silence. He did so in a sworn affidavit before the county clerk at Pioche. On 27 September 1872, the *Pioche Record* ran the confession on its front page. Residents not only learned gruesome details of the massacre but read that Klingensmith feared for his life and believed that he would have been assassinated had he made the same confession before any court in the Territory of Utah. Following this disclosure, the *Record* carried succeeding reports of Mormon retaliatory threats against Klingensmith, including news of his rumored death in 1881 at the hands of Mormon "Destroying Angels."[28]

Another disaffected Mormon, Charles Wesley Wandell, developed a connection to the massacre and likewise aired his views at Pioche. Wandell served as district attorney for Lincoln County and then as justice of the peace at Hiko. He had participated in the founding of Pioche, surveyed a portion of the town, and had one of its streets named in his honor. Wandell claimed that he was disfellowshiped from the LDS Church in 1864 for prospecting, but the main cause of his estrangement from Mormonism centered on the Mountain Meadows Massacre. He was not a participant in that event but had the misfortune of passing through the meadow shortly after the slaughter. The horrible scene prompted him to conduct his own investigation. He subsequently published a series of "open letters" to Brigham Young implicating him in the tragedy. He claimed to have evidence linking the prophet and his two counselors to events at the meadow, but he died before having a chance to share his findings at the Lee trials. Wandell did, however, deliver a paid lecture at Pioche about the massacre. Even though the attendance proved "select," those who came "left well satisfied with their evening's entertainment." Although Wandell had moved from southern Nevada before his passing in 1875, residents there still remembered him as a "favorably known" man.[29]

The town's other major connection to the massacre came through its "distinguished lawyer," William W. Bishop, who served as John D. Lee's attorney. Lee faced two trials, the first of which ended in a hung jury, with the eight Mormon jurors voting for acquittal and the others for conviction. At the second trial, however, an all-Mormon jury found Lee guilty of murder at Mountain Meadows, and the judge sentenced him to die. The best evidence suggests that Mormon leaders and federal prosecutors worked out an agreement whereby Mormon officials would ensure Lee's conviction in exchange for an end to prosecution of other Saints. As these events played out, the Pioche newspaper kept its readers informed of Bishop's activities at the trials and hinted at a conspiracy following news of the verdict. Bishop himself claimed that he was used by the Mormon priesthood "when they had need for him" and "kicked by them" when "they had need to drop him."[30]

After the trials, Lee entrusted Bishop with his autobiography and confession, a "brief synopsis" of which Bishop turned over to the *Pioche Record* for publication. The newspaper promised that Bishop would eventually print Lee's entire manuscript—over eight hundred pages—so that the public could have "a full and correct history of Mormonism," including "the accounts of numerous mysterious disappearances and murders."[31]

Clearly, the massacre and its aftermath shaped Piochers' views of their LDS neighbors. That was especially evident in between the two trials, when the *Record* struck Mormonism with perhaps its strongest venom. In an editorial aimed at plural marriage, the paper called polygamy "the national disgrace" and admonished that it be "summarily dealt with. . . . If a jury cannot be found in Utah that will convict, import one; if that procedure is unconstitutional amend the Constitution." The polygamists of Utah Territory, the newspaper thundered, "have defied the National Government for more than a quarter of a century, and it is quite time the foul blot was wiped out." It was not only polygamy that offended the *Record*, however; it was the southern Utah polygamists' connection to the Mountain Meadows Massacre: "When will justice be meted out to the worse than savages who took part in the wholesale butchery of defenseless men, women, and children?" the paper demanded. "And this in the name of polygamy."[32]

Besides Pioche's connection to the massacre and its paper's outspoken hatred of polygamy, the town also served as a haven for a few prominent men disgruntled with Mormonism. Patrick Edward Connor, a former commander at Fort Douglas in Salt Lake City and arch nemesis of Brigham Young, turned at least part of his attention to Pioche after leaving the military. Through his soldiers he had been involved in the organization of the Meadow Valley Mining District in 1864; he traveled there himself in 1870 to guard his interests and invest in additional mines. Connor built a saw mill to supply lumber to the town and owned and operated the Pioche Water Works for a time. He also served as director of the Salt Lake, Sevier Valley, and Pioche Railroad, a short-lived company that failed in its attempt to build a narrow-gauge road from Salt Lake to Pioche.[33]

Connor's anti-Mormon stance was well known in Nevada and elsewhere. He did little to hide his view of the Saints as "traitors, murderers, fanatics, and whores." In 1866 he even testified before the U.S. House Committee on Territories regarding what he termed "Mormon trickery" and its attendant "tyranny and oppressions." He charged the Mormons with treason, the unlawful practice of polygamy, a system of leader-dictated homicides, and a violent opposition to mining. In Nevada, such anti-Mormonism was deemed admirable, especially as Connor sought the Republican nomination for governor in 1878. Among the list of qualities his supporters touted were Connor's involvement in the development of Pioche and his executive ability in dealing with the Mormons: "He did more to give the Gentiles a foothold in Mormondom than any man living or dead," one newspaper bragged. Although he failed to gain his party's nomination, he had already left his mark at Pioche and must have shaped attitudes there against the Mormons.[34]

At least two other men disappointed with Utah and the Saints likewise were drawn to the mining town. William Godbe, the excommunicated dissenter who had lost his LDS membership partly over his opposition to Young's mining policy, played an active role at Pioche during the 1880s. Like Connor, he was an outspoken critic of the Mormon theocracy and must have found sympathetic ears in Pioche. The Lincoln County assessor, N. H. Carlow, was another apostate Mormon who made a home at Pioche.[35]

Apart from the mining town's magnetism for disenchanted Mormons, Piochers had opportunities of their own to formulate opinions of their LDS neighbors, likely on a daily basis. Mormons from throughout central and southern Utah freighted and traded at the mining camp. The interaction between the two groups was generally of an economic nature and primarily occurred in Piochers' space. In such a setting it was easy for the miners to poke fun at the Saints.

The perception that the trade at Pioche was controlled by Brigham Young to fatten his coffers no doubt created resentment. "Thousands of dollars of gold and silver coin pass every month from Pioche to the Utah settlements, never to return," the *Daily Record* complained in 1873. Thus the town's hard currency was "lost to local circulation forever, and goes to swell the capital of that monopolizing institution of Brigham Young." To combat such an unequal balance of trade, the *Record* encouraged its readers to develop the county's agricultural resources. "We must be self-sustaining before we can be truly prosperous," it prodded.

In a mining culture that honored the tenacious prospector, such a call to the plow likely fell on deaf ears. A day later, the *Record* flatly noted that "an unusually large number of produce wagons came in . . . from the Utah settlements, bringing chickens, eggs, potatoes, flour and grain." Piochers should not have been surprised by this, at least according to the *Salt Lake Tribune*. It responded to the *Record's* earlier complaint, advising Pioche residents that the Saints were simply doing as counseled: "[T]o milk the Gentiles and monopolize everything to their own advantage."[36]

The arrival of "teams from Mormondom" became a fact of life at Pioche and continued well past the turn of the century.[37] Piochers, therefore, found ways to cope. Bandits worked the roads leading from town, where they attacked returning traders and stole their cash profits. On one occasion, a thief even reportedly admonished his victim "to go and sin no more by dealing with Gentiles." In response, the newspaper advised the LDS teamsters to "carry arms and be always ready to defend themselves."[38] Attacks of a different sort occasionally occurred in town. One day Pioche youth pelted Mormon peddlers with eggs, while on another occasion the Mormon Orson Huntsman experienced similar intolerance. After Huntsman had unloaded his lumber at the Raymond and Ely mine, he asked the superintendent how long before the whistle would blow, explaining that the noise would spook his horses. The superintendent responded that it would not blow for another hour, but then promptly went in and "turned the whistle loose, loud as thunder." Huntsman's team and wagon bolted and did not stop until it crashed a quarter of a mile away.[39]

A derogatory air permeated the cultural interaction at Pioche, but the attitude was not entirely negative. In fact, one judge at Pioche, likely Mortimer Fuller, even gained favor with the Saints in Salt Lake City. In an 1871 editorial, the LDS-owned *Deseret News* touted the judge as "a sensible man" for impaneling two polygamists as jurors, as well as admitting as citizens of the United States several men who had more than one wife. The editorial was clearly meant as an attack on Judge James B. McKean, the federally appointed Chief Justice of Utah. McKean excluded Mormons who believed in polygamy from juries and refused to naturalize Mormon aliens on the same grounds. The *News* therefore contrasted McKean with the "sensible and impartial judiciary" at Pioche and concluded that "if a U.S. judge in Nevada will admit 'Mormons' to citizenship in that state without asking questions about religion; and will have men with more than one wife on their juries, it is safe to presume that there is nothing unconstitutional or unlawful in so doing." On this issue the *Pioche Record* proved somewhat sympathetic to the Mormon cause. Although it contended that "there are faults on both sides," it

called McKean unfit for office and advocated his removal, especially because his rulings "seem only successful in stirring up a bitter sectarian
feeling and causing a legal blockade."[40]

On an individual basis, there were other events that bridged the
cultural divide. Despite warnings to the contrary, at least a few Mormon women married miners. Emma Atchison, a Mormon from Panaca,
married John H. Ely, a partner in the Raymond and Ely mine. The union
proved influential in securing Mormon aid for Ely as he developed mines
at Pioche and a mill at Bullionville.[41] Romance brought another couple
together, too. A resident of Pioche evidently "fell in love with the Bishop's
daughter at Eagle Valley" and determined to marry her, but not before
becoming a Mormon himself. The *Record* made light of the affair: "Another nice young man has been saved from everlasting damnation," it
announced. The youth went to St. George and "was doused into the grease
vat in the temple and wears endowment duds." That was a consequence
of loving a Mormon: "[H]e either had to go through the vat or do without
the girl. . . . That's right, young sisters, make the boys get well greased
before you marry them," the paper jabbed. Hannah Hamblin, a Mormon
girl from Clover Valley, chose to disregard that advice, however. She married Thomas Logan at Pioche. Justice Young performed the ceremony in
what the newspaper deemed "quite a fashionable wedding."[42]

Baptism provided another link between the cultures, as at least a few
gentiles joined the Mormon faith. Stephen Sherwood, a founder of the
Meadow Valley Mining District, eventually attracted some of his family
to the area. A few of his sons operated a saw mill at Clover Valley and
a lumber yard on Main Street in Pioche. Mormons from Clover Valley
and Hebron freighted for the Sherwoods and must have had an influence
upon at least two of the brothers, John and William. According to one
Latter-day Saint, Church elders preached to the Sherwoods "time and
again" until John, William, and their families were converted. They were
baptized in March 1879 at Clover Valley and manifested a "good spirit,"
especially in regard to their tithing obligations.[43]

One miner at Pioche, however, did not have to get baptized to gain
an appreciation for the Mormons. In 1871, Franklin Buck visited among
the Saints at several southern Utah towns. Upon his return to Pioche,
he concluded that "the Mormons are the Christians and we are the Hea-
thens." He went on to compare Pioche with what he found at the Mormon towns: "In Pioche we have two courts, any number of sheriffs and
police officers and a jail to force people to do what is right. There is a
fight every day and a man killed about every week. About half the town
is whisky shops and houses of ill fame. In these Mormon towns there

are no courts, no prisons, no saloons, no bad women; but there is a large brick Church and they keep the Sabbath—a fine schoolhouse and all the children go to school. All difficulties between each other are settled by the Elders and the Bishop. Instead of every man trying to hang his neighbor, they all pull together. There is only one store on the co-operative plan and all own shares and it is really wonderful to see what fine towns and the wealth they have in this barren country. It shows what industry and economy will do when all work together." Polygamy, however, was difficult for Buck to swallow: "The Devil is not as black as he is painted. Take out polygamy from the Mormon system and I see nothing to object to and that will surely die out in the rising generation."[44]

By the 1880s, Pioche's boom years were over, the aftermath of the Mountain Meadows Massacre had largely played out, and the miners at Pioche and Bullionville had settled into a tentative tolerance of their Mormon neighbors. The newspaper continued to make light of Mormon ways, but it nonetheless employed a Panaca Saint to keep its readers appraised of happenings in town. In 1882, Bullionville elected a Latter-day Saint as justice of the peace "over their ungodly precinct," and in the 1890s Pioche and Panaca baseball teams competed.[45]

Polygamy, however, still created a chasm too wide to span. A growing national outrage over Mormon marital practices prompted Congress to pass the Edmunds Act in early 1882, which made it easier to convict polygamists by lowering the standard of proof. No longer would lawmen have to provide evidence of illegal marriage; they would simply have to prove "unlawful cohabitation." It also disqualified polygamists from voting, serving on juries, and holding public office.[46] As Congress debated the Edmunds bill, the *Pioche Weekly Record* weighed in on the issue in a lengthy editorial titled "Down with Polygamy." The paper began its argument in a somewhat sympathetic tone toward its polygamous neighbors, especially as it pointed out the hypocrisy of many easterners who denounced Mormons as immoral yet indulged in extramarital affairs themselves. Still, the paper's stance was decidedly antipolygamy, albeit with a sarcastic twist: "The people of Southeast Nevada have done more to blot out the practice of polygamy among the Mormons than all the balance of the inhabitants of the American continent combined," the *Record* bragged. Its method of "throttling this twin relic of barbarism" was simply for the miners to marry "the Utah girls" themselves. When a Mormon wed more wives than the law allowed, "the Navadians have eloped with the extra wives." "The Mormons must be taught that they have to cease the practice of polygamy," it wryly demanded, "even if every man in Lincoln county has to marry two dozen wives himself. Down with polygamy."[47]

Only a few months following this editorial, Panaca Saints made a friendly gesture toward their neighbors at Pioche and Bullionville in what turned out to be a public-relations ploy on polygamy. The Saints invited the miners to Sunday services to hear John D. T. McAllister, a regional Church leader from St. George, address the group. Residents from Pioche and Bullionville responded enthusiastically as several buggy teams full of visitors filled the Mormon chapel. McAllister used the occasion to explain the practice of polygamy to the outsiders—but to little avail. The editor of the *Record* joked that the truthfulness of the discourse caused the visitors to look "upon the seven beautiful young ladies who composed the choir" and to conclude "how happy we would be with all of them, and yet how miserable with only one." This dig aside, the editor complimented McAllister's preaching and noted that, "owing to the number of gentiles present, . . . those who spoke were all very careful not to utter a word which would offend any one in the house. . . . We were well satisfied with our trip to Panaca."[48]

Apart from polygamy, perhaps most telling of a shift in attitude toward the Latter-day Saints was the *Record's* coverage of significant events in Mormondom. In 1877 it gave nearly full-page attention to the execution of John D. Lee at Mountain Meadows but only curtly noted the death of Brigham Young that same year.[49] In contrast, on the event of Utah statehood in 1896, the paper devoted nearly two columns to its coverage under the headline, "Now the State of Utah." By that time the Mormons had renounced polygamy and adopted the national two-party system, and local Saints were embracing mining. To gain statehood, Mormons had abandoned the key principles—polygamy and theocracy—that divided them from the miners at Pioche and the rest of the nation. Those gone, it was easy for Pioche to welcome Utah into the sisterhood of states. Although the newspaper did not comment on the event, it ran a wire from the Washington press that noted, "The Mormon question was at one time thought to interpose insuperable obstacles to Statehood; but with the downfall of polygamy Mormonism has ceased to be viewed as a menace to the institutions of the land."[50]

Though painful, the Americanization of the Mormons was far less complicated than that of the Southern Paiutes. Broadly defined, the Mormons were Anglo-American Christians who, in appearance, were largely indistinguishable from their mining neighbors. To Americanize, they only had to shed offensive religious ideals. To find similar acceptance, the Paiutes would have had to shed their skin, an impossible task that would keep the Paiutes from ever enjoying the same benefits of mainstream American life that the Mormons slowly began to realize after the turn of the twentieth century.

Unlike the Mormons, the miners lacked a religiously motivated vision of Indian redemption. Racism largely permeated the exchanges between miners and Paiutes, which occasionally erupted into violence. Miner–Paiute interaction took on a variety of forms: the miners employed Paiutes, played poker with them, robbed, murdered, raped, and sometimes pitied them, but did little to understand them. Like the Mormons, the miners viewed Paiutes in an Anglocentric manner that required them to abandon Indian ways as a means of finding acceptance. The miners maintained a racially based perspective of the Paiutes as "red men," which persisted throughout the nineteenth century.

Overall, the miners saw Paiutes—and Native Americans in general—as troublesome, especially as they impeded access to western mineral wealth.[51] No doubt Piochers shared in the optimism of fellow resident George W. Arnold, who predicted that "the western prospecters will not be kept back very long by the murdering Indian."[52] In essence, guarding mining space at Pioche was tantamount to guarding the nation's wealth. Piochers called Indians who interfered with such a mission "skulking assassins" and "murdering savages," not only because they occasionally killed a prospector but because they "slaughter[ed] American citizens engaged in their lawful business."[53] As a right of citizenship, the miners were determined to find their fortune in the West and were unwilling to let Paiutes stand in their way.[54]

Early on, the town's opinion of Paiutes was largely shaped by reports of Indian troubles elsewhere, as well as those filtered through the tribe's Indian agent stationed at Pioche. In 1872, news reached town that Muddy Valley Paiutes allegedly had harassed several whites along the Muddy River. One account claimed that Paiutes chased a settler to his dwelling, fired several shots at him, and nearly cut off two of his fingers with a shovel. The county assessor likewise purported to have been "bothered going through the lower part of the country." The assessor concluded that "these Indians will put any man out of the way who they think will not be missed." In light of such circumstances, the paper recommended that the Indian agent George W. Ingalls, then living at Pioche, "make his permanent residence where the Indians are, instead of where they are not." The *Record* worried that "if something is not done, and that speedily, trouble will ensue. A large number of these 'Reds' have Henry rifles and six shooters and are much better armed than the Whites."[55] Two weeks later, when Ingalls left Pioche to investigate Indian affairs throughout the region, the newspaper hoped that "his mission among the Indians . . . will result in good to the settlers."[56]

By 1873, things had changed. In March, President U. S. Grant had created the Moapa Reservation, and supplies intended for the Paiutes began arriving through Pioche. A six-thousand-pound shipment of salt pork, however, never reached the reservation. It was auctioned at Pioche to cover the unpaid freight charges. The incident disillusioned the newspaper with regard to the government's handling of Paiute affairs. "Now, who will make up the loss of that 6,000 pounds of pork to the Indians?" the *Record* wondered.[57] By then, Pioche's boom times had attracted an Indian population to town, so interaction with the natives was no longer someone else's concern. When one "poor old Indian" was discovered abandoned by his tribe and lying on the mountainside near death, the paper demanded, "Where is the Indian Agent?" More importantly, it questioned, "[H]ow long shall an outraged people be exhorbitantly taxed to pay annuities to the Indians, to give them the means of providing themselves with a decent subsistence, and then see the money squandered in every possible manner except the legitimate one, while the poor Indian is paid in stinking hog meat that would poison a coyote, and blankets too coarse in the web to stop the career of a frightened rabbit. Once more in shame and disgust, we repeat the question, 'Where is the Indian Agent?'"[58]

Sympathy over the Indians' plight, however, was short-lived. A series of tragic episodes in 1874 and 1875 illustrates the wanton disregard for Indian life that permeated attitudes at Pioche and surrounding mining camps. The trouble began in June 1874, when two miners named Newton and Stevens attempted to capitalize upon the Native American geological knowledge of the region. Newton and Stevens were no doubt well aware of the role Paiutes played in the early discovery of silver at Pioche and Pahranagat. With dreams of finding similar wealth, the prospectors induced two Indians to serve as guides as they searched for outcroppings of ore. The rock they found, however, proved a disappointment, and the party began its return trip to Pioche. The elder Indian guide lagged behind on the trail and did not eat dinner with the other three. At camp, the guide's suspicious activities continued. Finally, at around two o'clock in the morning, he abruptly sat up from his sleep and "jumped on his feet and commenced to run." Without asking questions, Newton and Stevens opened fire. Three bullets entered the guide's body, and one struck him in the head. He fell dead in a pool of his own blood, while his companion escaped in a flight of panic. Back at Pioche the incident was highlighted as evidence of "the perils of prospecting in this wild country."[59]

This murder enraged other Native Americans, but it also seems to have created guilty paranoia at Pioche, which translated into additional atrocities. Rumors began to circulate of Indian attacks on mining parties or lone prospectors. A renegade band of Shoshone and Paiute warriors, whose reputation for violence grew with each new story, was known to operate in the region west of Pahranagat and north of Las Vegas.[60] In late 1874, when the Castera family and the William Honan prospecting party left Lincoln County for new strikes at Panamint Valley, two hundred miles west, the stage was set for tragedy. "Crooked Leg" and his band of Paiutes murdered two members of the Honan party and wounded Honan himself, who struggled back to Hiko with news of the attack. When weeks passed with no word from the Castera family, hearsay told of their death at the hands of savages. Officials at Pioche arrested a Paiute youth and questioned him as to the whereabouts of the missing group. When the boy denied knowledge of the travelers, Piochers clamored for federal troops to investigate and petitioned the governor for aid. The newspaper demanded that Paiutes at the Muddy Valley Reservation be interrogated: "[T]here is every reason to believe," the *Record* asserted, "that many solitary travelers have fallen victim to the lust for blood which is inborn in Indian nature. Knowing these things, we think it is about time that a measure of retribution should be dealt out to these murdering wretches, the severity of which will give them a lively fear of the vengeance of the whites." The paper fixed its anger upon Tem-piute Bill, a Paiute whom it claimed "is notorious for many rascalities, and strongly suspected of other murders."[61]

Aided by friendly Shoshones, deputy sheriff J. A. Bidwell soon arrested Tem-piute Bill. The sheriff brought him to Hiko but could not keep angry miners from harassing him. A hostile mob questioned Tem-piute Bill, who under violent and intense pressure not only confessed to several murders but named Johnny and Moquitch as accomplices. A party of men then retrieved Moquitch and hanged him alongside Tem-piute Bill from the second-story window of a building at Hiko. The mob next tracked down Johnny at a local Paiute camp and in the melee that ensued murdered him, along with six or seven other Indians who had the misfortune of being there. Somewhat satisfied, the *Record* gloated, "[T]hese bloodthirsty savages have had thus a lesson taught them that it is probable the survivors will not readily forget, and for a time, at any rate, will keep from imbruing their murderous hands in the blood of the unprotected prospector and traveler." Slightly concerned over the blood on the hands of the white vigilantes, the paper moralized, "[M]ob violence we at all times deprecate, but there are times and occasions when it seems to be justifiable." Ironically, in the middle of this frenzy, news of the Castera family's probable safe arrival at its destination circulated at Lincoln County, but by that time mob anger was already beyond control. Captain David Krause of the U.S. army, stationed at Fort Cameron, Utah, investigated the affair and concluded that "the killing was of the ordinary kind that happens on the frontier."[62]

Anxiety over the threat of Indian retaliation persisted at Pioche and grew to a fever pitch in September 1875, when a miner named Toland was reportedly murdered by Indians near Spring Valley, northeast of Pioche. Stories of a widespread Indian uprising soon alarmed miners throughout the region, who quickly appealed for help from the army's Pacific division at San Francisco. Before long, calvary troops under Captain E. V. Sumner were on their way to Spring Valley to suppress the supposed rebellion. Indian signal fires had been seen for weeks throughout the region, which put settlers on edge. Then a report reached army troops stationed at Cherry Creek, Nevada, that ranchers at Spring Valley were besieged by five hundred Indians. Stories also circulated that the whole affair was a Mormon–Indian conspiracy. According to some accounts, Mormons had been baptizing the Indians and promising them that "with water fixing they would be all the same as white men." LDS missionaries supposedly told their Indian converts that "they could kill the whites and be supported by the Mormons."[63]

By the time Captain Sumner arrived at Spring Valley, however, the episode was over. A company of armed volunteers from Pioche had already intervened and hanged the Indian whom they deemed responsible for Toland's death. The hanging seemed to satisfy the mob, despite some of its members' determination to "exterminate all Indians guilty or not guilty." Sumner did suggest that the Indians be taken to "a reservation at some distance, and away from Mormon or other influence." Nonetheless, final reports of the affair called the "magnitude of the difficulty . . . greatly exaggerated."[64]

At Pioche, however, this incident, combined with those of the recent past, created apprehension over the town's vulnerability in the midst of Native American territory: "Situated as we are in this wilde desert country," the *Daily Record* editorialized, "surrounded by the red imps who thirst for blood from the day of their birth until death; having suffered in every conceivable way from their cruelty and treachry [sic], we are prepared to judge of the Indian character without prejudice or passion." The *Record* then pronounced President Grant's Indian peace policy "a perfect failure, humbug and fraud" and demanded that instead of preaching and civilizing, "the Indians should all be placed under military rule; should be kept on their reservation or killed." If the government would not act, "[I]t is time that the people of Nevada took the matter in their own hands and put an end to the difficulty by exterminating the entire race." Such a solution, the news concluded, would allow settlers "to reclaim the desert wastes . . . in safety."[65]

Although Indian hating at Pioche never returned to the height it reached in 1874–75, discriminatory methods of frontier justice prevailed there for the remainder of the century. In cases involving whites wounding or killing Native Americans, the perpetrators literally got away with murder. In 1876, when one settler shot and wounded an innocent Indian over a missing suit of clothes, the *Record* declared that it was done "without any just or reasonable cause," but the settler still went unpunished.[66] Similarly, in 1882, when Pahranagat Valley Indians repeatedly herded livestock owned by a Mr. Frenchy out of their garden plot, a vengeful Frenchy shot and killed one of the Indians. The newspaper called it an "outrage," but the justice of the peace acquitted Frenchy on the basis of self-defense.[67] A year later, when an Indian was riddled with a dozen bullets at Bullionville in retaliation for his shooting a dog and wounding a white man, the inquest concluded that the Indian "came to his death from gun-shot wounds, at the hands of unknown parties." Although Paiutes "armed to the teeth" invaded Bullionville a week later, the chief of the Muddy Indians "managed to cool down his warriors," and nothing more came of the incident.[68]

Pioche authorities were similarly complacent on at least two occasions when murder occurred among Indians. In 1878, a Pahranagat Indian named Nick allegedly killed another Paiute known as Ice Cream, over his "squaw." Evidence suggested that Ice Cream's body had been thrown down a well, which prompted Sheriff McKee to investigate. McKee feared that the body at the bottom of the well "might be that of a white person instead of an Indian" and therefore went to the trouble of recovering it. After nearly two days' work, using ropes and grappling hooks, the sheriff and his crew managed to surface the dead person's remains, minus a leg. They identified it as Ice Cream. The Sheriff and his men buried the body near the well, informed the Indians of the death, and then simply dismissed the case. Ice Cream's brother came from the Moapa Reservation to conduct his own investigation. He concluded that indeed Nick had committed the crime and vowed vengeance upon him. Similarly, in the 1895 case of a Paiute murdering a Shoshone, white settlers at Pioche let tribesmen from both groups work it out themselves. After negotiations, the exchange of a "rickety buckboard and worn out harness" settled the affair.[69]

In sharp contrast, when Indians killed whites, Piochers advocated a different standard. In 1879, when Tem-piute Bill's old band allegedly killed a miner near Hiko, the paper recommended that the government station troops in the area to "teach these Indians that they must stop killing white men whenever they take a fancy to."[70] Even as late as 1890, when a Paiute allegedly murdered a mail carrier in southern Lincoln County, extralegal tactics still held sway. Local citizens offered a two-hundred-dollar reward for the suspect, dead or alive, and then threatened the local Paiutes that "if he was not captured every Indian in the vicinity would be exterminated." In response, Paiute tribesmen promptly tracked down and killed the accused man. The *Record* praised local whites for "dealing out summary justice to this red devil" and predicted that the settlers' actions would "have a salutary effect on the balance of the tribe."[71]

It was only in cases of rape of Indian women by white miners that a higher standard prevailed. In more than one incident, rapists served jail time for their crimes against Indian women. The newspaper even castigated as "creatures in the shape of men" six miners accused of gang raping an "old gray-haired [Indian] woman on the verge of the grave." Perhaps, as the anthropologist Martha C. Knack suggests, authorities at Pioche saw the Indian victims "first as women, and then secondarily as representatives of a scorned ethnic group." In punishing the perpetrators for raping Indians, they also may have been attempting to protect the town's Anglo women from similar violence.[72]

In the majority of interethnic exchanges at Pioche, however, prejudice prevailed. Paradoxically, the same Indians that the miners deemed savage and devilish when encountered outside of town became objects of ridicule and scorn when viewed from the security of Pioche.[73] "It is not unusual," the paper complained in 1873, "to see Indians, male and female, stretched out on the ground on the principal streets sunning themselves, forcing pedestrians to walk around their lazy carcases. Would it not be well enough to stop this aboriginal vagrancy?"[74] Despite the town's admitted dependency upon Indian labor for menial tasks, the newspaper still poked fun at the "noble redmen" who worked hauling wood, calling them "Jackasses."[75] In similar derogatory language it reported on "squaw fights" and noted several bouts between Indian men and women, concluding that "the mating season of the Indians must have arrived."[76]

Drunkenness was the other major vice for which Piochers castigated the Indians. The miners' own affinity for liquor was no secret, and drunken brawls were common. Several breweries, saloons, and liquor stores catered to the miners' thirst. The El Dorado Saloon, for example, promised "an excellent place to cool off, with some pleasant beverages, prepared according to the highest rules of the mixologist's art."[77] Some

Piochers in 1873 proposed a temperance society, but liquor remained an integral part of town life. As Franklin Buck explained, "[H]ere we have 35 whisky shops and very few praying women."[78]

Liquor and Native Americans, however, should not mix—at least according to prevailing nineteenth-century Anglo-American standards. From the colonial period onward, Anglos had fruitlessly attempted to control or prohibit the sale of alcohol to Native Americans.[79] At Pioche the story was no different. In April 1877 the newspaper reported on an "Indian Fandango" at the wickiups near town, which included "plenty of whisky." Despite a number of Piochers who joined in the celebration, the paper still encouraged law officers to prosecute those responsible for "the crime of selling whisky to Indians." In a similar article, the *Record* reported that Pioche lawmen had begun the practice of cutting off an Indian's hair when arrested for drunkenness. In a rare show of sympathy, the paper argued that "next to his life, an Indian values his hair," and recommended that "if the officers wish to be of some benefit to the community, let them arrest the men who violate the law by selling the liquor to the red men."[80] Such prodding apparently had little effect. As late as the 1890s the paper still reported on "Indian drunks." In one account it complained that "scarcely a night passes that Indians, both squaws and bucks, cannot be seen reeling past the smelter in a beastly state of intoxication." It again suggested that "the penitentiary is a fit home" for those selling "firewater" to the natives.[81]

Although the racism that permeated Pioche's attitude toward Paiutes never waned, evidence suggests that the miners at least accepted Indians into the lowest levels of Pioche society. The miners employed Paiutes at a variety of tasks, offering them opportunities for wage labor likely not available elsewhere. Like the Mormon traders, Native Americans were attracted to Pioche by the relative abundance of cash that circulated.[82] The Paiute known as Ice Cream, for example, came about his nickname by pushing a wheelbarrow along town streets, where he sold the favored summer treat for which he was named. Gambling also drew Native Americans to the mining camps: "There was an international game of poker played in one of the Bullionville saloons," the *Record* reported in 1882. "The players were a Chinaman, an Indian, a Scandinavian, a Mormon and a Gentile." Although "the wily Chinee got away with the pot," the Indian's participation still suggests that he possessed the cash to play and that he enjoyed a modicum of acceptance at the mining camp, albeit into one of the seamier sides of American life.[83]

At Pioche, exchanges with Mormons and Paiutes were steeped in paradox. Pioche deemed itself an "out-post of civilization" among the Mormons and Paiutes yet demonstrated little civility, especially during its boom years. Miners defended their space by employing notions of "abstract nationalism" centered on American ideals of progress, destiny, and individualism. Like the dramatic ups and downs of the Gilded Age economy, Pioche experienced a boom-and-bust cycle that offered little reward for the lonely prospector and minimal long-term sense of place. Pioche's garbage-strewn streets as well as the graft and corruption of county politicians suggest that individualism won out over community concern and reflect the broader trends of America's post–Civil War plunge into an urbanized industrial society.

Pioche valued the tenacious prospector and his untiring quest for wealth. That quest, however, kept the miners moving, always looking for the next big strike. It also created notions of space that stretched well beyond southeastern Nevada. "I thought I would stay in Pioche and ranch and take life easy," Franklin Buck wrote, "but as soon as the place gave out and no chance to make but a living I grew weary and sighed for new worlds to conquer." For Buck, chasing the American Dream, the search for El Dorado, and the myth of western mineral abundance came to shape his worldview and became his religion. Describing this lifestyle, he wrote, "We expect every day to find or get an interest in a rich mine. We are loose to go to Arizona, Sonora, Colorado or anywhere where we hear of a new town." Even when he decided to settle down and live on a farm in Napa Valley, California, Buck found it difficult to leave—not Pioche, but "this life of excitement, speculating in stock, rich strikes." In contrast, he predicted that "it will be a humdrum slow business to go to picking grapes and milking cows and raising chickens. . . . If I were years younger I would take the mining camps."[84]

The miners' incessant search for wealth brought them to southern Nevada by the thousands in the 1870s, but later it also took them away. By 1900 only a few hundred remained to keep the town alive. The Mormons and Paiutes, in contrast, held notions of space more permanently anchored to a specific place. They valued persistence, stability, and community above the acquisitiveness that permeated Nevada's mining camps and Gilded Age America as a whole. Pioche, in essence, became a lens of prevailing American values through which its residents viewed their Mormon and Paiute neighbors and found them wanting. To make sense of their own mobile and violent society, the miners "characterized the boundary between order and disorder as a cultural divide."[85] The miners therefore deemed Mormon theocracy un-American. Pioche's strong connection to the aftermath of the Mountain Meadows Massacre, as well as its string of residents who disliked Mormonism, offered ample proof of the hierarchical control and blind devotion to authority that the *Pioche Record* believed typified life among the Saints. Polygamy, too, appeared sordid to Piochers. Even Franklin Buck, who admired the unity and order that prevailed at the Mormon towns he visited, could not accept the polygamy that he found there.

Still, attitudes toward the Mormons changed over time according to differing circumstances and personalities. In the 1880s, miners from Pioche and Bullionville attended and enjoyed LDS Church services at Panaca. By 1900, Pioche residents seemed much more at ease with their Mormon neighbors than they had been forty years before—they had not necessarily changed, but Mormonism had more closely aligned itself with mainstream America. In contrast, Piochers' attitude toward the Paiutes barely softened over time. Negative images of "red men" permeated the exchanges. Piochers demonstrated little regard for Paiute life, especially in cases of interethnic murder. Even as late as the 1890s, white officials employed extralegal methods to resolve such episodes. In several instances, the *Pioche Record* decried what it deemed an innate thirst for blood among the Indians at the same time that it washed blood from the hands of mobbing whites. Only in cases of miners raping Indians did the demands of justice hold whites accountable at Pioche. When the interethnic exchanges occurred within the security of town, images of the Paiutes shifted from bloodthirsty to lazy, ignorant, and drunk. In general, Piochers found few things to like about the Paiutes, an attitude that altered little over time.

Piochers had much more in common with their Mormon neighbors than with the Paiutes. Of the Saints, the *Pioche Record* only demanded the eradication of polygamy, while of the Paiutes it called for the extermination of "the entire race." While Mormons could shed offensive religious ideals, the Paiutes could not shed their skin. Broadly speaking, as the Saints abandoned polygamy and theocracy and embraced mining, there was little to distinguish them from the miners at Pioche. Similar Americanization would be impossible for the Paiutes. Even though Piochers employed Paiutes and accepted them into the town's cash economy, racism still clouded the interactions. In the end, like the Mormons and the Paiutes, the miners at Pioche carved an intercultural world for themselves in which they rested on top.

7 *"Dead and Dying in the Sagebrush"*

On one occasion during his explorations of Southern Paiute country, John Wesley Powell came upon "three old women" crouched around the fire of an otherwise deserted camp. The rest of the band had moved on, but the women remained behind. They sat stoically staring into the fire of what would become their death camp. Alternating between sitting, dancing, chanting, and sleeping, they would starve themselves to death over the coming days. It was better that way, according to Southern Paiute belief, so that the women would not turn into *U-núpits*, or witches, and be doomed to live in snake skins.[1]

For the women it was a sacrifice they seemed willing to make. Their death would relieve the band of the burden of their care, which would be especially onerous during winter's meager months: "When the cold moons come," one Southern Paiute explained, "our children are hungry."[2] The Paiutes' cyclical journeys and subsistence economy no doubt required strength and endurance to survive. Sometimes, therefore, the elderly simply stayed behind. The old ones sacrificed themselves for the good of the whole. It was a gift of life for which the rest of the tribe honored them.

When Powell rode up to the three Paiute women, they paid no attention to him. They silently stared into the fire. Eventually, each one stood, aided by a staff, and joined in a dance. Together they circled the fire in a shuffling movement while they chanted:

Aí-ai aí-ai aí-ai
I-van tú ni-shump' 'pa-ní-gunt
U-ni-shump' ú-ni-shump'
I-aí Kwa-vwan' i-aí Kwa-vwan' i-aí

Alas, alas, alas,
Here long enough have I walked the earth
Enough, enough
I will die, I will die.[3]

For half an hour they continued this ritual before resting around the fire again. To Powell, the entire scene was "wild and weird in the extreme," yet it "made a deep impression upon" him. When he came across the rest of the band a few days later, he inquired about what he had witnessed. The band explained the practice to him and spoke of the elderly women's sacrifice in laudable tones.[4]

The Southern Paiutes clearly cherished as virtuous what Powell judged "wild and weird." It was another example of the multiplicity of meanings that had come to reshape life on the southern rim of the Great Basin. Mormons and miners would observe similar examples of Paiute death practices. Viewing such lonely scenes from across shifting cultural divides, it was easy for Anglo-Americans to denigrate the Paiutes. Nonetheless, Mormons and miners faced deaths among their own people that forced them to confront community standards of care for the sick and dying. In that process, the three groups stretched the intercultural space that they had created for themselves beyond the bounds of the physical world to encompass ritualistic notions of an afterlife.

Much like the rituals of possession that anchored each community in the dirt at the edge of the Great Basin to begin with, the death rituals dig deeply into that same dirt to complete the circle of life and thereby solidify the sacred nature of each group's space. Frontier Mormons, miners, and Southern Paiutes each performed distinct rituals designed to mitigate the effects of sickness and death. For the three groups these rituals created order out of tragedy and fostered a sense of community at a time of loss. The rituals likewise reflected and were shaped by each group's broader worldview. The true test of those worldviews, however, came in each community's willingness to stretch the bounds of its rituals to include outsiders. Mormons, miners, and Southern Paiutes were confronted with episodes of sickness and death that took place in each other's space. Their responses reflected their worldviews in action and thereby teach important lessons about the intercultural space that they created. The rites of passage of Mormons, miners, and Southern Paiutes were performed "not simply to *mark* transitions, but to *effect* them"—even across cultural borders.[5]

Exploring the rites of passage, what meanings they held for each group, and how each group dealt with sickness and death is essential to understanding the pervasive ways in which their lives intersected. The three death episodes that follow—a series of Southern Paiute abandonment cases treated as a group, the death of a Mormon sheepherder at Shoal Creek/Hebron, and the death of an Anglo-American miner at Pioche—also highlight defining elements of each group's space. Although sickness and death seemed to elicit cross-cultural sympathy and respect in ways that the difficulties of living together were unable to do, distrust and prejudice still animated exchanges. The stories of death told here speak loudly of the multiplicity of meanings each group brought to the southern rim of the Great Basin. They also serve as sober evidence of the gulf that existed between the Southern Paiute, Mormon, and miner worldviews—a gulf that cast a long shadow even over death.

In a series of incidents in 1873, miners at Pioche were confronted with unsettling moral dilemmas. They found several elderly Shoshones and Paiutes left to die in the sagebrush. Witnessing these scenes forced at least a few townspeople to grapple with a variety of emotions, some of which compelled them to respond. The outreach, however, was limited in scope and begrudged by the newspaper.

In March 1873, a Piocher named Myles A. Knapp came upon "an old Piute squaw" lying in the brush about a mile north of the city. She was between fifty and sixty years old and was "too weak to stand without assistance." She had no food or water and only "a little strip of rab[b]it skin robe" to "protect her from the chill night air." Knapp concluded that she had been "left there by her brutal tribal relations to die." He promptly reported her condition at the hospital, whereupon E. E. Williams, the steward, took "nourishment and necessary medicine" to the woman. Hospital authorities agreed to provide a couch for her and to feed and care for her until the Indian agent, then at the Muddy Valley, "has an opportunity to decide whether he will provide for the unfortunate being, or leave her to starve." Even that level of aid was too much for some. The newspaper complained that the poor fund at the hospital was not intended for Indians. Native Americans were "wards" of the government, it insisted; as such, the Indian agent should provide for their care.[6]

Only weeks later, another informant led Mr. Williams from the hospital and a reporter from the *Record* to two more Indians "dead and dying in the sagebrush." One elderly man lay dead at his camp, his body partly coiled under cedar boughs, resting against a stump, face downward. From the state of the body, Williams believed that the man had passed away two or three weeks previously. Without a shovel at hand to bury the body, the men covered it again with boughs and left "to acquaint the authorities."[7]

On their return to town, however, the men came upon "a scene more dreadful and heartrending than the last." It was "the living skeleton of an old squaw, gray-haired, wrinkled, and, with the exception of a pair of moccasins and a rabbit skin cloak, entirely nude." Williams made her as comfortable as possible, but "she appeared too far gone to realize any attention and too weak for removal." They left her "until an ambulance might be dispatched." Once again, however, the newsman concluded that such "deplorable misery" was not the responsibility of officials at Pioche. "The Indian question is beyond their jurisdiction," he argued.[8]

In another case of death later that month, the Indian agent George W. Ingalls did investigate. He and the coroner concluded that an elderly man found dead near town was a member of a band of Shoshones who had recently arrived at Pioche and that he died from natural causes.[9] Four months later, at the discovery of yet another elderly Indian dying, at least one resident responded with compassion. George Whalen took the Indian some water but reported that "he was hardly able to swallow." Whalen claimed to have known the Indian for three years and described him as an "industrious, hard-working fellow." This time the *Record* blamed the Native Americans: "[I]t is needless to comment on the heartless conduct of the Indians. We who live on the frontier know their habits—that they have less pity for the aged sick than for the beasts of the forest." Yet, besides Whalen, no one from Pioche intervened until two days later, when it was too late. The man died, unprotected from the fierce storm that had passed over a few days previous. Expressing some sense of responsibility for the first time, the *Record* suggested that it was the coroner's duty to "bury those who die indigent. . . . Thus far we have heard of no steps being taken for the burial," it prodded. "This poor old man died alone, naked, without friends, and his body is left to rot on the hillside. And yet Pioche is a civilized community."[10]

More than confronting Piochers with moral dilemmas, these death episodes underscore the horrific poverty of the Paiutes. Neither the Mormons nor miners were ever confronted with the difficult choice of leaving their elderly behind due to a lack of resources. For the Southern Paiutes, the necessity of making such a decision offers grim evidence of the tribe's spot on the lowest rung of the border region's hierarchy of power.[11]

Even though materially impoverished, the Paiutes remained culturally rich, a point abundantly evident in their approach to sickness and death. For them, matters of health were essentially concerns of the spirit. In common cases such as colds, coughs, fevers, stomach aches, rheumatism, sore eyes, swellings, or boils, the Paiutes used a variety of herbal remedies. However, they generally attributed unexplainable sickness to intrusions of material objects or evil spirits into the body, or to "soul loss." In difficult cases, a sick person's community of caregivers would summon a shaman. Paiute shamans could be either male or female tribal members who possessed keen spiritual awareness and came to their power through unsolicited dreams. Generally an animal or sometimes a human spirit appeared to the would-be shamans and instructed them in the art of healing. An owl, wildcat, eagle, badger, mountain sheep, porcupine, or coyote might become the shaman's tutelary spirit. If novices accepted the call to shamanism, the spirit animal would instruct them in the healing rituals of song, dance, and suck. These dreams might repeat themselves over several nights, during which time the newly called would announce the manifestations to the band. Over time shamans might continue to receive instruction from their spirit companion and could acquire additional spirit guides and a repertoire of songs.[12]

When summoned, shamans might wait for instruction from a guardian spirit before proceeding to a sick person's aid. With the spirit guide directing the action, shamans would approach a patient, perhaps carrying a staff and eagle feathers for use in the healing ritual. The ritual consisted of the shaman singing and dancing back and forth as directed by the spirit guardian. At the guardian's instruction, shamans would lay flat on the ground and pull the sick person on top of themselves and then suck the ailment, intruding object, or ghost from the patient. Some shamans might then dance and sing, while others might exhibit the disease object before dismissing it, sometimes through burial or by throwing it away. In particularly troublesome cases, the shaman might ceremoniously breathe a guardian spirit into the sick person so that the spirit could then suck the disease from the patient. The healing ceremony generally lasted all night, and if the ill person was not cured, it might continue over three nights.[13]

If a shaman proved repeatedly unsuccessful, he or she might be suspected of sorcery and could be murdered by bereaved relatives. Those who were effective, however, earned the respect of their patients. One Paiute who claimed to be "nearly dead" described his healing at the hands of Witatsi, a gifted healer: "'I was lying down when he came. As he neared camp he started to sing and dance. He told me there was a ghost in my belly but that he could get it out and that I should be well by morning. By sundown I felt better. He sang and danced all night, and in the morning he left. He took out the ghost and killed it.'"[14] Other shamans gained reputations as specialists. A rattlesnake shaman treated snake bites, a spider doctor specialized in insect bites, and a rock shaman worked with injuries received in falls from cliffs or trees.[15]

Even with common sicknesses Paiutes perceived otherworldly influences at work. In 1872, at a camp in northwest Arizona, John Wesley Powell observed such a belief. Sitting with a group of Paiutes around a fire one evening, the conversation suddenly hushed as the Indians gazed "into the darkness in great terror." The chief, Chu-ar-ru-um-peak, fired his pistol into the night sky, and another man shot an arrow. Other Paiutes scattered ashes from the fire into the wind and "puffed from their mouths." The Paiutes explained that they had heard an *U-ní-pits*, or evil spirit, and were driving it away.[16]

At the same camp a few nights later, Chu-ar-ru-um-peak complained of a piercing headache; or, as he described it, "there was an *U-nu-pits* [sic] in his head." As a remedy, a fellow Paiute rubbed ashes from the fire over his head and into his hair. This was accompanied by "much gesticulation and blowing," which eventually drove the spirit away. The chief announced that "the pain had entirely ceased." Powell seemed somewhat skeptical but noted that the chief reported his cure "with all apparent sincerity."[17]

Thomas D. Brown, a Mormon missionary among the Paiutes in the 1850s, could not help but express similar wonder at the apparent success of Paiute shamanism. When a Paiute woman gave birth and then became ill, she complained of pain running through her left breast to the left shoulder blade. Brown attempted to intervene using Mormon faith healing. He "anointed her breast and shoulder with oil" but wrote that afterwards she was "not much better." Abraham, the woman's husband, then went for a shaman to come and care for his wife. The next day the shaman arrived and began the healing ritual, singing, dancing, and sucking. Over the course of the ceremony he sucked "some nasty green stuff" from the woman as well as a variety of stones, about the size of beans, which he would carry off and hide among the bushes or in the earth. For Brown, it was hard to explain the Shaman's success: "Whether they induce faith in the patient, that by their songs, suction & carrying off the disease; or whether a healing spirit attends them in their administrations; or a magnetic stream passes from the whole through the diseased person—a mesmeric influence that heals, I know not but the general testimony is that often remarkable cures are affected."[18]

Much less sympathetic, the Indian agent A. J. Barnes wondered at the "strange tenacity" with which the Paitues clung to what he called "superstitions." He complained in 1875 that Paiute medicine men "practice the most hideous incantations over the sick." He also expressed dismay that "should the medicine-man . . . lose three patients in succession, they kill him. This they consider inexorable justice."[19]

Paiute death practices were equally difficult for Anglo-Americans to understand. Upon death, relatives placed a departed person's earthly possessions such as blankets, bows and arrows, guns, baskets, and rabbit-skin mantillas with the body. They might paint the corpse's face red with pigment and wrap the entire bundle in buckskin. Traditionally, Paiutes would then cremate the body and may have killed the dead person's dog, horse, and even a relative to serve as companions in the afterlife. This practice bothered Barnes the most. "When a member of a family dies," he wrote somewhat bewildered, "the surviving relatives kill one, two, and sometimes as many as four horses, perhaps to accelerate the departed to the 'happy hunting grounds.'"[20]

San Juan Paiutes continue cremation, while other bands have modified it over time. Perhaps coinciding with Anglo colonization, some Paiutes shifted from cremation to burial. They might use rocks to cover the corpse or deposit it in stone clefts or washes. At the death of a loved one, mourners would cut or singe their hair and abstain from salt and meat for four days. They also abandoned the wickiup where the death took place, and in cases of cremation, burned it along with the body.[21]

Over time, the Paiutes accepted Anglo medical practices and were open to cross-cultural borrowing. In 1875, Barnes commented optimistically that, "little by little, during the last four years, [the Paiutes] have acquired confidence in the mode of treatment practiced by the white man, and to-day . . . they no longer fear to place themselves under the treatment of a white physician."[22] Paiutes also incorporated Mormon faith healing into their health practices. Nevertheless, Paiute shamanism persisted throughout the nineteenth century, and tribal members clung tenaciously to traditional rituals. The Paiute seemed to focus on healing the sick no matter the source of the proposed cure.

The Paiutes held a sacred reverence for life and for the state of a soul in the afterlife, a reverence that became more pronounced when Anglo-Americans attempted to interfere with their funerary traditions. In 1854, when a Paiute child died, the Mormon missionary Rachel Lee tried to persuade the mother to let Lee wash and dress the body and place it in a coffin according to Mormon custom. The Paiute mother flatly refused and requested Lee to leave. Bothered at her inability to intervene, Lee reported that she could not determine "whether this corpse was burnt or hid away."[23] In 1883, citizens at Bullionville murdered an Indian. Following the coroner's inquest, the settlers interred the body. When Paiute tribal members learned of this, however, they dug up the corpse and carried it back to their camp, likely to conduct a proper ceremony.[24]

Even when confronted with bodies from across the ethnic divide, it seems that at least some Paiutes relied upon traditional rites of passage. Perhaps only in the event of murder were Paiutes faced with disposing of Anglo-American bodies. In such cases, Anglo-Americans naturally projected suspect motives onto the Paiutes. In 1879, Tem-Piute Bill's former renegade band allegedly killed a prospector at Pah Rock Springs, about eighteen miles from Hiko. After killing the man, the natives dragged the body among some pine trees and cremated it. The *Pioche Record* concluded that "the Indians have taken to burning the bodies of their victims, destroying all traces of their bloody deeds." Nonetheless, a search in the vicinity uncovered the bones of two additional men whom Paiutes had buried with rocks.[25] Similarly, when Okus murdered George Rogers, he "buried him with rocks in a narrow canyon."[26] While it is impossible to know the catalyst behind such actions, the burning of the body and burial with rocks were consistent with Paiute funerary practices. Even still, the only reason the Paiutes had these bodies in the first place was because they murdered them as outsiders.

The Cry was the final aspect of Paiute death rites and was traditionally separate from a funeral. The Paiutes likely adopted the Cry from their Mojave neighbors and incorporated it into their culture as an important ritual designed to revere the dead. In an annual Cry ceremony, several bands might gather at a central location to mourn those who had passed away that year. Over the course of a night, singers chanted in rhythmic tones, their voices rising and falling in a sacred cadence. The chants were designed to "sing the spirit of the deceased along a special route through traditional Paiute land to his or her dwelling place in the next world."[27]

At a Cry, Paiutes might first remember and mourn for the entirety of their ancestors who had ever lived. Then by name they would cry for those who had passed away in the previous year. Finally, they would pay respect to specific persons whom tribal members desired to venerate. Occasionally a speaker might interrupt the singing to talk to the dead: "We believe you are living in a good country," one chief explained to the deceased. "We think it is a better country than this one and that is why you do not come back. Over there it is always warm and the sun shines.

You have green grass and shady trees and fat game and plenty of food all the time." After such a speech the Paiutes would begin a new chant, gather in a tight circle, and rhythmically cry.[28]

For the Paiutes, rituals of sickness and death served important community functions. Shamans provided connections to the spirit world and offered meaning and cure for otherwise unexplainable illnesses. Death rituals helped Paiutes to find order in the loss of band members and knotted the band and its material goods into an eternal relationship with the deceased. Paiute Cry ceremonies further solidified that bond and demonstrated a devotion to the dead that stretched across time and space.

———————

Like the Paiutes, the Mormons held deeply spiritual notions of sickness, death, and an afterlife. Especially in the nineteenth century, Latter-day Saints relied heavily upon faith in Jesus Christ as the master healer. In 1831 Joseph Smith reported a revelation that established a pattern for Latter-day Saints. In it, the Lord instructed the Saints, "[W]hosoever among you are sick, and have not faith to be healed, but believe, shall be nourished with all tenderness, with herbs and mild food." He also advised that "the elders of the church, two or more, shall be called, and shall pray for and lay their hands upon [the sick] in my name; and if they die they shall die unto me, and if they live they shall live unto me."[29] Within such a context, the Saints adopted a variety of healing practices. Male priesthood holders administered to the sick in two main ways. They anointed an ill person with oil and pronounced a blessing through the laying on of hands; and they baptized the infirm by immersion for health. Mormon women were equally involved as healers; they performed washing and anointing rites and blessings through the laying on of hands. Some women practitioners became noted for their skill in herbal cures as well as for their service as midwives. The Saints also heavily relied upon Thomsonian herbal remedies. These cures, pioneered by the self-taught botanist Samuel Thomson, emphasized gentle treatments such as steam baths and herbs over the harsh bleeding or purging that regular physicians offered.[30]

For some Saints, faith-based practices took precedent over the treatments of secular practitioners. At Hebron there was no doctor, so as Carrie E. L. Hunt recalled, "[W]hen a person became ill, all the people offered their services to help. The Elders were called in to administer to the patient. This did more to cure them than usually doctors do and besides, the people had good tried and true remedies which were simple but effective."[31] Over time, however, Mormons, like the Southern Paiutes, became more accepting of secular medicine. At the same time, also similar to the Paiutes, they have never abandoned faith cures and view both as avenues to good health.

For nineteenth-century Mormons, administering to the sick was one of many areas of their lives in which they were encouraged, even commanded, to coalesce for the good of the whole. Mormon scripture included an injunction admonishing the Saints to "impart of your substance to the poor, every man according to that which he hath, such as feeding the hungry, clothing the naked, visiting the sick and administering to their relief, both spiritually and temporally, according to their wants."[32] At Hebron, John Pulsipher explained: "When one of our little settlement dies, we all drop our own work and furnish whatever is needed and attend to the burial without money or price."[33] Carrie E. L. Hunt added that a "spirit of helping neighbors was especially true at a death. I have watched my father make many caskets for the townspeople," she remembered. "He never charged a thing for his time or work."[34] As the medical historian Lester E. Bush Jr. observed, "Mormon communities long have been known for the extent to which they respond tangibly to the needs of 'their own.'"[35] On the frontier, opportunities to care for more than their own pushed Saints to define broadly their standards, and in a few situations led them to include Paiutes and miners in their circle of concern.

Even before the forced merging of Clover Valley and Shoal Creek, which eventually begot Hebron, Shoal Creek inhabitants endured a tragic incident that illustrates the settlers' grasp of communal ideals in caring for the sick. It also highlights their response when one of their number failed to live up to those ideals. The episode provided Hebronites a standard of care that they would strive to realize in future circumstances, including those that involved outsiders.

About a foot of snow fell at Shoal Creek in February 1865, followed by "the coldest we[a]ther ever known since the settlement of this country." The storm killed more of the Shoal Creek stock than any from the three previous winters. In the middle of this bitter weather, Thomas Fuller died while tending Edward Westover's sheep herd. John Pulsipher and Thomas Terry attended to his burial. Fuller, an Australian convert to Mormonism, apparently had no family, was about fifty years old, and was considered a "harmless, peaceable man."[36]

The incident, however, did not end with Fuller's interment. The following month, on 16 April 1865, Father Pulsipher conducted an investigation into the death of the shepherd, and in particular into Westover's role in that death. Rumor was that Fuller "came to his death for want of proper care" at the hands of Westover. As ecclesiastical head, Zera Pulsipher presided over the case with two visiting elders from St. George, "Bros. Lund & Moss," sitting with him as judges. Westover made opening remarks in which he described the usual amount of provisions used in his family and claimed that "the old man has had his share & more to[o], & these reports about the suffering of the late Tho[ma]s Fuller are false."[37]

Thomas S. Terry testified next. Terry recounted being called to the Westover camp and arriving with John Pulsipher. They found Fuller dead, "lying in his brush Wick[i]up in the sheep pen about ¼ of a mile from" the Westover place. The men had no provisions for his burial, so they secured his body for the night and returned four miles to their homes.[38]

The next day, Terry and Pulsipher made a coffin, found a suit of clothing, and traveled through a foot of snow to bury Fuller. By the time they arrived, Westover was on the scene. He began digging a grave while Terry and Pulsipher washed and dressed the body. As they removed Fuller's clothing, which Terry described as "very scanty & ragged," they were met with what Terry recalled as "the most horrible sight my eyes ever beheld! The man was literal[l]y cover[e]d with lice. I am doubtful," Terry continued, "whether a quart cup would have held them—the largest lice I ever saw." He then recounted calling Westover to take a look. Westover declared that he "knew the old man was lousy, but didn't suppose he was so bad as that." Terry and Pulsipher proceeded to brush the lice from the body and then scrub Fuller clean. "So much scurf & dirt had accumulated on him that it was an awful job," requiring six kettles of hot water. His hair, too, provided a challenge, as it "had not been cut or combed for so long . . . that it was matted into wads & covered with nits." Fuller's physical makeup was also poor. Terry described him as "very thin in flesh, but little more than skin & bones—a mere skelleton [sic]."[39]

After hearing Terry's testimony, Westover scrambled to defend himself. He claimed that Fuller had been sent away from his previous job because "he was lousy." Westover took him in because "no one else would have him." He then claimed that Fuller had done quite well in his employ as a shepherd, "til he froze his feet in the fore part of winter, & now because he is dead, you have got me up here to cat haul me, I believe, & I have a notion not to stay to hear it."[40]

Zera Pulsipher next questioned Westover about Fuller's appetite and health. He also inquired how often Westover allowed Fuller a change of clothing, to which Westover responded, "Why, he couldn't change at all, unles[s] I had given him mine & I went naked. He had a shirt washed last Aug. & after that he washed some in the creek & my wife mended a pair of Pants & got lice all over her apron[.] I told her not to wash or mend anymore for him—let him do it himself."[41]

Pulsipher then turned to spiritual matters and found justification for a decision against Westover. Pulsipher inquired if Westover had been attending to his prayers, to which Westover "final[l]y confest that he had not for considerable length of time." Pulsipher then blamed Westover for not reporting the situation to anyone, thus preventing the community from responding to the needs of a destitute brother. He stated that he personally would have divided his own clothing with Fuller had he known the need existed. The visiting elders also took their turns at chastening Westover, telling him that he had "not done his duty as an Elder in Israel." Why, they queried, "let that poor old man lie & perish with lice?"[42]

After conferring for a few minutes, the three judges handed down their decision. They instructed Westover that it was his duty "to make a confession before this meeting & at some convenient time be rebaptised [*sic*] to restore him to full fello[w]ship with the saints and with the Lord." Westover claimed he could not comply with the request for rebaptism and appealed the case to Erastus Snow.

This tragic incident illustrates the communitarian ideals for which nineteenth-century Mormons strove. Fuller's death and its aftermath became community concerns. When news of Fuller's condition was voiced among the locals, it became evident that Westover's level of care fell short of the understood standards for a Saint. Fuller's death and Westover's scolding offer a prime example of Mormonism's broader rejection of life as a Darwinian struggle of all against all and a clear reminder to Shoal Creek ranchers that community was more important than self-interest.

Other experiences of death at Hebron, while not as grievous, demonstrate a similar principle. In 1866, Father James Huntsman was appointed to a committee to survey and divide farmland at Shoal Creek. In accomplishing this task, his son Orson wrote, "The weather was wet and cold, [father] got his feet wet and then attended a meeting in the evening through which [he] took cold that terminated in his death." Father Huntsman's sickness lasted about twenty-five days and provided opportunity for community care. According to Orson, "[T]he elders came in from time to time and administered to him and we did all we could." The family even sent for a Dr. Higgans of St. George, who diagnosed the illness as typhoid fever, but Orson was apparently not impressed with the physician's skill. He reflected, "I can't help but feel that the doctor did more harm than good." In the end, Orson reconciled himself to the death of his father, writing, "[I]t seemed as though it was to be."[43]

John Pulsipher, acting as clerk, recorded his perspective on Huntsman's passing in the ward record, linking the death to a lack of faith on the part of the community: "Father Huntsman took cold while measuring land," Pulsipher penned. "Fever set in. He continued to get weaker & worse in spite of all we could do for him til he died. . . . *Our faith was not sufficient to keep him.* . . . Lord comfort and bless the family." This entry, juxtaposed against one on the following page in the ward record, makes it clear that at least in Pulsipher's mind, the physical health of individuals within the community largely hinged upon the spiritual health of the community as a whole. Pulsipher wrote: "Bad colds are coming, nearly all of us are affected with it & some are very sick. Mother Pulsipher has had a hard time—but through faith in the Lord & power of the Priesthood she is recovering."[44] The town's faith was insufficient to keep Huntsman, but faith in the Lord and the priesthood healed Mother Mary Brown Pulsipher.

When John Pulsipher's wife, Rozilla, developed what he called "a lingering sickness of 3 ½ years," he lamented just before her death, "[I]t seems impossible to get faith or medicine sufficient to cure her." He noted that "she begged of me to let her go." She was still young, only thirty-four when she died, but at times she had become so sick she could not turn over in bed without help. John enlisted broader community aid through priesthood administrations and baptism for health, but to no avail. When death finally came, John described the solemn passing this way: "[I]n the midst of family and friends she breathed her last as quietly as going to sleep." Rozilla's departure, preceded by three and a half years of ill health, was a somber communal occasion involving "family and friends."[45]

For frontier Mormons, the challenge came in extending the same solicitude to the Paiutes and miners. One winter in the 1870s, Dudley Leavitt's family had an opportunity to do just that. Leavitt had cultivated long-standing friendships among the Paiutes and had taken a Paiute named Janet as his fourth wife. Thus, when Leavitt encountered "an old squaw" left to die near his home at Gunlock, south of Hebron, he did not hesitate to help. He immediately set to work and "'fixed her a good solid wigwam of willows, covered it with bark, and banked it up around the bottom.'" One of Leavitt's daughters recalled her brothers chopping wood for the woman and the girls carrying food to her: "'We never thought of eating a meal until we had taken the old squaw hers,'" she remembered. "'We kept her all winter and when spring came, and it got warm, the tribe came back and took her with them.'"[46]

Elsewhere, Mormons found additional opportunities to care for outsiders. In 1866, Panaca Saints took responsibility for the body of a miner,

George Rogers, whom the Paiute Okus had killed and buried with rocks. The Saints retrieved the body from its Paiute internment and brought it back to Panaca. In a spot near what would become the Panaca cemetery, they buried Rogers and placed "a nice stone" at the head of the grave to mark his final resting place.[47] It was an act of compassion that suggested a sense of obligation to care for Rogers's body according to Mormon conventions.

At Hebron, residents took similar care when a Joseph Graham was discovered dead on the road eight miles east of town. Justice of the Peace J. W. Hunt held an inquest and learned that Graham was formerly a Mormon and had plied his trade for several years as a peddler at Pioche. Hunt determined that Graham likely had been pitched head-first from his wagon. He had a large gash on his forehead, and evidence suggested that his team and wagon had run over the length of his body. Hunt concluded that he died "without a struggle." Hebron authorities contacted his son, who arrived and with the aid of Hebronites buried Graham in the Hebron cemetery.[48]

Mormons also cared for Paiute corpses, although at times with less regard than that shown Rogers and Graham. When Muddy Saints executed Co-quap for his alleged involvement in stock raids, they only dug a shallow grave for his body and covered it with sand. The coyotes soon found it and ate the flesh.[49] At Clover Valley, when Mormon settlers killed an Indian in an attempted stock raid, they buried the body in a wash. Perhaps out of some fear for the dead, especially that of a Native American, Mary J. Bunker remembered avoiding that spot thereafter.[50]

The story at Hebron was a little different. When Brush-head's wife became ill, Hebronites prayed for her and tried to relieve the family's temporal wants. Despite such attempts, Brush-head's wife died. At her passing, Brush-head reportedly came to John Pulsipher and requested that she be buried "like the white people . . . , as he did not want her burned." Pulsipher and other townsmen built a casket for her and laid her to rest in the Hebron cemetery, next to the Pioche peddler, Joseph Graham.[51]

The Mormons, then, occasionally extended their circle of care to include people from other groups. The miners at Pioche, however, were more tentative in their outreach. They established methods for attending to their own, but Piochers struggled to spread their concern across cultural boundaries. Among themselves, miners found ways to set aside individualistic attitudes and demonstrate concern for the unfortunate, especially in matters of sickness and death. The Masonic Lodge and

Independent Order of Odd Fellows at Pioche helped channel residents' compassion. Those brotherhoods provided communities of caregivers to mitigate the loneliness of sickness and death so far from home and family. Outsiders did not benefit from this selective system, however.

Nineteenth-century medical practices at mining camps and across the West were primitive at best. Licensing and regulation were almost nonexistent, making it possible for anyone with an inclination to dabble in the healing arts to call himself a doctor and open for business. In some areas, "quacks" outnumbered credentialed physicians, so that public faith in the profession, even for those with the most sophisticated training, remained low. Doctors' treatments were not much more advanced than the herbal remedies practiced by the Mormons and Paiutes, and sometimes perhaps more harmful. Common prescriptions included purgatives and emetics. Doctors might also administer opium for pain and diarrhea, quinine for malaria, mercury for syphilis, and morphine for dysentery. Public hospitals were more often viewed as "refuges for the poor," or merely as "a place to die rather than be cured."[52]

At Pioche, the story was no different. Father Lawrence Scanlan, a Catholic priest, raised money to operate a hospital under the auspice of the Society of St. Vincent de Paul. County officers also opened a hospital, which in part operated from a citizen-donated "poor fund," designed to provide medical care to those who could not otherwise afford it. The county physician, Dr. Charles G. Foltz, attended to the hospital patients, while E. E. Williams served as steward. In November 1872, the hospital sheltered sixteen patients "afflicted with various diseases." It was reported to be "under good management" and "kept scrupulously clean."[53]

At least eight doctors and one dentist also practiced at Pioche in 1872. Dr. H. Bergstein described himself as a physician, surgeon, and accoucheur, while Quy Fung boasted that he had "a diploma from the Medical Institute in Canton, China." Fung specialized in "diseases of females and of the eye" and claimed a "long and successful practice in this state." Dr. D. H. Whelpley guaranteed "a sure cure," promising that "in cases of venereal diseases, piles of long standing, chronic diseases, etc., a cure is effected without the use of mercury." He kept consultations strictly confidential and could be reached at "Mrs. Pyles's Lodging House—Room No. 5." Dr. F. C. Nichols, the only advertising dentist in town, promoted preventative dental care. He urged Piochers to avoid sleepless nights by attending to their teeth. He warned, "Don't wait until they ache and then in language of regret say you would give most anything to save them."[54]

During the economic downturn of the early 1880s, Pioche went without a physician for a time. Dr. G. R. Alexander, a druggist, handled the town's medical needs as best he could, but residents still petitioned for a doctor to move to Pioche. By the 1890s, a Dr. Campbell opened a practice in town and provided medical care to residents throughout the region.[55]

Townspeople themselves also demonstrated a broad-based concern for the sick and dying. In 1873, when Dennis Downey lost both his feet to amputation, an anonymous but well-known gentleman in town responded. The kindhearted man started a subscription to raise the necessary three hundred dollars to "procure a set of patent feet for Downey." The newspaper was optimistic that the money could "easily be raised in Pioche for so worthy an object." Similarly, when John D. Randolph suffered the effects of "cancer in the neck," he was unable to work and soon became indigent. Three townsmen, T. C. Poujade, Jonas Cohn, and Peter Hientzelman, acknowledged his plight and formed a committee to collect funds for his relief. In 1889, when Edward Kewley, better known as Old Ned, was found dead in his cabin, the town again took action. Ned was about eighty years old, had been ailing for some time, and was "somewhat of a hermit, living for many years . . . completely alone in a very deserted place." Nonetheless, he was well known at Pioche, and residents promptly took up a collection. From the proceeds, Ned's "body was decently buried . . . in the public burying ground."[56]

Besides such general goodwill, some Piochers benefitted from their membership in either the town's Masonic lodge or its Independent Order of Odd Fellows. Both were chartered in the early 1870s and continued to serve the community as important social and charitable institutions through the remainder of the nineteenth century. Masons and Odd Fellows provided for the care and interment of their deceased members, and the two groups worked together to fence and organize a cemetery for that purpose. By 1873, they had enclosed a plot of ground with a "neat and substantial piling fence" and had already provided a final resting spot for eleven bodies.[57]

Fundamental tenets of Odd Fellowship included caring for the sick and a "solemn inunction to 'bury the dead.'" To prevent any member from suffering "an unpitied death and a pauper's grave," Odd Fellows "bound themselves together in mutual helpfulness." They "entered into a solemn covenant to provide each member and his wife, at their death, with the means of decent Christian sepulture." To that end, Odd Fellows were instructed in the proper manner of visiting the sick, as well as in prescribed speeches, prayers, songs, and rituals for funeral ceremonies.[58]

In January 1873, when two members of the Odd Fellows lodge died of pneumonia, the brotherhood provided services for them. Obediah Brown, a native of Worcester, Massachusetts, was about fifty-seven years old at the time of his passing. He left no family, but he did have "many friends in the wilds of the Pacific coast who honor his memory." The newspaper reported that "in his last illness he received every care and attention which fraternal sympathy and sincere friendship could suggest." The same month, John Bibinger died at Pioche, but no one was sure of his history. Even still, the paper consoled, "in his last moments his fraternal brother Odd Fellows ministered to his every want." A year later William Bremner, another Odd Fellow, died of "consumption, contracted by exposure while prospecting." He left no property and only a few personal effects, yet the order provided an "impressive funeral" on his behalf.[59]

This brotherhood served to mitigate the harshness of death on the mining frontier. Nonetheless, if John W. Erisman's passing is any indication, even the Odd Fellows could not completely assuage the longing to be amidst familiar surroundings in one's final days. Erisman arrived in southern Nevada in late 1872 and soon found work as a woodcutter for the Sherwood brothers at Clover Valley. On 12 December, only weeks into his new job, his ax slipped and cut his knee. "Don't know how bad it will be," he wrote, "but hope it will not be serious."[60]

The next day the wound started to drain, and before long Erisman was in bed unable to move. "Very cold nights and I am here sick," he lamented four days after the accident. "Almost penniless and none that care to attend on me much." Within three weeks Erisman was transported to the Society of St. Vincent de Paul Hospital at Pioche, where he spent a "miserable" New Year's Day. He quickly lost confidence in Dr. D. L. Deal, his attending physician. Eventually Erisman sent for a Chinese doctor, perhaps Dr. Fung, who promised to relieve his suffering within a few days. This new physician plastered the wound and gave Erisman two cups "full of nasty bitter dope," none of which seemed to help. On 3 January, Erisman "passed a fearful night burning with fever and pains racking my body." Over the next two weeks his diary became a chronicle of his slow, painful, and lonely death.[61]

During that time, members of the Odd Fellow brotherhood, to which Erisman belonged, visited him nearly every day. "Had two callers that helped to pass away the time a little," he recorded one day. Even on days with visitors, however, he felt isolated. He described 8 January as "a very lonesome day," even though "McKenzie called. Johnson and Mitchell also. All talk encouraging. But none realize how bad it is." On one day without callers Erisman complained, "Oh I do get so discouraged sometimes when all alone and suffering intense pain. And no way to relieve it. The Brothers are rather going back on me in the watch business, and now is just my time of need."[62]

For the most part, Erisman missed his home and family, something the Odd Fellows could not replace. "Oh that I were back in old Illinois," he wrote on New Year's Day. Two days later he expressed a similar thought, adding that in Illinois, "I know I would get well." Pining away on a bed "not made up for two weeks," he again bemoaned his circumstances. "Oh, but this is a horrible country where a man can get no medical aid worth a cent. Afternoon very lonesome. No callers and I was mostly alone." His thoughts also frequently turned to his parents, both of whom were sick at the time of his departure to the West: "[W]ould like very much to hear from home," he hoped one day. He wrote a letter to his father another day and yearned, "[O]h that I could see him again." In the final entry of his diary, Erisman had learned of his parents' passing: "Troubles never come singly," he philosophized. "Had a letter from Hiantie and it tells me of the death of my father and mother, both within 2 months. Oh but this has been a terrible year for me, 1872 and 1873. . . . They say it is always darkest just before day. Would to God that day would break soon." Over a month later the newspaper reported that "the remains of John W. Erisman were . . . consigned to their last resting place by his brother Oddfellows." The paper described the ceremony as "unusually impressive," complete with a band and "the beautiful burial service of the Episcopal Church."[63]

Even with the brotherhood of Odd Fellows or the benefit of collections, death at Pioche could be terribly lonely. Erisman's slow decline and forlorn passing underscores the cost of pursuing the American Dream in the nineteenth-century West. It was a quest that led individuals away from the meaningful relationships of family, friends, and community in search of an ever illusive treasure. For Erisman the quest ended in an agonizing way. His Odd Fellow visitors were poor substitutes for the companionship of loved ones at such a crucial time, a bitter reality he was forced to confront alone.

For those without such aid, death must have been lonelier still. In November 1872, A. Grinell, a forty-five-year-old native of Spain, died at the hospital, "friendless and without means." He had languished for several weeks from an abscess of the liver before finally passing away. Samuel Dysant, a thirty-eight-year-old native of Ireland, parted in a like manner. He suffered in the hospital for six weeks before "heart disease" claimed his life. The newspaper described him as "destitute" and noted that he "had no friends here that we are aware of." Henry L. Campbell was not as bad off as that, but he still died distant from family care. A native of San Antonio, Texas, he froze his feet in February 1873. He deteriorated over the next three months with gangrene and pneumonia until he finally succumbed. A "large number of his friends" followed his casket to the city cemetery, where he was remembered as "a steady, hard-working, temperate man."[64]

Internment at the city cemetery was by no means privileged. As early as 1873, over one hundred graves filled the common lot that lay adjacent to the Masonic–Odd Fellows cemetery. A few women and children were interred there, but most of those graves marked the final resting place of adult males. Only about twenty-five graves had proper headstones to note the names of the dead. "Rude headboards, with inscriptions written in pencil," marked some graves, while others had "nothing to indicate the name or nativity of the dead." One marker crudely carved in wood simply noted, "Shot by a coward while working his claim no one even knew his name. Pioche Nev." The cemetery largely included victims of mining accidents as well as victims of violence. Many of the latter reportedly died with their boots on, earning the graveyard the nickname "Boot Hill." A legend developed early that seventy-five men died at Pioche before the first person passed away from natural causes. Adding to the stark and fateful feel of the spot, nothing had been done by 1873 "to preserve the resting place of the dead from the depredations of domestic animals." As the *Record* protested, "[T]he public cemetery ought to be enclosed, for it is no credit to our camp that its dead should be interred in an open field."[65]

Clearly, miners at Pioche developed expected levels of care for their sick and dying. As the newspaper put it, "[O]ur people are not wanting in the virtue of charity, contributing cheerfully for the relief of the distressed and for the burial of those who die without means." At times, Piochers even extended such charity to others. In 1893, when an Indian fell from a load of hay at Panaca and broke his leg, Dr. Campbell treated him at Pioche. Residents then provided for his recovery "in one of the vacant cabins back of Main street." Three years later, Dr. Campbell also treated George Edwards, a Mormon from Panaca. Edwards suffered from a broken collarbone and injuries to his head and shoulder after being thrown from his horse. The Woods family at Clover Valley also recalled sending for a doctor from Pioche in emergency cases.[66]

Nonetheless, the intercultural charity at Pioche had its limits, especially as Pioche maintained its stance as guardian of American progress. As such, it was difficult for at least some of its residents to accept healing practices beyond secular medicine. In 1883, the *Record* reported on what it mockingly called "a remarkable cure." When an Indian child at Spring Valley came down with "a bad case of the measles," Bishop Millet, the Mormon leader for the region, offered to perform a priesthood blessing. As the newspaper described it, the bishop "proceeded to the wickiup where the child was, and kneeling down by its side, placing his hands on the sick child, and with his eyes cast heaven-wards, the good Bishop mumbled something to his God. A miracle had been performed," the *Record* jeered. "Shortly after Bishop Millett removed his hands from the child, the little babe passed quietly to sleep—the sweet sleep of death. . . . Now, after the performance of this miracle, who dare say that the Lord is not with the Mormon Church and people."[67]

The border region's hierarchy of power cast a long shadow, even over death. Paiutes again stood at the bottom of the power structure. Anglo-Americans treated their rituals with suspicion and sometimes derision. When John Wesley Powell came upon a camp of abandoned elderly Paiutes, he called the scene "wild and weird." The *Pioche Record* attributed the same practice to the "heartless conduct of the Indians." The Mormon missionary Thomas D. Brown had a hard time explaining the success of Paiute shamanism, and the Indian agent A. J. Barnes simply labeled Paiute medicine as superstition.

As a bastion of American progress, Pioche boasted of two hospitals and at least eight doctors during its boom years. Although the miners at Pioche clearly set individualism aside in matters of health, especially among their own, there is little to suggest that they accepted Mormon or Paiute methods. Pioche doctors were open to treating Mormons and Paiutes, yet the exchanges appear limited. When confronted with a string of Native American deaths, Piochers struggled to respond. A few residents and the county hospital did provide assistance, but the newspaper begrudged even that little aid.

In matters of health and rituals of death, the miners emerged the least affected by the intercultural space that they shared with the Mormons and Southern Paiutes. The latter two groups turned to herbal remedies and faith-based healing, while the miners relied upon doctors who practiced secular medicine. As in life, a hierarchy of death emerged, with the miners least accepting of Mormon and Paiute ways. Mormons and Paiutes were more open to cross-cultural sharing, with both groups embracing regular medical practices, yet never abandoning their traditional cures. The Paiutes especially accepted Mormon faith healing and the miners' secular medicine, while still relying upon Paiute shamanism.

For the Mormons and miners, the treatment of Paiute elderly was most difficult to understand. Yet, indigent Mormons and miners faced equally lonesome and unsettling deaths among their own people. Thomas Fuller's lice-covered body at Shoal Creek and John Erisman's languishing death at Pioche offer striking evidence of that. All three groups thus struggled to deal with caring for the poorest of the poor even among their own. For the Paiutes, leaving the elderly behind was a difficult economic choice designed to preserve the strength of the band. For the elderly themselves, if Powell's observation is indicative, it was a profound personal sacrifice for the good of the group. In any case, it underscores the Paiutes' poverty and in a tragic way emphasizes their position at the bottom of the region's power structure. Mormons used Fuller's dreadful death as a means to shore up levels of care expected of a Latter-day Saint and to reinforce notions of community concern over individualism. Erisman's death at Pioche, in contrast, illustrates the individualism bound up in the search for wealth in the American West. Pioche embodied that quest, and although the miners there made attempts to soften the most difficult of life's passages, they were poor substitutes for family and friends at the dying hour. These three striking stories of death, therefore, underscore the distinctive qualities of each community. They also serve as evidence of the expansive gap separating Southern Paiute, Mormon, and miner worldviews.

Perhaps the greatest evidence pointing to a discrepancy in the valuation of lives on the southern rim of the Great Basin rests among the deceased themselves. The graveyard at Hebron suggests an intercultural divide that persisted even in death. Certainly, Hebronites stretched the confines of compassion in caring for the body of Joseph Graham, the lapsed Mormon peddler, and equal regard for Brush-head's wife. Townspeople built caskets, dug graves, and otherwise cared for the bodies of these outsiders. They even found space for them within the bounds of their burial place. They laid Graham and Brush-head's wife next to each other in the far northwest corner of the Hebron cemetery, albeit thirty feet from the grave of the nearest Hebronite. In death, as in life, Mormons, miners, and Southern Paiutes created an interethnic and cross-cultural space for themselves—although they simultaneously kept their distance.

8 Transformations

The morning of 17 November 1902 dawned "clear and beautiful" at Hebron. It was unseasonably pleasant weather, and even the typically chilly north wind decided not to blow that day. Chris Ammon, a Norwegian stone mason, was eager to take advantage of the sunshine to finish work on Frank Hunt's house. Everything seemed normal as Ammon methodically laid the last rocks on one of the gable ends of the Hunt home, but sometime after the noon hour something peculiar happened. The rock Ammon was placing began to bounce in his hand and refused to lie still. It took a split second for Ammon to realize that not only the rock but the earth was shaking—Hebron was being rattled by an earthquake.

Ammon did not bother to climb down the ladder; he jumped from the scaffold and ran. Orson Welcome Huntsman was also working outside that day. He was laboring at his workbench under a willow shed when he heard what he thought was a whirlwind, but as he began to "teeter to and fro," and the willows over his head started to shake, he realized there was no wind. He was being jarred by the quake.[1]

Settlers for hundreds of miles felt similar rumblings. Pioche reported three distinct shocks at 12:45 P.M. and suggested that the oscillations ran north to south and came at five-second intervals, with an aftershock twenty minutes later. In St. George, rocks and bricks fell from the chimneys of several homes, and plaster fell like rain from the ceiling at a local school, where the frightened children were excused for the day. Nearby at Santa Clara, one resident reported that "hardly a building in the town escap[ed] without some injury." Townsfolk at Lund and Toquerville also felt the shockwaves, which put residents throughout the region on edge.[2]

Hebron, however, was hardest hit. Huntsman witnessed "chimneys falling from house tops in every direction" and porches crashing to the earth. Terrified women and children came running and screaming from their homes to gather in the streets. One woman ran outside with her two little girls, one tucked securely under her arm and the other clutched tightly by the hand. Upon reaching safety she told a concerned friend that she and her children were unharmed but "every dam[ned] deash [dish] in the house was broken." Almost every home in Hebron was damaged, some so extensively that they were no longer safe. Aftershocks continued at intervals throughout the afternoon and persisted for several weeks thereafter, so that many residents felt hesitant to sleep in their homes. The first night after the quake, Huntsman's eleven-by-fourteen-feet temporary "slab house" became shelter to over thirty persons who made their beds on the floor. Others sought shelter in the Mormon tithing granary, which was made of wood. Huntsman recalled that the young women made the first night almost "laughable," as any small tremor caused them to "crowd up together like sheep, as if one would save the other."[3]

Beyond its effects on local residents, the earthquake symbolized a more widespread rumbling of change that had been transforming the region for some time. In many ways, the earthquake struck a different world than that which the Mormons, miners, and Paiutes had inhabited almost forty years earlier, when the death of George Rogers brought them together in confrontation. The intensity of the competition for land and silver had long since diminished. The three groups had learned to share their space, although begrudgingly, over the ensuing forty years, as each community developed its own defensive tactics and methods of interacting with the others. By the early twentieth century, new forces pulled Mormons, miners, and Paiutes in different directions. While they continued to intermingle, the world-between-worlds that they had created for themselves had largely disappeared. Its demise was primarily due to economic pressures, but it also reflected a shift in ideas about sacred space away from the values that had infused earlier interactions.

For the Mormons, the intense need for Zion land had disappeared with the passing of Brigham Young. By 1900, the Mormon ranching outposts at Clover, Eagle, and Spring Valleys still contained an LDS family or two but were largely abandoned. Only Panaca remained, the lone survivor

of the Saints' anxious attempts in the 1860s to outflank the gentiles and
"to hold in check outside influences."[4]

After the earthquake struck Hebron in 1902, its residents also began
to move. It was only the latest in a series of difficult events to challenge
the tenacity of Hebron's citizens. They had struggled with droughts,
floods, sicknesses, leaky flumes, battles over land, power conflicts, and
the enticements of Pioche. Now most of their homes were damaged and
questionably safe. It was a watershed moment in Hebron history from
which the town did not recover. On 11 January 1903, the men of Hebron
met to discuss the fate of their town. Some spoke in favor of moving to
a budding new community eight miles to the east. Orson Huntsman
had formed a reservoir and canal company and spent considerable time
and energy attracting investors to his venture. He surveyed a town site
at the mouth of Shoal Creek, and people began moving there in 1896. It
was in June 1903, however, that the new town received its biggest boost.
Edward H. Snow (son of the apostle Erastus Snow) and Thomas Cottom,
local Mormon leaders from St. George, met with Hebron residents to
consider moving the town. All in attendance agreed that relocating offered the best future for them and their children.[5]

By 1905, most Hebronites had torn down their homes and rebuilt at
Huntsman's new town site. Even though Hebronites moved only a few
miles east, in many ways they moved an entire world away. The transfer
symbolized for Mormons a revised vision of sacred space on the frontier.
On the one hand, it ended Hebron's forty-year struggle to define and defend its space, while on the other hand, it marked a shift for Mormonism
as a whole away from earlier communitarianism and the reification of
ancient Israel toward a new worldview more tolerant of differences and
more closely aligned with mainstream definitions of what it meant to
be an American. Perhaps the name Huntsman chose for his new town is
most telling of that shift in values: he called it Enterprise.[6]

The financial doldrums at Pioche factored into the Mormons' move
from the frontier. Pioche, as a regional economic force, had diminished
significantly by 1900. Its population dipped to a low of 242, as silver
extraction ground to a halt and the miners moved away. Pioche largely
owed its existence at the turn of the century to its status as county
seat. Reflecting that view, the *Pioche Record* changed its name after the
turn of the century to the *Lincoln County Record*; by then it was only
a weekly publication. Far from the raucous camp that typified Pioche's
boom days, by 1905 meetings of the board of county commissioners and
the convening of district court provided most of the excitement in town:
"Rooms will likely be scarce this term of court," the *Record* suggested

in January 1905. "Fellows coming to serve as jurymen would do well to bring along their covered wagons and beddings. They might be able to rent them out at good profit." There was obviously an economic advantage to housing the district court at Pioche. It attracted outsiders to town, which generated income for local businesses. "Of course court business is rather expensive," the *Record* explained, "but the good feature of it is that it brings people from the various parts of the county together and we all get acquainted, while otherwise we would have never met." Even with court in session, Pioche hardly resembled the lively camp it once was, and while court was in recess it was quieter still.[7]

There was little left at Pioche to generate the type of nationalistic fervor that typified its boom years. Piochers were still proud Americans, but the ardor of the earlier Independence Day celebrations cooled significantly by the turn of the century. In 1905, for example, the Fourth of July festivities began with a salute of thirteen anvil guns at sunrise, followed by the brass band parading through the streets, the reading of the Declaration of Independence, recitations, sports competitions, a choir comprised of "ten voices, some of which were really good," and a dance that lasted until two o'clock in the morning. It was, according to the *Record*, "a day's pleasure such as we seldom are fortunate enough to meet."[8] Missing in such an assessment, however, is the bigger vision of Pioche's role in the nation's "growing greatness" that had permeated the town's earlier identity.[9] Perhaps it was a Chinese resident at Pioche who best accounted for the reason behind the difference: Following a "very quiet observance" of the Chinese New Year in 1900, marked only by the hoisting of a yellow flag and "some popping of crackers," the Chinese man explained, "Too muchee hard time, not muchee man now."[10]

Despite those hard times, however, one thing did not change at Pioche: an undying optimism that the next strike was just around the corner. The *Record* assumed the role of booster press and churned out glowing reports of the town's potential. It frequently described the activities of outside capitalists who visited the town in search of wealth. "There have been several mining men in town going through the mines during the week and investigating," the *Record* noted in February 1905.[11] Much more exciting, however, was the announcement the previous month of the formation of the Utah-Nevada Company, capitalized at a reported fifteen million dollars. The new corporation purchased mines and tailings in Utah and Nevada, including at Pioche and Bullionville.[12] Within a month the *Record* reported that considerable real estate had recently changed hands and suggested that "altogether the outlook is exceedingly encouraging."[13] Another account that same month noted additional investors coming and going and then promised, "[I]n about three months the population of Pioche will begin to increase."[14] Other headlines announced "Pioche Will Boom," "Not an Idle Man in Town," and "The Future of Pioche Looks Good."[15] By the end of 1905 the *Record* concluded that "Old Pioche is looking brighter than it has for many years. The big Nevada-Utah company are commencing operations in A No. 1 shape and before six months . . . the monthly payroll of that company is expected to reach in the neighborhood of $50,000." With that and other ventures in the works, the *Record* predicted, "Pioche will be [the] leading camp in the county, both in population and votes."[16]

As was typical of mining in the West, such predictions rarely came true. Pioche never returned to the glory days of its boom years. Boosters, nonetheless, celebrated those years and used them to suggest the town's future potential. A 1923 promotional pamphlet for the Prince Consolidated Mining Company lauded Pioche's prosperity in its bonanza days and bragged that its population had once totaled ten thousand. It concluded that the town's early history is "an indication of what the future undoubtedly has in store." Pioche did rebound in the 1940s and ranked among the top ten lead-zinc producers in the nation. By 1958, however, this second boom ended. The only thing left for Pioche to capitalize upon was its raucous reputation as "the baddest town in the old west."[17]

The Paiutes also experienced forces pulling them in new directions. The first two decades of the twentieth century saw the creation of reservations at Kaibab, Chemehuevi, Las Vegas, San Juan, and Indian Peaks, as well as an effort to revive the reservation at Moapa. Reservations were later added at Kanosh and Koosharem, and the Mormon Church created a land reserve for the Cedar City Paiute band. Still the Paiutes continued to fend for themselves as off-reservation seasonal laborers. As the anthropologist Martha C. Knack contends, "[N]one of the reservations set aside for Paiute use could possibly support the resident populations by means of . . . sedentary agriculture." With Pioche in decline and the Mormon frontier nearly abandoned, the Paiutes found work elsewhere. Harvesting cantaloupe at Moapa Valley or sugar beets at Richfield provided migratory wage labor. Farm and ranch work continued to offer employment opportunities, as did domestic chores for women.[18]

By 1905, at least one Native American had even turned to prospecting. In January of that year, an Indian located a ledge from which he broke off several pieces of "fine looking quartz." It assayed $121 in gold and four ounces of silver. He then led two local men to the site of his discovery. They located several claims, the two non-Indians "giving the redman an equal interest."[19] Although nothing likely came of the find, the Native

American's inclusion as a claimant marked progress over Moroni's role in the opening of the mines at Pioche forty years earlier. It also suggests that Native Americans had adapted to the realities of their altered space and, like the Mormons, sought some of the material rewards for themselves.

The Paiutes had suffered the most from the influx of Mormons and miners into their world, with disease and poverty taking a tremendous toll. The ethnographer Robert C. Euler argues that by the first decade of the twentieth century, "any semblance of native Paiute life was a thing of the past."[20] The Paiutes nonetheless adapted to their new realities with remarkable flexibility. Though Mormons and miners relegated Paiute bands to the economic margins, they remained spiritually rich. The long-standing psychic connection to their land diminished little, despite a large-scale alienation from it. At a tribal council meeting at the Shivwits Reservation in 1935, one Paiute leader explained that tie in terms of his concern for future generations. Pointing to several Paiute youngsters playing in the dirt, he wondered, "Will the children of these little children have sand to play in?"[21] It was a haunting concern that echoed the sentiments expressed by an earlier Paiute headman in 1871: "Our children play in the warm sand. We hear them sing and are glad."[22] Sacred space to the Paiutes was basic. Dirt for Paiute children to play in would ensure that future generations of Paiutes would develop the same affinity for spiritual ground that had sustained their ancestors. In 1874, Taú-gu (Coal Creek John) had told residents of Pioche that the Paiutes could "manage better for themselves" than Indian agents could do for them.[23] Out of necessity, the Paiutes did just that.

While the "drama of life on the edges" is compelling in its own right, it teaches lessons that reach well beyond the American West.[24] Placing the Mormons, miners, and Southern Paiutes within the broader context of Gilded Age America argues against western exceptionalism. The frontier on the southern edge of the Great Basin experienced several national political, economic, and cultural trends that typified the post–Civil War era. The growth of federal power, corrupt politics, laissez-faire capitalism, and cultural Americanization played out larger than life among the Mormons, miners, and Southern Paiutes.

The federal government wielded significant power in the map-drawing controversy of 1866. It used that power to redraw the Utah/Nevada/Arizona borders in favor of mining interests. In the process, it treated the West much like the South, where Radical Republicans were supervising the readmission of southern states into the Union. One of those radicals, James M. Ashley, used his power as chair of the house committee on territories to guard admission of western states into the Union. He even attempted to eradicate Utah from the map and reconstruct the West into something more to his liking.

Laissez-faire capitalism and corrupt politics also characterize the Gilded Age, and the southern rim of the Great Basin witnessed its share of both. Nevada's Governor Blasdel, Utah's carpetbag Governor Durkee, the Indian agents Sale and Fenton, jurors, and local officials used their public roles for private gain. Outside capitalists also took advantage of unregulated opportunities. George Hearst engaged in courtroom mining and walked away richer for it. Individual miners tended to lose out, relegated to wage labor and poor working conditions, much like their counterparts employed at urban factories in the East. In addition, the mud, garbage, and filth that littered the streets of Pioche were little different from the descriptions that late nineteenth-century reformers offered of Chicago slums.

Finally, the Mormons and Southern Paiutes experienced a forced cultural homogenization over time that fits well within a broader national framework of Americanization. In 1915, Theodore Roosevelt gave expression to this in a speech that denounced "hyphenated Americanism." He said, "[T]he one absolutely certain way of bringing this nation to ruin . . . would be to permit it to become a tangle of squabbling nationalities, an intricate knot of German-Americans, Irish-Americans, English-Americans, French-Americans, Scandinavian-Americans or Italian-Americans." "There is no such thing," Roosevelt added, "as a hyphenated American who is a good American."[25]

Roosevelt's words are best understood within the context of the First World War. He was fearful of Americans taking sides in the conflict according to their country of origin and thereby leading to a deterioration of unity at home. Even still, it speaks to a broader trend in American history that attempted to define what it meant to be an American.[26] That trend had excluded people of Chinese ancestry altogether and severely limited immigration of peoples from southern Europe. Even though the Mormons and Southern Paiutes do not fit within either of those categories, the Americanization process forced upon them over the last half of the nineteenth century still resonates with the nation's broader efforts to define itself. Those who fell outside of prevailing notions of citizenship were either suppressed or forced to conform. For the Mormons that meant eradicating polygamy and theocracy. For the Southern Paiutes it meant subjugation followed by consignment to the geographic, economic, and social margins. In Utah, Southern Paiutes would later be forced through the federal government's termination program in the 1950s, another attempt to Americanize them that failed with devastating consequences.[27]

Beyond echoing national trends, however, there are specific principles bound up in this frontier story. What, in the end, does it mean to be a good neighbor, especially to peoples with drastically different values? For the Mormons, miners, and Southern Paiutes, the answer was elusive. The 1860s and 1870s brought a flood of Mormons and miners into Paiute lands, forcing the Paiutes to interact with the outsiders in a new interethnic space where the rules that governed exchanges within the Paiute community changed. Mormons and miners introduced competing worldviews into a growing entanglement of space, and federal officials intervened to complicate matters. As Congress sought solutions to the Mormon Question and the Indian Problem, it privileged progress, industry, and destiny over Paiute sacred space and the LDS Zion. A hierarchy of power emerged that sorted the three groups according to conformity to prevailing standards of Americanism. On a local level, this hierarchy framed interactions between the three groups and shaped the prejudices that emerged. The frontier proved a bewildering mixing ground of peoples, places, and values that forced each group to resolve its own identity and find new meaning in the mess.[28] Mormons, miners, and Southern Paiutes largely did so in ways that defined each other in negative terms.

Ironically, the spiritual nature of the space that they created seemed to justify the disparaging characterizations. The rituals of possession that each group employed brought conflicting meanings to the same desert soil. It linked that soil to three different cosmologies and in the process seemed to justify the making of enemies out of culturally distinct "others." With disparate gods on each group's side, the Mormons, miners, and Southern Paiutes competed, sometimes violently, not only over land but over whose worldview would imbue that land with purpose. Tabuts carried the Southern Paiutes to "the very best place," at the center of the world, and placed them there. They became "the people." Next, the god of Abraham, Isaac, and Jacob led Mormon settlers to that same spot, where they sought to honor Him as they set out to reify ancient Israel and to build a modern-day Zion. Finally, the god of America in the cloak of Manifest Destiny, individualism, progress, industry, and the quest for wealth lured hard-rock miners there too. The miners at Pioche were just as sure as the Mormons and Southern Paiutes that *they* were fulfilling the designs of Providence and in fact pushing them forward. It was not simply an economic, political, or cultural contest but a spiritual one, with otherworldly implications.

As they intermingled, each group failed to see weaknesses in itself that were at least as great as those that it projected onto its neighbors. This was especially true as the Mormons, miners, and Southern Paiutes attempted to deal with sickness and death among their own, let alone across the cultural divide. Miners and Mormons viewed the abandonment of Paiute elderly with little understanding of the underlying implication that the Paiutes' destitute economic circumstances forced such difficult choices upon them. At the same time, the lice-laden death of the Mormon sheepherder Thomas Fuller and the languishing demise of John Erisman highlight the struggle that Mormons and miners faced in caring for the poorest of the poor of their own. The three groups' responses to these deaths, as well as their rituals designed to affect sickness and dying, highlight in haunting ways the sometimes expansive cultural gap that separated each community from the other two.

There were moments, nonetheless, of enlightened understanding in which members of each group looked past ethnic and cultural differences to view broader commonalities. Brush-head's family shared space with Hebronites, and over time the two communities enjoyed a close relationship. After getting to know his Paiute neighbors, John Pulsipher described them as "good honorable people."[29] Likewise, Franklin Buck from Pioche decided, after visiting several Mormon towns, that "the Devil is not as black as he is painted."[30] It was easy, in other words, for Mormons, miners, and Paiutes to disparage each other from across deep cultural divides, but when they took time to develop relationships, perceptions generally changed.

Almost in spite of themselves, Mormons, miners, and Southern Paiutes not only created an interethnic and cross-cultural space but an interdependent one as well. As much as the miners resented it, they were largely reliant upon Mormon produce and Paiute labor to keep their community functioning. Even though the Mormons castigated Pioche as Babylon, they still welcomed its cash payments, a significant flow of which no doubt made it possible for their colonization effort in the south to succeed. Likewise, the Mormons sometimes killed and denigrated the Southern Paiutes but still benefitted from their labor and intelligence networks. The Southern Paiutes, although suffering the most, also used the Mormons and miners to their advantage. They worked for both groups, traded with them, and found access to material goods that made their lives easier. The points of intersection for these three groups also became points of reliance. Even though each group changed as a result of its encounter with the other two and even arrived at a degree of mutual understanding, the remarkable nature of this story is the cultural persistence each community maintained in the face of these interactions. It seems evident that the story of any one of these three groups cannot be fully understood without the other two. It was a reality that the three groups largely ignored, preferring instead to entrench themselves behind walls of differences.

In the twentieth century, divisions persist, but members of each group have become more tolerant. Bennjamin Pikyavit, a Southern Paiute spiritual leader at the Kaibab Reservation in northern Arizona, has adopted a worldview much more accepting of outsiders. He borrowed a Lakota-style sweat-lodge ceremony and brought it home to Kaibab, where he regularly conducts sweats that are open to all people. "'It is my way of being a part of the spirit that moves in all things,'" Pikyavit explains. "'It is my job to do these things, to help people whenever I can, to be responsible for them, because I am a spiritual leader.'"[31] At Pioche, too, things changed over time, so that the Latter-day Saints established a congregation there in the 1930s and have constructed several chapels throughout eastern Nevada since. As the historian James W. Hulse sees it, "Mormon Country is extending into [eastern Nevada] more successfully than it was ever able to do in the era of Brigham Young."[32] More tolerant attitudes on both sides of the Utah/Nevada border have certainly facilitated that change.

What prevented such amicability in the nineteenth century? The answer seems more complex than the triumph of an enlightened, more tolerant present over a backward past. These three cultural groups no longer compete for the same geographic place—a contest in which each group believed God was on its side. The wealth at Pioche is used up, and Mormonism has grown from a persecuted minority into a respected, global, and financially stable church. It no longer faces a precarious future, a situation that dictated that it defend Zion's borders. The Southern Paiutes maintain a long-term spiritual connection to their land, but do so from the margins, no longer a threat to anyone. In other words, the things that drew them to conflict—riches, land, the gods, shifting power, and competing notions of sacred space—have either disappeared or transformed drastically. In the end, the threats from across the cultural divide were not as great as each group initially made them out to be.

Although celebrating diversity is important, in doing so, cultures, ethnic groups, religions, and even nations risk obscuring their commonalities and the interdependent nature of their space. Perchance the Mormons possessed a beneficial guiding principle all along but failed to appreciate fully its applicability to their frontier struggle. Mormon scripture suggests that "all are alike unto God," black and white, bond and free, male and female, heathen, Jew, and Gentile.[33] It was a verse that nineteenth-century frontier Mormons too quickly overlooked in their zeal to cast themselves in an Old Testament dichotomy, with Zion on the one side and Babylon on the other. The miners at Pioche also failed to find common ground, choosing instead to divide their space between civilized Pioche and the uncivilized Mormons and Indians. Out of necessity, the Southern Paiutes were the most flexible. Even still, as To-go-av admonished, they remained wary of outsiders and largely relied upon each other. They initially defended their space vigorously but over time withdrew to preserve their worldview against the press of forces bearing down upon them.

The true test of values for the Mormons, miners, and Southern Paiutes was not in their ability to coexist but in their willingness to stretch the bounds of community responsibility to include people who were drastically different from them. Sadly, in the forty years that these three disparate cultural groups shared their space, they made little opportunity to do so.

NOTES

Chapter 1: Intersections

1. Patricia Nelson Limerick, "What on Earth Is the New Western History?" in *Trails toward a New Western History,* ed. Patricia Nelson Limerick, Clyde A. Milner II, and Charles E. Rankin (Lawrence: University Press of Kansas, 1991), 86.

2. This version of the incident is taken from the Journal History of the Church of Jesus Christ of Latter-day Saints (chronology of typed entries and newspaper clippings, 1830 to the present), 29 March 1866, 2–3 (hereafter cited as Journal History), Family and Church History Department, Church of Jesus Christ of Latter-day Saints, Salt Lake City; James G. Bleak, St. George, to Erastus Snow, Salt Lake City, Journal History, 2 April 1866, 6–9.

3. The Danites were a loosely organized group of Mormon vigilantes, active only in Missouri in the fall of 1838, who generally acted independently of church leaders. Non-Mormons in the West frequently laid deaths and other violent and mysterious occurrences within the Utah Territory at their feet; tales of their exploits often assumed mythic proportions. See David J. Whittaker, "Danites," in *Encyclopedia of Mormonism,* ed. Daniel H. Ludlow (New York: Macmillan Publishing, 1992), 356–57.

4. Journal History, 29 March 1866, 2–3; Bleak to Snow, Journal History, 2 April 1866, 6–8.

5. At the end of the nineteenth century, the historian Frederick Jackson Turner looked back over American history and found tremendous significance in the western frontier. Turner saw the frontier as a line between savagery and civilization that stripped the European of his Old World vestiges and re-created him an American. To Turner, the frontier became an active agent in defining American development. It acted on the western pilgrim in successive waves, as wilderness gave way to civilization and the frontier pushed farther west. Frederick Jackson Turner, "The Significance of the Frontier in American History," in *The Frontier in American History* (New York: Henry Holt and Co., 1921), 1–38. New Western historians such as Patricia Nelson Limerick, Donald Worster, and Richard White dismiss Turner's triumphal explanation. In their stories, capitalistic Anglo males were the conquerors who, in the guise of national progress, exploited western lands and minority peoples. See, for example, Richard White, *"It's Your Misfortune and None of My Own": A New History of the American West* (Norman: University of Oklahoma Press, 1991); Patricia Nelson Limerick, *The Legacy of Conquest: The Unbroken Past of the American West* (New York: W. W. Norton and Co., 1987); Donald Worster, *Rivers of Empire: Water, Aridity, and the Growth*

of the American West (New York: Pantheon Books, 1985); and Patricia Nelson Limerick, Clyde A. Milner II, and Charles E. Rankin, eds., *Trails toward a New Western History* (Lawrence: University Press of Kansas, 1991).

6. For examples of this type of thinking regarding the frontier, see David J. Weber and Jane M. Rausch, Introduction to *Where Cultures Meet: Frontiers in Latin American History,* ed. David J. Weber and Jane M. Rausch (Wilmington, Del.: Scholarly Resources Inc., 1994), xiii-xli; John Mack Faragher, "The Frontier Trail: Rethinking Turner and Reimagining the American West," *American Historical Review* 98 (February 1993): 106–17; and Richard White, *The Middle Ground: Indians, Empires, and Republics in the Great Lakes Region, 1650–1815* (Cambridge: Cambridge University Press, 1991). Elliott West's exceptional work, *The Contested Plains: Indians, Goldseekers, and the Rush to Colorado* (Lawrence: University Press of Kansas, 1998), was especially influential in conceptualizing this study.

7. This study treats Mormons as a distinct nineteenth-century ethnic group. See Dean L. May, "Mormons," in *The Harvard Encyclopedia of American Ethnic Groups,* ed. Stephan Thernstrom (Cambridge, Mass.: Belknap Press of Harvard University Press, 1980), 720–31; Patricia Nelson Limerick, "Peace Initiative: Using the Mormons to Rethink Culture and Ethnicity in American History," in *Something in the Soil: Legacies and Reckonings in the New West* (New York: W. W. Norton and Co., 2000), 235–55; and Armand L. Mauss, *All Abraham's Children: Changing Mormon Conceptions of Race and Lineage* (Urbana: University of Illinois Press, 2003), 1–16.

8. David J. Weber, *"The Legacy of Conquest,* by Patricia Nelson Limerick: A Panel of Appraisal," *Western Historical Quarterly* 20 (August 1989): 316.

9. White, *"It's Your Misfortune,"* 316.

10. Eric Foner, *Reconstruction: America's Unfinished Revolution, 1863–1877* (New York: Harper and Row, 1988), 18–34.

11. James M. McPherson, *Battle Cry of Freedom: The Civil War Era* (New York: Ballantine, 1989), 861.

12. Foner, *Reconstruction,* 233; Sean Dennis Cashman, *America in the Gilded Age: From the Death of Lincoln to the Rise of Theodore Roosevelt* (New York: New York University Press, 1984), 215. Republicans, from the election of Lincoln to McKinley (1860–1900), won nine of eleven presidential campaigns with candidates from three pivotal states—Indiana, Illinois, and Ohio. Even still, as Cashman notes, "In this period of Republican ascendancy the Democrats were not weak." Republicans, from 1875–97, generally controlled the Senate, while Democrats usually held the House (216–17).

13. John C. Gerber, *Mark Twain* (Boston: Twayne, 1988), 58–60; Mark Twain and Charles Dudley Warner, *The Gilded Age* (Hartford, Conn.: American Publishing Co., 1873).

14. See Charles W. Calhoun, "The Political Culture: Public Life and the Conduct of Politics," in *The Gilded Age: Essays on the Origins of Modern America,* ed. Charles W. Calhoun (Wilmington, Del.: Scholarly Resources, 1996), 185–213, for a revisionist approach to the Gilded Age that suggests that politics of the time were no more corrupt than in other ages.

15. Alexis de Tocqueville, *Democracy in America,* trans. George Lawrence, ed. J. P. Mayer (New York: HarperCollins, 2000), 532, 536.

16. Cashman, *America in the Gilded Age*, 10–13.

17. Ibid., 86–109; Frank Van Nuys, *Americanizing the West: Race, Immigrants, and Citizenship, 1890–1930* (Lawrence: University Press of Kansas, 2002).

Chapter 2: Making Space

1. The religious historians David Chidester and Edward T. Linenthal contend that "sacred space is significant space, a site, orientation, or set of relations subject to interpretation because it focuses crucial questions about what it means to be a human being in a meaningful world." To "understand the symbolic orderings of American sacred space," they continue, "considerable attention will have to be paid to the interpretive labors that have gone into making space significant." David Chidester and Edward T. Linenthal, Introduction to *American Sacred Space*, ed. David Chidester and Edward T. Linenthal (Bloomington: Indiana University Press, 1995), 12.

2. Mircea Eliade, *The Sacred and the Profane: The Nature of Religion, the Significance of Religious Myth, Symbolism, and Ritual within Life and Culture*, trans. Willard R. Trask (New York: Harper and Row, 1961), 29–36.

3. David B. Madsen, "Dating Paiute-Shoshoni Expansion in the Great Basin," *American Antiquity* 40 (January 1975): 82–86.

4. There is little agreement among scholars as to Paiute band names. Those cited here are gleaned from a variety of sources. See Catherine S. Fowler and Don D. Fowler, "Notes on the History of the Southern Paiutes and Western Shoshonis," *Utah Historical Quarterly* 39 (Spring 1971): 98–99; Robert C. Euler, *The Paiute People* (Phoenix: Indian Tribal Series, 1972), 1–3; Ronald L. Holt, *Beneath These Red Cliffs: An Ethnohistory of the Utah Paiutes* (Albuquerque: University of New Mexico Press, 1992), 4–11; Inter-Tribal Council of Nevada, *Nuwuvi: A Southern Paiute History* (Salt Lake City: University of Utah Printing Service, 1976), 5–11; Gary Tom and Ronald Holt, "The Paiute Tribe of Utah," in *A History of Utah's American Indians*, ed. Forrest S. Cuch (Salt Lake City: Utah State Division of Indian Affairs/Utah State Division of History, 2000), 124–27; and Isabel T. Kelly, "Southern Paiute Bands," *American Anthropologist* 36 (1934): 548–60.

5. John Wesley Powell, *The Exploration of the Colorado River and Its Canyons* (1895; reprint, New York: Dover, 1961), 299–300, 322–33.

6. As the cultural historian Joseph G. Jorgensen contends, "Sentiments and ideas attached to practices of using and inheriting soil . . . are cultural phenomena, and the understanding of those phenomena requires the analysis of cultural organization, not soil." Joseph G. Jorgensen, "Land Is Cultural, So Is a Commodity: The Locus of Differences among Indians, Cowboys, Sod-Busters, and Environmentalists," *Journal of Ethnic Studies* 12 (Fall 1984): 1.

7. Quoted in Robert S. McPherson and Mary Jane Yazzie, "The White Mesa Utes," in *A History of Utah's American Indians*, ed. Forrest S. Cuch (Salt Lake City: Utah State Division of Indian Affairs/Utah State Division of History, 2000), 225.

8. Don D. Fowler and Catherine Fowler, *Anthropology of the Numa: John Wesley Powell's Manuscripts on the Numic People*, Smithsonian Contributions to Anthropology 14 (Washington, D.C.: Smithsonian Institution, 1971), 38. When Powell uses the word "Indian" in this context, he is generalizing about all Numic-

speaking tribes that he studied, of whom the Southern Paiutes occupied a great deal of his time.

9. See Jorgensen, "Land Is Cultural," 15; and Robert S. Michaelsen, "Dirt in the Court Room: Indian Land Claims and American Property Rights," in *American Sacred Space*, ed. David Chidester and Edward T. Linenthal (Bloomington: Indiana University Press, 1995), 49.

10. Quoted in Powell, *Exploration of the Colorado*, 323.

11. Quoted in Donald Worster, *A River Running West: The Life of John Wesley Powell* (New York: Oxford University Press, 2001), 270–71.

12. Versions vary from teller to teller and are similar among Paiute and Ute Indians. This is a synthesis of several versions. See Tom and Holt, "Paiute Tribe of Utah," 123; McPherson and Yazzie, "White Mesa Utes," 225; LaVan Martineau, *Southern Paiutes: Legends, Lore, Language, and Lineage* (Las Vegas: K.C. Publications, 1992), 22–24; Fowler and Fowler, *Anthropology of the Numa*, 78; Robert J. Franklin and Pamela A. Bunte, *The Paiute* (New York: Chelsea House, 1990), 13; and Toney Tillohash, oral interview by Kay Fowler, 16 June 1967, St. George, Utah, Doris Duke Oral History Project, No. 119, typescript, special collections, J. Willard Marriott Library, University of Utah, Salt Lake City.

13. Euler, *Paiute People*, 1.

14. Martineau, *Southern Paiutes*, 154–66; Isabel T. Kelly, *Southern Paiute Ethnography* (1964; reprint, New York: Garland Publishing, 1976), 31–32, 142–43, 175.

15. Powell, *Exploration of the Colorado*, 303–11; Kelly, *Southern Paiute Ethnography*, 120–21; Inter-Tribal Council of Nevada, *Nuwuvi*, 18; Franklin and Bunte, *The Paiute*, 33–35; Fowler and Fowler, *Anthropology of the Numa*, 73, 144; Edward Sapir, "Song Recitative in Paiute Mythology," *Journal of American Folklore* 23 (October–December 1910): 455–72.

16. Tom F. Driver, *Liberating Rites: Understanding the Transformative Power of Ritual* (Boulder, Colo.: Westview Press, 1998), 16.

17. John Lewis Pulsipher, *The Life and Travels of John Lewis Pulsipher, 1884–1963: The Autobiography of a Southern Nevada Pioneer* (N.p., n.d.), 2. This must have been a story that John Lewis Pulsipher heard growing up and therefore could be subject to embellishment. John Pulsipher did not record it in his journal. Joseph Fish, a turn-of-the-twentieth-century chronicler of Hebron history who was acquainted with many Pulsipher descendants, wrote of the encounter: "There were a number of Indians here, whom they met, and made a treaty with them. They were friendly and willing for the Pulsiphers to bring their stock, come and live with them, thus helping the Indians to live better by paying them for services when they worked for the whites." See Joseph Fish, "History of Enterprise and Its Surroundings," 33–34, typescript in possession of Kay Reeve, Hurricane, Utah.

18. Hebron Ward Historical Record, vol. 1 (1862–67), 6–7, microfilm, Historical Department, Church Archives, Church of Jesus Christ of Latter-day Saints, Salt Lake City (hereafter cited as CA).

19. Mormon leaders established the Iron Mission in 1850, but settlers did not arrive until early 1851. See Morris A. Shirts and Kathryn H. Shirts, *A Trial Furnace: Southern Utah's Iron Mission* (Provo, Utah: Brigham Young University Press, 2001).

20. Richard Lyman Bushman, *Making Space for the Mormons*, Leonard J. Ar-

rington Mormon History Lecture Series No. 2 (Logan: Utah State University Press, 1997), 5.

21. Ibid., 13.

22. Ibid., 25.

23. Leonard J. Arrington, *Great Basin Kingdom: An Economic History of the Latter-day Saints, 1830–1900* (1958; reprint, Lincoln: University of Nebraska Press, 1966), 38.

24. Joseph Smith Jr., *History of the Church of Jesus Christ of Latter-day Saints,* vol. 5, ed. B. H. Roberts, 2d ed. (Salt Lake City: Deseret Book Co., 1971), 85. For additional accounts of Joseph Smith's prophecies regarding a Mormon move West, see Lewis Clark Christian, "Mormon Foreknowledge of the West," *BYU Studies* 21 (Fall 1981): 403–15.

25. Isaiah 2:2. The meaning of the phrase "the mountain of the LORD's house" is amplified for Mormons because ancient temples were thought of as mountains. For a recent reference to this prophecy, see Gordon B. Hinckley, "This Great Millennial Year," *Ensign* 30 (November 2000): 67–71. Hinckley, as president and prophet of the Church of Jesus Christ of Latter-day Saints, quotes this verse in Isaiah, adding, "I believe that prophecy applies to the historic and wonderful Salt Lake Temple."

26. Eliade, *Sacred and the Profane,* 26–28.

27. For a discussion of the contested nature of sacred space that challenges some of Eliade's ideas, see Chidester and Linenthal, Introduction, esp. 16–18.

28. Hebron Ward Historical Record, vol. 1, 5–6.

29. Hebron Ward Historical Record, vol. 2 (1867–72), 35 (emphasis added).

30. Hebron Ward Historical Record, vol. 1, 1–2.

31. Ibid., vol. 1, 78–81.

32. Orson Welcome Huntsman, Diary of Orson W. Huntsman, typescript, vol. 1, 29–31, L. Tom Perry Special Collections Library, Harold B. Lee Library, Brigham Young University, Provo, Utah.

33. Ibid.; Hebron Ward Historical Record, vol. 2, 34–35.

34. Huntsman, Diary, vol. 1, 32; Hebron Ward Historical Record, vol. 2, 39.

35. The Doctrine and Covenants of the Church of Jesus Christ of Latter-day Saints, 21:1; 85:1.

36. Hebron Ward Historical Record, vol. 1, 2.

37. Hebron Ward Historical Record, vol. 2, 34–35.

38. Fish, "History of Enterprise," 55.

39. Carrie Elizabeth Laub Hunt, *Memories of the Past and Family History* (Salt Lake City: Utah Printing Co., 1968), 12.

40. Richard V. Francaviglia, *Hard Places: Reading the Landscape of America's Historic Mining Districts* (Iowa City: University of Iowa Press, 1991), xviii, 214–15.

41. *Pioche Daily Record,* 3 October 1872.

42. *Weekly Ely Record* (Pioche, Nev.; precursor to the *Pioche Daily Record*), 1 September 1872.

43. *Pioche Daily Record,* 1 April 1873.

44. *Pioche Daily Record,* 28 January 1873.

45. Rossiter W. Raymond, *Statistics of Mines and Mining in the States and Territories West of the Rocky Mountains,* U.S. Treasury Department, annual report

(Washington, D.C.: Government Printing Office, 1872), 177. See also James W. Hulse, *Lincoln County, Nevada, 1864–1909: History of a Mining Region* (Reno: University of Nevada Press, 1971), 24 (see 23–27 for a discussion of crime at Pioche).

46. The founding story was told from the witness stand as trial testimony in *Raymond and Ely Company v. the Hermes Mining Company,* described below. Apart from that, the most comprehensive recounting of the founding at Pioche is in John Michael Bourne, "Early Mining in Southwestern Utah and Southeastern Nevada, 1864–1873: The Meadow Valley, Pahranagat, and Pioche Mining Rushes" (Master's thesis, University of Utah, 1973), chaps. 3, 4, and 6. See also Hulse, *Lincoln County,* chaps. 1 and 2; James W. Abbott, "The Story of Pioche," in *The Arrowhead: A Monthly Magazine of Western Travel and Development* (Los Angeles: San Pedro, Los Angeles, and Salt Lake Railroad, 1907): 3–11; Brigham D. Madsen, *Glory Hunter: A Biography of Patrick Edward Connor* (Salt Lake City: University of Utah Press, 1990), 108–11; Lloyd K. Long, "Pioche, Nevada, and Early Mining Developments in Eastern Nevada" (Master's thesis, University of Nevada at Las Vegas, 1975); and Andrew Karl Larson, *"I Was Called to Dixie," the Virgin River Basin: Unique Experiences in Mormon Pioneering* (Salt Lake City, Deseret News Press, 1961), 159–65. For statistics on Pioche's silver production in the 1870s, see Bourne, "Early Mining," 113–22.

47. From the trial testimony in *Raymond and Ely v. Hermes,* it is difficult to piece together the exact timing of events, especially surrounding William Hamblin's initial visit to the ore. A letter from Edward Bunker, bishop at Santa Clara, to Brigham Young (20 January 1864, Brigham Young Collection, Office files, 1832–78, microfilm, reel 40, box 29, folder 17, CA) indicates that the first visit took place in the fall of 1863. Stephen Sherwood testified that Hamblin, in 1862, had located a claim at what would become Pioche, but Sherwood must have been mistaken in his recollection. Other testimony, particularly that by William Pulsipher, suggests that it was not until 1863. Captain Hempstead's report of the founding as printed in the *Daily Union Vedette* at Salt Lake City, 2 July 1864, supports Pulsipher's testimony, although it does not include Pulsipher as a participant in the first visit. The context of Pulsipher's testimony suggests that he was with Hamblin when Moroni led them both to the ore. The reconstruction of those early events presented here is based most heavily upon Pulsipher's testimony and Hempstead's report as well as Judge Pitzer's closing argument as a lawyer for the Hermes Company. See *Pioche Daily Record,* 29 March, 12 April, and 24 April 1873; *Daily Union Vedette,* 2 July 1864.

48. *Pioche Daily Record,* 17 April 1873.

49. Irving Telling, "History of William Haynes Hamblin," in *A Preliminary Study of the History of Ramah, New Mexico* (N.p., n.d.), Family History Library, Church of Jesus Christ of Latter-day Saints, Salt Lake City (hereafter cited as FHL). According to Telling, Hamblin spent two years in California attempting to recover in the gold fields a significant loss of wealth he experienced when a business partner swindled and then abandoned him (4). While he was in California, Hamblin's two wives did not hear from him for two years and "thought he must be dead." He returned, however, without much money, but he did have "three wagons loaded with everything."

50. Red, blue, yellow, and black were colors used in Paiute face painting. The

paint was especially used for "squaw" and bear dances, as it "frightened away evil spirits." Powell recorded, "Red paint signifies joy. The face painted from the lower point of the ear to the middle of the nose above and black below signifying war." See Fowler and Fowler, *Anthropology of the Numa*, 162; and Kelly, *Southern Paiute Ethnography*, 66–68.

51. This was a moment of historical irony that paralleled the experience of Joseph Smith, the first Mormon prophet. Smith claimed that an angel named Moroni led him to a very different buried treasure—golden plates, which he then translated into the Book of Mormon. The Paiute Moroni's involvement in locating the original Meadow Valley claim is only hinted at in the court case. See, for example, *Pioche Daily Record*, 28 March 1873. The version rendered here is gleaned from a report written by Captain Hempstead, published in the *Daily Union Vedette* (Salt Lake City), 2 July 1864. Hempstead was at the claims in 1864 and likely learned the information in his report firsthand. In any case, his is the most detailed and a close chronological retelling of the first location by Hamblin, with Moroni as guide. There is, however, another version of the discovery in a 20 January 1864 letter from Bunker to Young. According to Bunker, the Paiutes had been trying to persuade Hamblin "to go with them to a lead mine as they said the Mormons wanted lead. Last fall he [Hamblin] consented to go with them. He found the mine situated about 12 miles from Meadow Valley lying about northwest from here and about 120 miles distant. He brought [*sic*] some of the ore home with him." Bunker also mentions Hamblin giving a gun to a Paiute, not as inducement to show him the spot but as incentive to keep the spot secret, especially from a group of California prospectors then searching for wealth in the area. Edward Bunker to Brigham Young, 20 January 1864, Brigham Young Collection, Office files, 1832–78, microfilm, reel 40, box 29, folder 17, CA. It is difficult to know which version is more accurate. I have relied upon Hempstead's account because it seems more plausible that Hamblin would be twisting Moroni's arm to show him the ore, rather than the other way around. Given Hamblin's two-year search for gold in California, it is difficult to imagine him resisting Indian enticements to find wealth nearby. Bunker's telling is perhaps suited to Brigham Young as audience in that it makes Hamblin a reluctant participant instead of an active prospector, much more in line with Young's general policy against mining.

52. The Bunker group consisted of William Pulsipher, William Hamblin, Alsen Hamblin, Daniel C. Cill, Andrew Gibbons, Benjamin Brown Crow, Jeremiah Leavitt, A. Chamberlain, and the county surveyor, Israel Ivins. See Daniel Bonelli to George A. Smith, 30 April 1864, and Edward Bunker to Brigham Young, 20 January 1864, Brigham Young Collection, Office files, 1832–78, microfilm, reel 40, box 29, folder 17, CA; Bourne, "Early Mining," 22–23.

53. Brigham Young to Edward Bunker, 6 February 1864, Brigham Young Collection, outgoing correspondence, CA.

54. Ibid.

55. *Pioche Daily Record*, 28 March, 24 April 1873.

56. *Pioche Daily Record*, 30 March, 24 April 1873.

57. Madsen, *Glory Hunter.*

58. *Pioche Daily Record*, 28, 29, 30 March 1873.

59. Bunker to Young, 20 January 1864.

60. Bonelli to Smith, 30 April 1864.

61. *Pioche Daily Record,* 30 March 1873.

62. The reconstruction of these events is taken from *The Raymond and Ely vs. The Kentucky Mining Co.: Judge Beatty's Decision* (Pioche: Record Publishing Co., 1873), Nevada Historical Society, Reno. Information also came from the testimonies of Thomas Box, Thomas M. Box Jr., Stephen Sherwood, Jacob N. Vandermark, Peter Shirts, and from Judge Pitzer's closing argument in *Raymond and Ely v. Hermes,* all of which were reported in the *Pioche Daily Record,* 28, 29, 30 March, 17, 24 April 1873. Bonelli to Smith, 30 April 1864, fills in some detail; and Bourne, "Early Mining," 21–28, thoroughly chronicles the same events.

63. Bonelli to George A. Smith, 30 April 1864; Panaca Ward, Uvada Stake, manuscript history and historical reports, microfilm, CA.

64. P. Edw. Connor, Brigadier-General, Commanding, to Capt. David J. Berry, 30 April 1864, and Micajah G. Lewis to Capt. David J. Berry, Camp Douglas, Utah Ter., 13 May 1864, in *The War of the Rebellion: A Compilation of the Official Records of the Union and Confederate Armies,* series 1, vol. 50, pt. 2 (Washington, D.C.: Government Printing Office, 1897), 845.

65. *Daily Union Vedette,* 8 July 1864.

66. Erastus Snow to Brigham Young, 19 June 1864, Brigham Young Collection, Office files, 1832–78, microfilm, reel 55, box 42, folder 18, CA.

67. *Daily Union Vedette,* 1 July 1864.

68. *Daily Union Vedette,* 8, 11 July 1864.

69. *Pioche Daily Record,* 1 April 1873; Panaca Ward, manuscript history and historical reports.

70. *Pioche Daily Record,* 28, 30 March, 1 April 1873.

71. *Pioche Daily Record,* 28, 29 March 1873.

72. *Pioche Daily Record,* 28, 29, 30 March 1873.

73. Mel Gorman, "Chronicle of a Silver Mine: The Meadow Valley Mining Company of Pioche," *Nevada Historical Society Quarterly* 29 (Summer 1986): 71; *Judge Beatty's Decision,* 4.

74. See W. Turrentine Jackson, *Treasure Hill* (Tuscon: University of Arizona Press, 1963), 20; Bourne, "Early Mining," 85–92.

75. David G. Dalin and Charles A. Fracchia, "Forgotten Financier: François L. A. Pioche," *California Historical Quarterly* 53 (Spring 1974): 17–24; Philip S. Rush, "The Strange Story of F. L. A. Pioche," typescript, Lincoln County Museum, Pioche, Nevada.

76. Gorman, "Chronicle of a Silver Mine," 71.

77. Court Order Book, book B, vol. 2, 187–88, County Clerk's Office, Lincoln County Courthouse, Pioche, Nevada (hereafter cited as LCC). From testimony of Sherwood and Vandermark, it seems evident that Raymond and Ely purchased their claims as well. See also *Judge Beatty's Decision,* 4.

78. See Gorman, "Chronicle of a Silver Mine," 71; Hulse, *Lincoln County,* 9–10 and chap. 1 n.11.

79. For theories surrounding Pioche's death, see Dalin and Fracchia, "Forgotten Financier," 17, 24. Ideas included: "[H]is depression over France's humiliation at its quick loss of the Franco-Prussian War in 1870, severe headaches as a result of an injury received from a fall from a horse, his guilt over his role in the vigilante hangings of the 1850s, business problems known only to himself and a few associates."

80. *Pioche Daily Record*, 29 March 1873.
81. *Pioche Daily Record*, 28, 29 March 1873. The day after this report the newspaper recanted, apologizing to the "Sheriff and all concerned." The sheriff had made it clear that the courtroom was swept "perfectly clean twice a day, and the jurymen, who under an order of Court, sleep in the room, have no complaint to find of its condition."
82. *Pioche Daily Record*, 25 April 1873. Judge Pitzer, arguing on behalf of the Hermes Company, suggested that Raymond "seeks to influence witnesses and jurymen by threatening to close his mine if he loses this case," thereby injuring the "entire community if his private interests should be hurt by the result of the suit."
83. Telling, "History of William Haynes Hamblin," 4–5; Naida R. Williamson, "William Haynes Hamblin, 1830–1872," 4–5, typescript, FHL; *Pioche Daily Record*, 2 April 1873; Court Order Book, book B, vol. 2, 181, County Clerk's Office, LCC.
84. *Pioche Daily Record*, 23, 24 April 1873.
85. *Pioche Daily Record*, 24, 26 April 1873.
86. The "By-Laws of the Meadow Valley Mining District" were printed in the *Daily Union Vedette*, 4 June 1864.
87. *Pioche Daily Record*, 1, 22, 24 April 1873.
88. *Pioche Daily Record*, 24, 25, 27, 29 April 1873.
89. Court Order Book, book B, vol. 2, 198–99, County Clerk's Office, LCC; *Pioche Daily Record*, 2 May 1873; Abbott, "Story of Pioche," 10.
90. Court Judgement Record, book 445, vol. A, 1868–79, 242, County Clerk's Office, LCC.
91. Court Order Book, book B, vol. 2, 199, 224, County Clerk's Office, LCC.
92. *Pioche Daily Record*, 29 June, 1 July 1873.
93. *Pioche Daily Record*, 19 August 1873; Abbott, "Story of Pioche," 10; Hulse, *Lincoln County*, 26; Fremont Older and Cora M. Older, *George Hearst: California Pioneer* (Los Angeles: Westernlore, 1966), 142.

Chapter 3: Power, Place, and Prejudice

1. *Annual Report of the State Mineralogist of the State of Nevada for 1866* (Carson City: Joseph E. Eckley, State Printer, 1867), 64; *Daily Union Vedette* (Salt Lake City), 31 January 1866; Journal History of the Church of Jesus Christ of Latter-day Saints (chronology of typed entries and newspaper clippings, 1830 to the present), 6 July 1866 (hereafter cited as Journal History), Family and Church History Department, Church of Jesus Christ of Latter-day Saints, Salt Lake City; Michael Bourne, "Early Mining in Southwestern Utah and Southeastern Nevada, 1864–1873: The Meadow Valley, Pahranagat, and Pioche Mining Rushes" (Master's thesis, University of Utah, 1973), 55–56.
2. *Mining and Scientific Press* 13 (21 July 1866): 38–39; *Mining and Scientific Press* 13 (8 September 1866): 151; *American Journal of Mining, Milling, Oil-Boring, Geology, Mineralogy, Metallurgy, etc.* 1 (12 May 1866): 100.
3. James P. Ronda, "Coboway's Tale: A Story of Power and Places along the Columbia," in *Power and Place in the North American West*, ed. Richard White

and John M. Findlay (Seattle: Center for the Study of the Pacific Northwest and University of Washington Press, 1999), 19.

4. Quoted in William L. Riordon, *Plunkitt of Tammany Hall* (New York: Mc-Clure, Philipps, and Co., 1905), 3.

5. Kirk H. Porter and Donald Bruce Johnson, comps., *National Party Platforms, 1840–1956* (Urbana: University of Illinois Press, 1956), 27.

6. Edward Leo Lyman, *Political Deliverance: The Mormon Quest for Utah Statehood* (Urbana: University of Illinois Press, 1986), 7–11.

7. Richard D. Poll, "The Legislative Antipolygamy Campaign," *BYU Studies* 26.4 (1986): 107–21.

8. For further analysis of Utah's nineteenth-century political struggle, see Sarah Barringer Gordon, *The Mormon Question: Polygamy and Constitutional Conflict in Nineteenth Century America* (Chapel Hill: University of North Carolina Press, 2002); Lyman, *Political Deliverance;* Gustive O. Larson, *The "Americanization" of Utah for Statehood* (San Marino, Calif.: Huntington Library, 1971); Howard R. Lamar, "Statehood for Utah: A Different Path," *Utah Historical Quarterly* 39 (Fall 1971): 307–27; and Richard D. Poll, "The Americanism of Utah," *Utah Historical Quarterly* 44 (Winter 1976): 76–93.

9. William P. MacKinnon, "'Like Splitting a Man up His Backbone': The Territorial Dismemberment of Utah, 1850–1896," *Utah Historical Quarterly* 71 (Spring 2003): 100–124. MacKinnon places the Utah story within a broader framework of territorial border changes throughout American history. He finds that in that context, the massive realignment of Utah's borders was not unusual, but the circumstances and reasoning for some of those changes perhaps were. In some cases, hostility of "the most intense, punitive character" to Mormonism had an impact upon Utah's shrinking borders.

10. D. W. Meinig, "American Wests: Preface to a Geographical Interpretation," *Annals of the Association of American Geographers* 62 (June 1972): 170.

11. Gordon Morris Bakken, *Rocky Mountain Constitution Making, 1850–1912* (New York: Greenwood Press, 1987), 6–11.

12. David Alan Johnson, *Founding the Far West: California, Oregon, and Nevada, 1840–1890* (Berkeley: University of California Press, 1992), 72–75.

13. "Territory of Nevada," 35th Cong., 1st Sess., House Report No. 375, 12 May 1858, serial set 966, 4. See Johnson, *Founding the Far West,* 74–75; and Michael W. Bowers, *The Nevada State Constitution: A Reference Guide* (Westport, Conn.: Greenwood Press, 1993), 1–4, for additional references to appeals for separation.

14. U.S. District Court, Utah (Second District), *Report of the Grand Jury of the Second District of Utah Territory, September Term, 1859,* Beinecke Library, Yale University, New Haven, Conn.

15. Johnson, *Founding the Far West,* 72–77.

16. Frankie Sue Del Papa, ed., *Political History of Nevada,* 9th ed. (Carson City: State Printing Office, 1990), 79; James W. Hulse, *The Silver State: Nevada's Heritage Reinterpreted,* 2d ed. (Reno: University of Nevada Press, 1998), 89; George F. Brightman, "The Boundaries of Utah," *Economic Geography* 16 (January 1940): 87–95.

17. Johnson, *Founding the Far West,* 189–90, 315; Del Papa, *Political History,* 86.

18. Hubert Howe Bancroft, *History of Nevada, Colorado, and Wyoming, 1540–1888* (San Francisco: The History Company, 1890), 158.

19. Del Papa, *Political History*, 96. Article 14, Section 1 of the Nevada Constitution reads: "And whensoever Congress shall authorize the addition to the Territory or State of Nevada of any portion of the territory on the easterly border of the foregoing defined limits, not exceeding in extent one degree of longitude, the same shall thereupon be embraced within and become a part of this state."

20. *Annual Report of the State Mineralogist of the State of Nevada for 1866*, 64; *Daily Union Vedette*, 31 January 1866; Journal History, 6 July 1866; Bourne, "Early Mining," 55–56.

21. *Annual Report of the State Mineralogist of the State of Nevada for 1866*, 64; *Daily Union Vedette*, 31 January 1866; *American Journal of Mining* 1 (12 May 1866): 100; Journal History, 6 July 1866, 2–3.

22. *Daily Union Vedette*, 18 November 1865. Sale resigned his post as recorder in October 1865. *Annual Report of the State Mineralogist of the State of Nevada for 1866* notes that the number of mining locations on record for Pahranagat "probably reaches one thousand" (64).

23. Thomas C. W. Sale, Meadow Valley, Utah Territory, to O. H. Irish, Salt Lake City, 4 May 1865, microfilm roll 901, National Archives, Letters Received by the Office of Indian Affairs, Utah Superintendency, 1863–65 (hereafter cited as OIA-UT); Hulse, *Silver State*, 53.

24. *Mining and Scientific Press* 11 (23 September 1865): 182.

25. James W. Hulse, "Boom and Bust Government in Lincoln County, Nevada, 1866–1909," *Nevada Historical Society Quarterly* 1 (November 1957): 66.

26. Quoted in Hulse, "Boom and Bust," 66.

27. *Daily Union Vedette*, 1 November 1865, 31 January 1866.

28. *Daily Union Vedette*, 30 May 1866.

29. Hulse, "Boom and Bust," 78–79 n.5.

30. Ibid., 65–66; James W. Hulse, *The Nevada Adventure: A History*, 6th ed. (Reno: University of Nevada Press, 1990), 137–39.

31. Myron Angel, *History of Nevada* (Oakland, Calif.: Thompson and West, 1881), 477; Samuel P. Davis, ed., *The History of Nevada*, vol. 2 (Reno: Elms Publishing Co., 1913), 928; James W. Hulse, *Lincoln County Nevada, 1864–1909: History of a Mining Region* (Reno: University of Nevada Press, 1971), 15–16; Hulse, "Boom and Bust," 66–67; John M. Townley, *Conquered Provinces: Nevada Moves Southeast, 1864–1871*, Charles Redd Monographs in Western History No. 2 (Provo, Utah: Brigham Young University Press, 1973), 18–19; *American Journal of Mining* 1 (21 July 1866): 260.

32. See Hulse, *Lincoln County*, 15–16; and Townley, *Conquered Provinces*, 18.

33. *American Journal of Mining* 1 (21 July 1866): 260.

34. Hulse, "Boom and Bust," 68.

35. Journal History, 14 January 1870, 2.

36. Journal History, 3 October 1865, 1–2.

37. Charles Durkee, "Governor's Message," 11 December 1865, in Governors' Messages to the Utah Legislature, 1851–76, 108, Utah State Historical Society Library, Salt Lake City (hereafter cited as USHS).

38. Thomas Callister to George A. Smith, Journal History, 1 April 1866, 1;

see also George A. Smith to Thomas Callister, Journal History, 28 March 1866, 2–3.

39. *American Journal of Mining* 1 (21 July 1866): 259. It is difficult to pinpoint the time of Durkee's visit. From the context of Mormon letters noting the governor's movements, it was likely in early to mid April 1866. He was clearly back at work in Salt Lake City by early May. See Daniel H. Wells to Erastus Snow, Journal History, 3 May 1866, 3–5; and Townley, *Conquered Provinces*, 19.

40. Governor Charles Durkee, Salt Lake City, to President Andrew Johnson, Washington, D.C., 18 May 1866, in U.S. Department of State, State Department Territorial Papers, Utah Series, microfilm, vol. 2, no. 629.

41. *Mining and Scientific Press* 13 (3 November 1866): 279.

42. "Governor's Message," in Journal History, 10 December 1866, 2–4.

43. Journal History, 4 July 1865, 6–7.

44. Journal History, 5 July 1865, 1a; 6 July 1865, 1. Ashley had introduced statehood bills for Nevada, Nebraska, Utah, and Colorado during the Thirty-seventh Congress. Ashley won reelection in 1864 by over eight hundred votes; clearly, more than Utah's statehood bill led to the narrow margin. A group of Republican conservatives threw their support behind Ashley's Democratic opponent. See Robert F. Horowitz, *The Great Impeacher: A Political Biography of James M. Ashley* (New York: Brooklyn College Press, 1979), 85, 101.

45. *Daily Union Vedette*, 4, 13, 14 July 1865.

46. Orson F. Whitney, *History of Utah*, vol. 2 (Salt Lake City: George Q. Cannon, 1893), 137–40; *Congressional Globe*, 39th Cong., 1st Sess. (Washington, D.C.: F. and J. Rives, 1866), pt. 3, 2368–70. When Ashley noted his return from Nevada via the "southern route," he was likely referring to the Old Spanish Trail, which would have carried him through the heart of the contested land soon to be transferred to Nevada, although he would have missed the future Pahranagat District itself, passing to the south.

47. Donald Bufkin, "The Lost County of Pah-Ute," *Arizoniana: The Journal of Arizona History* 5 (Summer 1964): 7. There had been an attempt to extend the boundary in early 1865, which passed the Senate but died on the floor of the House (see 7–8). See also "Resolution of the Legislature of the State of Nevada, in Favor of the Passage of a Law Fixing as the Eastern Boundary of the State of Nevada the Thirty-Seventh Degree of Longitude West from Washington," 38th Cong., 2d Sess., Misc. Doc. No. 43, 24 February 1865, serial set 1210. The justification given in this resolution was simply that the Nevada Constitution provided for expansion eastward, whereas in 1866, when Congress passed the boundary change, the Pahranagat silver mines clearly became the motivating factor.

48. *Congressional Globe*, pt. 3, 2368–70. In the House debate over the boundary shift, Congressman James Ashley argued in favor of giving Nevada the proposed corner of Arizona, stating that "the annexation of this territory to Nevada makes the boundary line of that State a navigable river. The head waters of navigation will then be within the State of Nevada; they will have an outlet to the Gulf and to the sea; and as they have less arable land susceptible of cultivation than either Arizona or Utah, I think it due that we should annex this territory to the State of Nevada" (2370). On Call's Landing, or Callville, as a supply port and shipping point for Pahranagat, see *Daily Union Vedette*, 1 November 1865; 31 January, 9 July 1866. For the Arizona perspective on the border shift, see Bufkin, "Lost

County of Pah-Ute." The Arizona section did not officially become a part of Nevada until 1867, even though Congress passed it in 1866. Congress required that the Nevada legislature ratify the transfer from Arizona, which it did when it met in 1867. The Utah portion became part of Nevada automatically, by virtue of the Nevada Constitution making provision for additions from Utah. See Del Papa, *Political History*, 96–100.

49. For negative reports on Pahranagat from early 1866, see Hulse, *Lincoln County*, 14–15; and Townley, *Conquered Provinces*, 19–20.

50. The house debate over the bill is contained in *Congressional Globe*, pt. 3, 2368–70; all subsequent quotes from the debate are found therein. To trace Senate Bill No. 155 through the Senate and House, see *Congressional Globe*, pt. 1, 645; pt. 2, 1386, 1401, 1535; pt. 3, 2358, 2377, 2381.

51. Thomas Jefferson, *Notes on the State of Virginia*, ed. Thomas Perkins Abernethy (New York: Harper and Row, 1964), 157.

52. Donald Henriques Dyal, "The Agrarian Values of Mormonism: A Touch of the Mountain Sod" (Ph.D. diss., Texas A&M University, 1980), 1–4 and chaps. 5 and 6. For more on Jefferson's agrarianism, see James P. Ronda, *Jefferson's West: A Journey with Lewis and Clark* (Monticello, Va.: Thomas Jefferson Foundation, 2000), 28–29.

53. Paul W. Gates, *The Jeffersonian Dream: Studies in the History of American Land Policy and Development*, ed. Allan G. Bogue and Margaret Beattie Bogue (Albuquerque: University of New Mexico Press, 1996), chap. 3. For a discussion of the primacy of agriculture in the West and the Mormon influence upon John Wesley Powell's agrarian vision for the West, see Richard White, *"Its Your Misfortune and None of My Own": A New History of the American West* (Norman: University of Oklahoma Press, 1991), 147–54; and Marc Reisner, *Cadillac Desert: The American West and Its Disappearing Water* (New York: Penguin, 1987), chap. 1.

54. U.S. Treasury Department, *Statistics of Mines and Mining in the States and Territories West of the Rocky Mountains*, 1st annual report of Rossiter W. Raymond, U.S. Commissioner of Mining Statistics, 40th Cong., 3d Sess., 1868, House Ex. Doc. No. 54, 114–15; U.S. Treasury Department, *Statistics of Mines and Mining in the States and Territories West of the Rocky Mountains*, 2d annual report of Rossiter W. Raymond, U.S. Commissioner of Mining Statistics, 41st Cong., 2d Sess., 1869, House Ex. Doc. No. 207, 194–95.

55. For a general overview of the reservation system and its evolution during the Civil War and after, see Arrell Morgan Gibson, *The American Indian: Prehistory to the Present* (Lexington, Mass.: D. C. Heath and Co., 1980), 354–55, 392–97, and esp. chap. 17; Francis Paul Prucha, *The Great Father: The United States Government and the American Indians*, vols. 1 and 2 (Lincoln: University of Nebraska Press, 1984), 315–409, 437–78.

56. Gibson, *American Indian*, 379–80, 387, 393–95; Prucha, *Great Father*, 479–581.

57. Gibson, *American Indian*, 396–97; Prucha, *Great Father*, 527–33.

58. Petition, Meadow Valley, Washington Co., Utah Territory, to O. H. Irish, Salt Lake City, 27 August 1864, roll 901, OIA-UT; James Duane Doty and Amos Reed to O. H. Irish, 7 September 1864, roll 901, OIA-UT.

59. O. H. Irish to Wm. P. Dole, 9 September 1864, roll 901, OIA-UT.

60. Thomas C. W. Sale, Meadow Valley, Utah Territory, to O. H. Irish, Salt Lake City, 18 November 1864 and 15 December 1864; O. H. Irish, Salt Lake City, to William P. Dole, Washington, D.C., 22 November 1864, roll 901, OIA-UT.

61. Sale to Irish, 18 November 1864, 15 December 1864, 4 May 1865, roll 901, OIA-UT.

62. Petition, Panaca City, Utah Territory, to James D. Doty, Governor of Utah, Salt Lake City, 28 April 1865, roll 901, OIA-UT.

63. Sale to Irish, 15 December 1864; petitions, 27 August 1864, 28 April 1865, roll 901, OIA-UT. Among the names on the second petition identifiable as Mormons are Francis Lee, John N. Lee, George W. Lee, Francis C. Lee, Samuel Lee, John B. Atchison, William S. Atchison, and Samelson Atchison.

64. Sale to Irish, 19 May 1865, roll 901, OIA-UT.

65. Sale to Irish, 4 May 1865, roll 901, OIA-UT. For a good explanation of the Indian slave trade in Utah and the long-standing Ute raids upon the Paiutes, see Sondra Jones, *The Trial of Don Pedro León Luján: The Attack against Indian Slavery and Mexican Traders in Utah* (Salt Lake City: University of Utah Press, 2000); and Stephen P. Van Hoak, "And Who Shall Have the Children? The Indian Slave Trade in the Southern Great Basin, 1800–1865," *Nevada Historical Society Quarterly* 41 (Spring 1998): 3–25.

66. Irish to Dole, 15 May 1865, roll 901, OIA-UT.

67. "Articles of Agreement and Convention Made and Concluded at Pinto Creek," 18 September 1865, Ronald L. Holt Papers, box 3, folder 9, Special Collections, J. Willard Marriott Library, University of Utah, Salt Lake City.

68. For the connection of Sale, Conger, and McCurdy to the Pahranagat District, see *Daily Union Vedette*, 1 November, 18 November 1865; 30 May 1866; Townley, *Conquered Provinces*, 20. Following the Pinto Creek Treaty, Conger and McCurdy visited Pahranagat for a time. Conger represented eastern capital and apparently tested some of the ore of the region, with one account describing him as a "scientific mineralogist." He went on to become involved as an officer in the mining district organization. His role at the Pinto Creek Treaty, if any, is not clear.

69. As previously noted, the Paiutes were also victims in the Indian slave trade, with Navajos and Utes stealing their women and children to sell to Euro-Americans. See Jones, *Trial of Don Pedro León Luján*, 44–52; Inter-Tribal Council of Nevada, *Nuwuvi: A Southern Paiute History* (Salt Lake City: University of Utah Printing Service, 1976), 36–51; Van Hoak, "And Who Shall Have the Children?" 3–25.

70. Inter-Tribal Council of Nevada, *Nuwuvi*, 86–87. Sale estimated the Paiute population in 1865 to be between two and three thousand. See Sale to Irish, 4 May 1865, roll 901, OIA-UT.

71. R. N. Fenton, St. Thomas, Nev., to F. S. Parker, Washington, D.C., 14 October 1869, *Report of Commissioner of Indian Affairs*, House Exec. Doc. No. 37, 1869, serial set 1414, 645–46; Fenton, Pioche, Nev., to H. Douglas, Superintendent Indian Affairs of Nevada, 22 September 1870, *Report of Commissioner of Indian Affairs*, House Exec. Doc. No. 1, 1870, serial set 1449, 577–78; Charles F. Powell, Saint George, Utah Territory, to H. R. Clum, Acting Commissioner of Indian Affairs, Washington, D.C., 20 October 1871, *Report of Commissioner of Indian Affairs*, 1871 (Washington, D.C.: Government Printing Office, 1872),

561–63. For additional accounts of agent neglect, see J. C. Foster, Register, U.S. Land Office, Pioche, Nev., to C. Delano, Secretary of the Interior, Washington, D.C., 23 September 1874; A. J. Barnes, Saint George, Utah, to Edward P. Smith, Commissioner of Indian Affairs, Washington, D.C., 17 November 1874; Barnes, St. Thomas, Nev., to Smith, 3 December 1874; Daniel Cram, Assistant Special Detective, Salt Lake City, to George H. Williams, U.S. Attorney General, Washington, D.C., 8 December 1874, all in National Archives, Letters Received by the Office of Indian Affairs, Nevada Superintendency, 1874–75, microfilm roll 541 (hereafter cited as OIA-NV); Donald Worster, *A River Running West: The Life of John Wesley Powell* (New York: Oxford University Press, 2001), 266–67, 591 n.9; and Inter-Tribal Council of Nevada, *Nuwuvi*, 96–105.

72. Economic and environmental factors also contributed to the demise of the Muddy Mission (see chapter 5 of this volume).

73. Letter from the Acting Secretary of the Interior, Relative to the Condition of the Pi-Ute Indians, 42nd Cong., 3d Sess., 1873, House Ex. Doc. No. 66, serial set 1565, 2–3.

74. Ibid.

75. Ibid. Charles Powell reported in 1871 that the Paiutes along the Muddy "raise good corn, beans, melons, squashes, pumpkins, &c." Powell to Clum, 20 October 1871. When Mormon settlers founded West Point, their cattle threatened the Indian wheat planted along the upper Muddy. See Pearson Starr Corbett, "A History of the Muddy Mission" (Master's thesis, Brigham Young University, 1968), 82. For additional references to Paiute farming dating back to 1776, the first recorded Euro-American contact with the Paiutes, see Robert C. Euler, *Southern Paiute Ethnohistory*, University of Utah Anthropological Papers Number 78 (Salt Lake City: University of Utah Press, 1966), 111–13. As Euler sees it, Paiute irrigation and farming practices predated Euro-American contact.

76. H. R. Clum, Acting Commissioner of Indian Affairs, to C. Delano, Secretary of the Interior, 7 March 1873; C. Delano to Ulysses S. Grant, 12 March 1873; Ulysses S. Grant, Executive Order, 12 March 1873; Ulysses S. Grant, Executive Order, 12 February 1874, holograph photocopies in Maryellen Vallier Sadovich Collection, Manuscript x45, folder 3, Special Collections, Lied Library, University of Nevada at Las Vegas; Inter-Tribal Council of Nevada, *Nuwuvi*, 94–95.

77. *Pioche Daily Record*, 16 April, 18 April 1873. For the government evaluation of land claims and offering price for each claim, see J. W. Powell and G. W. Ingalls, *Report of Special Commissioners J. W. Powell and G. W. Ingalls on the Condition of the Ute Indians of Utah; the Paiutes of Utah, Northern Arizona, Southern Nevada, and Southeastern California; the Northwestern Shoshones of Idaho and Utah; and the Western Shoshones of Nevada; and Report Concerning Claims of Settlers in the Mo-a-pa Valley, Southeastern Nevada*, in *Annual Report of the Commissioner of Indian Affairs*, 1873, serial set 1601, 437–42.

78. Daniel Bonelli, St. Thomas, Nev., to E. P. Smith, Commissioner of Indian Affairs, Washington, D.C., 10 September, 5 October, 23 October 1874, roll 541, OIA-NV; A. J. Barnes, Indian Agent, St. Thomas, Nev., to E. P. Smith, 20 December 1874, roll 541, OIA-NV.

79. Barnes to Smith, 20 December 1874, roll 541, OIA-NV.

80. Barnes to Smith, 19 January 1875, roll 541, OIA-NV.

81. Bonelli to Smith, 10 September 1874, roll 541, OIA-NV.

82. Bonelli to Smith, 23 October 1874, roll 541, OIA-NV.

83. Henry P. Geib, M.D., Physician to Pai-Ute Reservation, to Smith, 26 October 1874, roll 541, OIA-NV.

84. Barnes to Smith, 20 December 1874, roll 541, OIA-NV; *Muddy or Moapa Indian Reservation*, Resolution of the Legislature of the State of Nevada, 4 February 1875, 43d Cong., 2d Sess., Misc. Doc. No. 61, 1–2.

85. Charles J. Kappler, comp. and ed., *Indian Affairs: Laws and Treaties*, vol. 1 (Washington, D.C.: Government Printing Office, 1904), 157.

86. The original reservation did include salt mines, which Ingalls argued should be kept in Paiute hands, and they were allowed to mine and market the salt. The cost of doing so, however, made the mines valueless, and the salt did not factor heavily into the reservation debate. See G. W. Ingalls to Smith, 25 January 1874; Bonelli to Smith, 20 September 1874, roll 541, OIA-NV.

87. For the proposed boundaries and the initial debate over the bill, see *Congressional Globe*, pt. 1, 363–64.

88. George A. Smith, Salt Lake City, to William H. Hooper, Washington, D.C., 24 January 1869, Historian's Office, Letterpress Copybooks, vol. 2, p. 764, Church Archives, Church of Jesus Christ of Latter-day Saints, Salt Lake City.

89. Horowitz, *Great Impeacher*, 144.

90. Quoted in Journal History, 17 March 1869, 3.

91. Horowitz, *Great Impeacher*, 158–69.

92. "Extension of Boundaries, Speech of Hon. William H. Hooper, of Utah, Delivered in the House of Representatives, February 25, 1869," *Congressional Globe*, pt. 3, appendix, 242.

93. Powell and Ingalls, *Report of Special Commissioners*, 414. Smith did allow that "in case it should be found impossible to induce them to look with favor upon a removal" to the Uintah Valley, Powell and Ingalls should "make a thorough examination as to the condition of affairs on the Muddy reservation." For Powell's activities as special commissioner, see Worster, *River Running West*, 261–96.

94. Powell and Ingalls, *Report of Special Commissioners*, 412–14.

95. Ibid., 414–16.

96. "Territory of Nevada," 35th Cong., 1st Sess., House Report No. 375, 12 May 1858, serial set 966, 4.

97. *Daily Union Vedette*, 1 November 1865.

98. Powell and Ingalls, *Report of Special Commissioners*, 424.

99. George M. Wheeler and Daniel W. Lockwood, *Preliminary Report upon a Reconnaissance through Southern and Southeastern Nevada, Made in 1869*, U.S. Army, Engineer Department (Washington, D.C.: Government Printing Office, 1875), 23–24.

100. Patricia Nelson Limerick, *Legacy of Conquest: The Unbroken Past of the American West* (New York: W. W. Norton and Co., 1987), 27.

Chapter 4: "Listen Not to a Stranger"

1. Richard White, *"It's Your Misfortune and None of My Own": A New History of the American West* (Norman: University of Oklahoma Press, 1991), 317.

2. John R. Alley Jr., "Prelude to Dispossession: The Fur Trade's Significance for

the Northern Utes and Southern Paiutes," *Utah Historical Quarterly* 50 (Spring 1982): 104–23; Stephen P. Van Hoak, "And Who Shall Have the Children? The Indian Slave Trade in the Southern Great Basin, 1800–1865," *Nevada Historical Society Quarterly* 41 (Spring 1998): 3–25.

3. Don D. Fowler and Catherine Fowler, *Anthropology of the Numa: John Wesley Powell's Manuscripts on the Numic People,* Smithsonian Contributions to Anthropology 14 (Washington, D.C.: Smithsonian Institution, 1971), 50.

4. This list is not complete but includes the major leaders and bands that the Mormons and miners primarily interacted with. It is gleaned from J. W. Powell and G. W. Ingalls, *Report of Special Commissioners J. W. Powell and G. W. Ingalls on the Condition of the Ute Indians of Utah; the Paiutes of Utah, Northern Arizona, Southern Nevada, and Southeastern California; the Northwestern Shoshones of Idaho and Utah; and the Western Shoshones of Nevada; and Report Concerning Claims of Settlers in the Mo-a-pa Valley, Southeastern Nevada,* in *Annual Report of the Commissioner of Indian Affairs,* 1873, serial set 1601, 418; and James G. Bleak, "Annals of the Southern Utah Mission," vol. B, typescript, 126–27, Special Collections, J. Willard Marriott Library, University of Utah, Salt Lake City.

5. Robert J. Franklin and Pamela A. Bunte, *The Paiute* (New York: Chelsea House, 1990), 37–38.

6. Ibid., 37–39; Isabel T. Kelly, "Southern Paiute Bands," *American Anthropologist* 36 (1934): 548–60.

7. Franklin and Bunte, *The Paiute,* 41–42.

8. Fowler and Fowler, *Anthropology of the Numa,* 94.

9. Isabel T. Kelly, *Southern Paiute Ethnography* (1964; reprint, New York: Garland Publishing, 1976), 31; Martha C. Knack, *Boundaries Between: The Southern Paiutes, 1775–1995* (Lincoln: University of Nebraska Press, 2001), 74–76; Sondra Jones, "Saints or Sinners? The Evolving Perceptions of Mormon-Indian Relations in Utah Historiography," *Utah Historical Quarterly* 72 (Winter 2004): 46. David J. Whittaker, "Mormons and Native Americans: A Historical and Bibliographical Introduction," *Dialogue: A Journal of Mormon Thought* 18 (Winter 1985): 35–36, notes that beginning with the earliest Mormon Indian mission in 1830–31, charges of a Mormon-Indian conspiracy dogged the Saints. Juanita Brooks, "Indian Relations on the Mormon Frontier," *Utah Historical Quarterly* 12 (January–April 1944): 16–18, chronicles the continuation of the accusations in Utah. As explained in chapter 6 of this volume, the Mountain Meadows Massacre gave credence to the charge in the minds of some anti-Mormons. See Andrew Karl Larson, *"I Was Called to Dixie," the Virgin River Basin: Unique Experiences in Mormon Pioneering* (Salt Lake City, Deseret News Press, 1961), 22–23, for an air of Mormon superiority in the Paiutes distinguishing between Mormons and Americans.

10. Ira Hatch, Eagle Valley, to James G. Bleak, St. George, Journal History of the Church of Jesus Christ of Latter-day Saints (chronology of typed entries and newspaper clippings, 1830 to the present), 26 January 1866, 3–5 (hereafter cited as Journal History), Family and Church History Department, Church of Jesus Christ of Latter-day Saints, Salt Lake City.

11. Ibid.

12. Bleak, "Annals," vol. A, 184.

13. Pearson H. Corbett, *Jacob Hamblin: The Peacemaker* (Salt Lake City: De-

seret Book Co., 1968), 223, 264; James G. Bleak St. George, to Erastus Snow, Salt Lake City, Journal History, 2 April 1866, 6; Bleak, "Annals," vol. A, 129, vol. B, 114. Tut-se-gav-its's death sent Mormons scrambling to find a chief among the Paiutes who would be equally as influential among his own people while still friendly to the Mormon cause. See Bleak, "Annals," vol. B, 114–17, 126. On Tut-se-gav-its's ordination, see Lawrence Coates, review of *Blood of the Prophets*, by Will Bagley, *BYU Studies* 42.1 (2003): 156.

14. *Union Vedette*, 9 July 1866.

15. Knack, *Boundaries Between*, 2, contends that "Paiute interracial relations were not dominated by warfare." As evidence, she contends that Paiutes lacked "a centralized political structure to organize large numbers of fighting men" and that they did not have "economic surpluses to sustain those men for prolonged military ventures." Therefore, "Paiutes were compelled to meet non-Indian immigrants peacefully." The meetings were not always peaceful, however; the Paiutes resorted to raiding in the mid to late 1860s and early 1870s.

16. Stephen P. Van Hoak, "Waccara's Utes: Native American Equestrian Adaptations in the Eastern Great Basin, 1776–1876," *Utah Historical Quarterly* 67 (Fall 1999): 309–30; John Alton Peterson, *Utah's Black Hawk War* (Salt Lake City: University of Utah Press, 1998), 195–208. Even before Waccara, the fur trade had introduced Anglo-American material goods to Paiutes. Besides Waccara's slave trade, the Paiutes had been victims of an extensive Spanish/New Mexican system, which increased after the 1830 opening of the Spanish Trail between New Mexico and California. Waccara successfully capitalized upon this trade during the 1840s and early 1850s. See Alley, "Prelude to Dispossession," 104–23; Van Hoak, "And Who Shall Have the Children?" 3–25.

17. Bleak, "Annals," vol. B, 117.

18. Peterson, *Utah's Black Hawk War*, 2.

19. Ibid., 182–84; *Daily Union Vedette*, 9 July 1866. One additional report suggests that the miners at Pahranagat were aware of Indian depredations in southern Utah during the Black Hawk War. The miners may have linked their own troubles with the Paiutes to that of the broader conflict. See *American Journal of Mining* 1 (8 September 1866): 372.

20. O. H. Irish to William P. Dole, 26 September 1864, *Report of Commissioner of Indian Affairs*, House Exec. Doc. No. 1, 38th Cong., 2d Sess., serial set 1220, 313.

21. Bleak, "Annals," vol. A, 169; *Pioche Daily Record*, 30 March, 1 April 1873.

22. Hebron Ward Historical Record, vol. 1 (1862–67), 29–30, microfilm, Historical Department, Church Archives, Church of Jesus Christ of Latter-day Saints, Salt Lake City (hereafter cited as CA); Erastus Snow to John D. L. Pearce, Meltiar Hatch and Samuel F. Lee, Journal History, 27 August 1864, 1–3; Bleak, "Annals," vol. A, 170–71.

23. Panaca Ward, Uvada Stake, manuscript history and historical reports, microfilm, CA; Bleak, "Annals," vol. A, 171–72; Journal History, 31 August 1865, 2.

24. *Daily Union Vedette*, 18 August 1865.

25. *Annual Report of the State Mineralogist of the State of Nevada for 1866* (Carson City: Joseph E. Eckley, State Printer, 1867), 64; Bleak, "Annals," vol. A, 196.

26. *Daily Union Vedette,* 30 May 1866.

27. *Daily Union Vedette,* 9 July 1866.

28. Bleak, "Annals," vol. A, 182, 187.

29. Pearson Starr Corbett, "A History of the Muddy Mission" (Master's thesis, Brigham Young University, 1968), 120–21.

30. Brigham Young, Salt Lake City, to Erastus Snow and the bishops and saints of Washington and Kane Counties, 2 May 1866, in Bleak, "Annals," vol. A, 226–27.

31. Journal History, 31 December 1866, 1; 10 July 1868, 2; Peterson, *Utah's Black Hawk War,* 330. Peterson lists Shoal Creek as one of the abandoned settlements. Shoal Creek, however, became the site of a fort where its settlers combined with those from Clover Valley for protection. For more detail, see W. Paul Reeve, "Cattle, Cotton, and Conflict: The Possession and Dispossession of Hebron, Utah," *Utah Historical Quarterly* 67 (Spring 1999): 161–62.

32. Violence took its toll upon innocent Paiutes, however. Due to the general war atmosphere that permeated southern Utah and Nevada, Mormons and miners retaliated against Indians in general, not only against the aggressive Paiutes. See Peterson, *Utah's Black Hawk War,* 218–24, for a description of "the Pipe Springs murders and Mormon retaliation"; and Franklin and Bunte, *The Paiute,* 51, for an account of vengeance at the hands of Pahranagat miners.

33. Bleak, "Annals," vol. A, 196, 220–21; vol. B, 115.

34. Bleak to Snow, Journal History, 2 April 1866, 6.

35. Juanita Brooks, *On the Ragged Edge: The Life and Times of Dudley Leavitt* (Salt Lake City: Utah State Historical Society, 1973), 108–9.

36. *Pioche Daily Record,* 1 April 1873.

37. For Paiute rites of passage and hunting rituals, see Isabel T. Kelly and Catherine S. Fowler, "Southern Paiute," in *Great Basin,* ed. Warren L. D'Azevedo, vol. 11 of *Handbook of North American Indians,* ed. William C. Sturtevant (Washington, D.C.: Smithsonian Institution, 1986), 370, 379–80; and Franklin and Bunte, *The Paiute,* 41.

38. *Pioche Daily Record,* 1 April 1873; Bleak, "Annals," vol. A, 220; Henry H. Lee, "The Murder of George Rogers," in *A Century in Meadow Valley, 1864–1964,* ed. Ruth Lee and Sylvia Wadsworth (Salt Lake City: Deseret News Press, 1966), 21.

39. David Chidester and Edward T. Linenthal, Introduction to *American Sacred Space,* ed. David Chidester and Edward T. Linenthal (Bloomington: Indiana University Press, 1995), 8.

40. Fowler and Fowler, *Anthropology of the Numa,* 51.

41. Ibid., 161; William R. Palmer, "Pahute Indian Government and Laws," *Utah Historical Quarterly* 2 (April 1929): 35–42.

42. Bleak, "Annals," vol. A, 222. Brooks, *On the Ragged Edge,* 109, suggests that the Paiutes hanged Bush-head themselves. Contemporary accounts clearly indicate otherwise.

43. Bleak, "Annals," vol. A, 217; Bleak to Snow, Journal History, 2 April 1866, 6; Corbett, "History of the Muddy Mission," 122–25.

44. Bleak, "Annals," vol. A, 234–35; Corbett, "History of the Muddy Mission," 123.

45. Bleak, "Annals," vol. A, 274–76; vol. B, 34; Corbett, "History of the Muddy

Mission," 81–82, 86–87. For an example of one Paiute's continuing hostility, see A. R. Mortensen, ed., *Utah's Dixie: The Cotton Mission* (Salt Lake City: Utah State Historical Society, 1961), 110–12.

46. Bleak, "Annals," vol. B, 57–59; John Wesley Powell, *The Exploration of the Colorado River and Its Canyons* (1895; reprint, New York: Dover, 1961), 323. For the historical controversy surrounding this event, see Donald Worster, *A River Running West: The Life of John Wesley Powell* (New York: Oxford University Press, 2001), 190–96, 212–15. Jon Krakauer, *Under the Banner of Heaven: A Story of Violent Faith* (New York: Doubleday, 2003), 233–45, speculates that Powell's men were actually murdered by Mormons in a conspiracy carefully orchestrated from the top. Worster's version is consistent with Powell's, and his reasoning is more sound than Krakauer's.

47. Robert C. Euler, *Southern Paiute Ethnohistory*, University of Utah Anthropological Papers Number 78 (Salt Lake City: University of Utah Press, 1966), 93.

48. "Journal of Stephen Vandiver Jones, April 21, 1871–December 14, 1872," ed. Herbert E. Gregory, *Utah Historical Quarterly* 16–17 (1948–49): 121.

49. A. J. Barnes to Edward P. Smith, 11 September 1875, *Annual Report of the Commissioner of Indian Affairs* (Washington, D.C.: Government Printing Office, 1875), 337. For a much earlier indication of the Paiute desire for government assistance, see Jack D. Forbes, ed., *Nevada Indians Speak* (Reno: University of Nevada Press, 1967), 35. In 1856, a Muddy River chief reportedly told the Indian agent George W. Armstrong that "he had heard of the great chief of the American people sending presents to the Utah Indians, and he often wondered why he and his band were overlooked. . . . The white people had for years been passing through his land to and from California, and he had never received anything for the privilege."

50. Mormons believe that a child becomes accountable for his or her choices at eight years of age. They therefore baptize beginning at that age.

51. Bleak, "Annals," vol. B, 401, 403–4, 407–16. For accounts of mass baptisms among Muddy Valley and Las Vegas Paiutes in the 1850s, see Knack, *Boundaries Between*, 66–67.

52. Bleak, "Annals," vol. B, 402–3. Young alludes to a Book of Mormon prophesy concerning the redemption of Native Americans into "white and delightsome" people.

53. "St. George Items," *Latter-Day Saints' Millennial Star* (Liverpool, U.K.) 37 (19 April 1875): 247.

54. Barnes to Smith, 11 September 1875, 338.

55. C. A. Bateman, Pyramid Lake Reserve, Nev., to Hon. E. P. Smith, Commissioner of Indian Affairs, 10 September 1875, *Annual Report of the Commissioner of Indian Affairs* (Washington, D.C.: Government Printing Office, 1875), 342. As explained in chapter 6, the Mountain Meadows Massacre involved Mormons and Paiutes slaughtering a California-bound immigrant company at Mountain Meadows in southern Utah.

56. "St. George Items," 247; Larson, *"I Was Called to Dixie,"* 24 n.18; Bleak, "Annals," vol. B, 416.

57. *Pioche Weekly Record*, 13 April 1878.

58. Martha C. Knack, "Nineteenth-Century Great Basin Indian Wage Labor," in *Native Americans and Wage Labor: Ethnohistorical Perspectives*, ed. Alice

Littlefield and Martha C. Knack (Norman: University of Oklahoma Press, 1996),
153, 174–75.

59. Ibid., 156.

60. *Pioche Daily Record,* 22 August 1875.

61. Quoted in Knack, "Nineteenth-Century Great Basin Indian Wage Labor,"
156.

62. Ibid., 148–53.

63. *American Journal of Mining* 1 (18 August 1866): 324.

64. *Deseret News,* 31 May 1866, 205; Journal History, 31 August 1865, 3.

65. Dale L. Morgan, ed., "The Reminiscences of James Holt: A Narrative of the
Emmett Company, Part II" *Utah Historical Quarterly* 23 (April 1955): 178.

66. Hebron Ward Historical Record, vol. 1, 34, 86.

67. Orrilla Woods Hafen, Mary R. Edwards, and Elbert B. Edwards, comps., *The
Woods Family of Clover Valley, Nevada, 1869–1979* (Boulder City, Nev.: Woods
Family Genealogical Committee, 1979), 8–9; Charles P. Mathews, "The Death
of Railroad Jim," in *A Century in Meadow Valley, 1864–1964,* ed. Ruth Lee and
Sylvia Wadsworth (Salt Lake City: Deseret News Press, 1966), 21.

68. *Pioche Daily Record,* 25, 27 March 1873.

69. See *Pioche Daily Record,* 9 February, 26 March, 12, 20, 22 April, 12 August
1873; 4 August 1876. Martha C. Knack found over 150 articles in the *Pioche Record* between 1872 and 1900 referencing an Indian presence. See Martha C. Knack,
"Newspaper Accounts of Indian Women in Southern Nevada Mining Towns,
1870–1900," *Journal of California and Great Basin Anthropology* 8.1 (1986):
83–98, specifically p. 84 for reference to the Indian population and newspaper
accounts. For archaeological evidence of Indian attachment to Nevada mining
towns, see Rolla Lee Queen, "Historical Archaeology and Historic Preservation
at Candelaria and Metallic City, Nevada" (Master's thesis, University of Nevada
at Reno, 1987).

70. For reports of Indian "vagrancy" and scavenging at Pioche, see *Pioche Daily
Record,* 10 May, 20 April 1873; 4 August 1876; and Hulse, *Lincoln County,* 27–
28.

71. A. J. Barnes to Edward P. Smith, 19 January 1875, roll 541, National Archives, Letters Received by the Office of Indian Affairs, Nevada Superintendency,
1874–75.

72. James E. Spencer to Commissioner of Indian Affairs, 30 August 1880, *Report
of Commissioner of Indian Affairs,* 46th Cong., 3d Sess., House Exec. Doc. No.
1, 1880, serial set 1959, 247–48.

73. John Wesley Powell and G. W. Ingalls had counted 379 Moapa Paiutes in
1873, whereas by 1906 the agent at Moapa found 129, a decline of about two-thirds
in thirty years. However, the 1906 number was likely underrepresentative because most Paiutes did not attach themselves to an agency and were not counted.
Powell and Ingalls, *Report of Special Commissioners,* 418; InterTribal Council of
Nevada, *Nuwuvi: A Southern Paiute History* (Salt Lake City: University of Utah
Printing Service, 1976), 105.

74. Ronald L. Holt, *Beneath These Red Cliffs: An Ethnohistory of the Utah
Paiutes* (Albuquerque: University of New Mexico Press, 1992), 35–38.

75. Sale to Irish, 4 May 1865, National Archives, Letters Received by the Office
of Indian Affairs, Utah Superintendency, 1863–65, microfilm roll 901.

76. Euler, *Southern Paiute Ethnohistory*, 93; Powell and Ingalls, *Report of Special Commissioners*, 411.

77. *Pioche Daily Record*, 22 September 1874.

78. Powell and Ingalls, *Report of Special Commissioners*, 411; Fowler and Fowler, *Anthropology of the Numa*, 21–22.

79. Inter-Tribal Council of Nevada, *Nuwuvi*, 98–101.

80. Quoted in Fowler and Fowler, *Anthropology of the Numa*, 22.

81. Quoted in Knack, "Nineteenth-Century Great Basin Indian Wage Labor," 157 (emphasis added).

82. For a more complete description, see ibid., 156–62.

83. Quoted in ibid., 156.

84. Knack, *Boundaries Between*, 130–34.

85. This list of reservations and dates is taken from Kelly and Fowler, "Southern Paiute," 389. See also Knack, *Boundaries Between*, 130–79. In addition, there were Indian villages at Cedar City and Richfield where the Paiutes lived on Mormon-owned land. The San Juan Paiutes live on the northern portion of the Navajo Reservation. Because the Paiutes remained largely "off-reservation" Indians, the creation of at least some of their reservations, apart from Moapa, followed a different path than was common across the West. For an explanation of the Kanosh example, see Martha C. Knack, "Utah Indians and the Homestead Laws," in *State and Reservation: New Perspectives on Federal Indian Policy*, ed. George Pierre Castile and Robert L. Bee (Tucson: University of Arizona Press, 1992), 63–91.

86. Knack, "Nineteenth-Century Great Basin Indian Wage Labor," 158–62; Knack, *Boundaries Between*, chap. 7.

87. Juanita Brooks, *Quicksand and Cactus: A Memoir of the Southern Mormon Frontier* (Logan: Utah State University Press, 1992), 84–86.

88. Patricia McCormack, "Native Homelands as Cultural Landscapes: Decentering the Wilderness Paradigm," in *Sacred Lands: Aboriginal World Views, Claims, and Conflicts*, Occasional Publication Series No. 43, ed. Jill Oakes, Rick Riewe, Kathi Kinew, and Elaine Maloney (Alberta: Canadian Circumpolar Institute and University of Manitoba, 1998), 27.

89. Louise V. Jeffredo-Warden, "Perceiving, Experiencing, and Expressing the Sacred: An Indigenous Southern Californian View," in *Over the Edge: Remapping the American West*, ed. Valerie J. Matsumoto and Blake Allmendinger (Berkeley: University of California Press, 1999), 334.

90. O. H. Irish to William P. Dole, 15 May 1865, roll 901, OIA-UT.

Chapter 5: "To Hold in Check Outside Influences"

1. Erastus Snow, St. George, to Brigham Young, Salt Lake City, Journal History of the Church of Jesus Christ of Latter-day Saints (chronology of typed entries and newspaper clippings, 1830 to the present), 22 July 1869, 1–2 (hereafter cited as Journal History), Family and Church History Department, Church of Jesus Christ of Latter-day Saints, Salt Lake City.

2. Quoted in Leonard J. Arrington, *Great Basin Kingdom: An Economic History of the Latter-day Saints, 1830–1900* (1958; reprint, Lincoln: University of Nebraska Press, 1966), 47.

3. Heber C. Kimball, 19 February 1865, *Journal of Discourses*, vol. 11 (London: LDS Booksellers Depot, 1867), 82.

4. Dean L. May, *Three Frontiers: Family, Land, and Society in the American West, 1850–1900* (Cambridge: Cambridge University Press, 1994), 89–91.

5. James G. Bleak, "Annals of the Southern Utah Mission," typescript, vol. A, 161–66, Special Collections, J. Willard Marriott Library, University of Utah, Salt Lake City; Panaca Ward, Uvada Stake, manuscript history and historical reports, microfilm, Historical Department, Church Archives, Church of Jesus Christ of Latter-day Saints, Salt Lake City (hereafter cited as CA).

6. Bleak, "Annals," vol. A, 162–66; Erastus Snow, St. George, to Brigham Young, Salt Lake City, Journal History, 19 June 1864, 2–5.

7. Ira Hatch, Eagle Valley, to Erastus Snow, St. George, Journal History, 26 January 1866, 3, 5.

8. James G. Bleak, St. George, to Erastus Snow, Salt Lake City, Journal History, 2 April 1866, 8–9; Bleak, "Annals," vol. A, 223–24.

9. Bleak, "Annals," vol. A, 309.

10. Ibid., vol. B, 23.

11. Snow to Young, Journal History, 22 July 1869, 2.

12. John M. Townley, *Conquered Provinces: Nevada Moves Southeast, 1864–1871*, Charles Redd Monographs in Western History No. 2 (Provo, Utah: Brigham Young University Press, 1973), 44. Nevada taxes became payable in coin beginning 1 January 1869. See Pearson Starr Corbett, "A History of the Muddy Mission," (Master's thesis, Brigham Young University, 1968), 146.

13. Erastus Snow, Salt Lake City, to James G. Bleak, St. George, 2 February 1870, in Bleak, "Annals," vol. B, 34; Erastus Snow, Salt Lake City, to James Henrie, Panaca, 6 February 1870, in Bleak, "Annals," vol. B, 35–36; Andrew Karl Larson, *"I Was Called to Dixie," the Virgin River Basin: Unique Experiences in Mormon Pioneering* (Salt Lake City, Deseret News Press, 1961), 164–65. Among other things, the citizens of Panaca, Clover Valley, Dry Valley, Rose Valley, Eagleville, and Spring Valley sent a petition of protest to the governor, Senate, and House of Representatives of Nevada over the boundary tax issue. See Bleak, "Annals," vol. B, 40.

14. Journal History, 11 August 1870, 1.

15. On Carlow's apostate status, see Townley, *Conquered Provinces*, 63 n.117.

16. Lincoln County tax roll, 1868–70, Treasurer's Office, Lincoln County Courthouse, Pioche, Nevada. In every Mormon settlement that Carlow visited (St. Joseph, St. Thomas, West Point, Overton, Clover Valley, and Panaca) he recorded on the tax roll his reception, generally either as "protest" or "refuses to give list."

17. Bleak, "Annals," vol. B, 39.

18. Quoted in Journal History, 10 July 1868, 2.

19. One Muddy colonizer, Warren Foote, wrote, "'Some of the brethren on this mission were not satisfied and never had been, but were staying because they were called to come here. Their hearts was not in the mission, consequently they hailed with delight anything that would be calculated to release them, even to the breaking up of their settlements.'" Quoted in S. George Ellsworth, *Mormon Settlement on the Muddy* (Ogden, Utah: Weber State College Press, 1987), 24.

Ellsworth also lists environmental circumstances that factored into the difficulty of the Muddy Mission (2). Also see Townley, *Conquered Provinces*, 43–51.

20. For local reaction and quotes concerning Young's visit, see Ellsworth, *Mormon Settlement on the Muddy*, 20–21. For additional narrative on abandonment of the Muddy, see Corbett, "History of the Muddy Mission," 145–59; Leonard J. Arrington and Richard Jensen, "Panaca: Mormon Outpost among the Mining Camps," *Nevada Historical Society Quarterly* 18 (Winter 1975): 210; L. A. Fleming, "The Settlements on the Muddy, 1865 to 1871: 'A Godforsaken Place,'" *Utah Historical Quarterly* 35 (Spring 1967): 168–72; and Townley, *Conquered Provinces*, 43–51. See also Brigham Young, George A. Smith, and Erastus Snow, St. George, to Bro. James Liethead and the Brethren and Sisters residing on the Muddy, 14 December 1870, in Bleak, "Annals," vol. B, 78–80.

21. Erastus Snow, St. George, to Bishop James Henrie and the Brethren of Panaca and Eagleville Wards, 19 December 1870, in Bleak, "Annals," vol. B, 80–82. The Mormons who stayed pursued a legal defense against the Nevada back taxes. After several protracted court cases, in December 1871, Lincoln County officials dropped their attempts at recovering the "delinquent taxes." For an in-depth chronology of this legal wrangling, see Barbara S. Mathews, "The Boundary Tax Dispute," in *A Century in Meadow Valley, 1864–1964*, ed. Ruth Lee and Sylvia Wadsworth (Salt Lake City: Deseret News Press, 1966), 9–15.

22. Larson, *"I Was Called to Dixie,"* 163–65.

23. Bleak, "Annals," vol. B, 146.

24. James Stephens Brown, *Life of a Pioneer: Being the Autobiography of James S. Brown* (Salt Lake City: G. Q. Cannon, 1900), 121–22.

25. Quoted in Ardis E. Parshall, "Marysvale: Mormons, Miners, and Methodists," 5, Paper presented at the Mormon History Association conference, Cedar City, Utah, May 2001, copy in possession of author. I am indebted to Parshall for the idea of control being at the heart of Young's mining policy, a point that she develops in her paper (3–6).

26. See, for example, the Book of Mormon, Alma 4:6–9.

27. Arrington, *Great Basin Kingdom*, 61, 71–76, 122–29, 223, 473 n.41; Leonard J. Arrington, "Abundance from the Earth: The Beginnings of Commercial Mining in Utah," *Utah Historical Quarterly* 31 (Summer 1963): 192. Young's California gold mission was very limited and tactical, while he was much more dedicated to the other extractive enterprises.

28. Journal History, 5 June 1870, 6.

29. For further consideration of Connor's impact upon Young's mining policy, see Arrington, *Great Basin Kingdom*, 201–3, 242–43, 473–74 n.41; and Brigham D. Madsen, *Glory Hunter: A Biography of Patrick Edward Connor* (Salt Lake City: University of Utah Press, 1990), chaps. 7 and 8.

30. Bleak, "Annals," vol. B, 208.

31. For the complete story of the Godbeite dissent, see Ronald W. Walker, *Wayward Saints: The Godbeites and Brigham Young* (Urbana: University of Illinois Press, 1998). For specifics on Godbe's disfellowshipment and excommunication, see chaps. 1 and 9, and for Walker's argument on the new approach toward mining, see pp. 363–64.

32. Bleak, "Annals," vol. A, 196–97.

33. Hebron Ward Historical Record, vol. 2 (1867–72), 42, microfilm, Historical

Department, CA. The following year, local leaders instructed the Hebron congregation "to cease trading with and sustaining gentiles—don't run after the mining or rail roads, but stick to the farms and business at home and you will be richer and have more of the spirit of the gospel" (vol. 2, 63).

34. Bleak, "Annals," vol. B, 132–35.

35. Ibid., vol. B, 168–70.

36. James W. Hulse, *Lincoln County, Nevada, 1864–1909: History of a Mining Region* (Reno: University of Nevada Press, 1971), 22–23, 28; Michael Bourne, "Early Mining in Southwestern Utah and Southeastern Nevada, 1864–1873: The Meadow Valley, Pahranagat, and Pioche Mining Rushes" (Master's thesis, University of Utah, 1973), 114. Washington County's 1870 population totaled 3,064, while by 1880 it had grown to 4,235. See Allan Kent Powell, "Population," in *Utah History Encyclopedia*, ed. Allan Kent Powell (Salt Lake City: University of Utah Press, 1994), 432.

37. Bleak, "Annals," vol. B, 173–75, 179–82. Hebron leaders similarly complained about the Clover Valley Saints' poor tithing record. See Hebron Ward Historical Record, vol. 3 (1872–97), 14, holograph photocopy, Enterprise Branch, Washington County Library, Enterprise, Utah. For an analysis of the type of strain such trade likely placed on the Utah economy, see May, *Three Frontiers*, 173, esp. n.55.

38. Bleak, "Annals," vol. B, 197. For similar speeches at St. George, much of which were directed at Pioche, see vol. B, 183–97 and 419–23. During the same visit to St. George, Young convened a meeting of the priesthood brethren. He asked the assembled men to arise and, with their "right arms raised to the square," he put them under covenant "to hence forward build up Zion with all the ability which God would give them" (vol. B, 182). Bishop Crosby, Orson Huntsman, John Pulsipher, and Charles Pulsipher of Hebron were at the 15–16 February meeting and made the covenant. Hebron Ward Historical Record, vol. 3, 12.

39. Ibid., vol. B, 188.

40. Brigham Young, 1 January 1877, *Journal of Discourses*, vol. 18 (London: LDS Booksellers Depot, 1877), 305. Young further warned southern Utah men against "putting their wives and daughters into their [gentile] society."

41. After citing Erastus Snow's 1865 order to cut off "'any man that would go to the western mines as a miner,'" Arrington argues that "there are no discoverable instances of such excommunications" (Arrington, *Great Basin Kingdom*, 474 n.42). Close scrutiny of local records indicates otherwise. See examples below.

42. Hebron Ward Historical Record, vol. 2, 36, 44; *Rio Virgen Times* (St. George, Utah), 12 May 1869.

43. Hebron Ward Historical Record, vol. 1 (1862–67), 62; Bleak, "Annals," vol. A, 282; *Daily Union Vedette*, 21 November 1865. In 1865 Burgess was also found guilty of larceny. The former Indian agent Thomas C. W. Sale worked as his attorney in the case. Their relationship likely stemmed from interaction at Pahranagat. For the court case, see Fifth District Court, Washington County, Probate Records, book A, 1856–67, pp. 141–44, microfilm, series 3168, reel 1, Utah State Archives, Salt Lake City (hereafter cited as USA).

44. Hebron Ward Historical Record, vol. 3, 35.

45. *Daily Union Vedette*, 31 January 1866.

46. Bleak, "Annals," vol. B, 1. The Josephites were dissenters who followed Joseph Smith's son, Joseph III, as prophet rather than Brigham Young.

47. Bleak, "Annals," vol. B, 206; Hebron Ward Historical Record, vol. 2, 108. In 1865 William Hamblin faced charges of larceny in district court with William Pulsipher as key witness for the prosecution. The jury found Hamblin not guilty. Unfortunately, surviving court records do not offer details of the action. However, Pulsipher's testimony in the Raymond and Ely case in 1873 gives a hint of his discontent with Hamblin over disregard for Pulsipher's original mining claim. See Fifth District Court, Washington County, Probate Records, book A, 1856–67, pp. 155–56, microfilm, series 3168, reel 1, USA; and *Pioche Daily Record* 12 April 1873. Hamblin's extended absence at the California gold fields was also contrary to Church teachings. Those events, however, preceded the 1870 apostasy charge by several years. From the context of the Raymond and Ely court case, Hamblin clearly became involved with Raymond and Ely at Pioche in 1870, in negotiations over his original claim. While the timing fits with Hamblin's excommunication, it is impossible to know whether or not that association cost him his membership. After being poisoned at Pioche in 1872, Hamblin was rebaptized, only two days before he died. Hebron Ward Historical Record, vol. 3, 6. Shirts, too, had a rocky relationship with authority years before his excommunication. His testimony at the Raymond and Ely trial makes that clear, as does his involvement in an Indian affair at Paria in 1866. For details, see Journal History, 15 January 1866, 1; 10 March 1866, 1–2; 11 March 1866, 1–2.

48. *Pioche Daily Record,* 17, 24 April 1873.

49. Bleak, "Annals," vol. B, 106–8.

50. Larson, *"I Was Called to Dixie,"* 262–65; Douglas D. Alder and Karl F. Brooks, *A History of Washington County: From Isolation to Destination* (Salt Lake City: Utah State Historical Society and Washington County Commission, 1996), 111.

51. Brigham Young, Salt Lake City, to Erastus Snow, St. George, 7 June 1871, in Bleak, "Annals," vol. B, 109–13, 127; Whitney, *History of Utah,* vol. 4 (Salt Lake City: George Q. Cannon, 1904), 275.

52. Journal History, 23 October 1871, 4.

53. Journal History, 25 November 1872, 1.

54. Orson Welcome Huntsman, Diary of Orson W. Huntsman, typescript, vol. 1, 53–54, L. Tom Perry Special Collections Library, Harold B. Lee Library, Brigham Young University, Provo, Utah.

55. For examples of Huntsman's work at Pioche and Bullionville, see ibid., vol. 1, 74, 81, 82, 94, 96, 110, 111.

56. Ibid., vol. 1, 94.

57. Hebron Ward Historical Record, vol. 2, 56.

58. Ibid., vol. 2, 134.

59. Arrington and Jensen, "Panaca," 213–14.

60. Spring Valley Branch, Panaca Ward, Uvada Stake, manuscript history and historical reports, microfilm, CA; Eagle Valley Ward, St. George Stake, manuscript history and historical reports, microfilm, CA.

61. Arrington and Jensen, "Panaca," 214.

62. Hebron Ward Historical Record, vol. 3, 18–19.

63. Ibid., vol. 3, 22.

64. Ibid., vol. 3, 4–5.

65. Arrington and Jensen, "Panaca," 214.

66. Hebron Ward Historical Record, vol. 3, 69.

67. Ibid., vol. 3, 108–9. For similar advice given at St. George in 1873, where one speaker "alluded to the influence of strangers over our unsuspecting females," see Bleak, "Annals," vol. B, 185.

68. Hebron Ward Historical Record, vol. 3, 114.

69. John Taylor made positive statements about mining, and he, along with other Church leaders such as Wilford Woodruff, George Q. Cannon, and Joseph F. Smith, invested in silver and gold mines in the 1880s and 1890s. This, however, did not ease the "problems of conscience" that some Mormon miners experienced. See Leonard J. Arrington and Edward Leo Lyman, "The Mormon Church and Nevada Gold Mines," *Nevada Historical Society Quarterly* 41 (Fall 1998): 191–205; Philip F. Notarianni, "Mining," in *Utah History Encyclopedia*, ed. Allan Kent Powell (Salt Lake City: University of Utah Press, 1994), 367; Donald Q. Cannon, "Angus M. Cannon: Frustrated Mormon Miner," *Utah Historical Quarterly* 57 (Winter 1989): 36–45.

70. Walker, *Wayward Saints*, 334–35; Hulse, *Lincoln County*, 41–42, 45–48. According to Walker, Godbe did not profit from his Lincoln County enterprises. By 1892, "[P]rofits began to accrue—just as the bottom fell out of the international price of silver. The project was abandoned. One moment, Godbe seemed certain to be a millionaire. The next, he was financially ruined" (335).

71. *Pioche Weekly Record*, 27 January 1883.

72. *Pioche Weekly Record*, 23 July 1881; 4 February 1882; 8 February 1900.

73. For detail on DeLamar, see Hulse, *Lincoln County*, chap. 6.

74. *St. George Union*, 22 February 1896.

75. *St. George Union*, 12 March 1896.

76. *St. George Union*, 25 January 1896. For other favorable reports at St. George regarding mining activity at DeLamar, see *St. George Union*, 16 April, 21 May 1896; and 27 February 1897. For other evidence of Mormon prospecting around the turn of the twentieth century, see Carrie Elizabeth Laub Hunt, *Memories of the Past and Family History* (Salt Lake City: Utah Printing Co., 1968), 47.

77. In the 1890s, the Church itself even looked to Nevada's mineral wealth as a potential solution to its financial difficulties. The Church's first presidency, consisting of President Wilford Woodruff, George Q. Cannon, and Joseph F. Smith, all sat on the board of directors of the Sterling Mining and Milling Company, which owned mines in Nye County, Nevada, immediately west of Lincoln County. See Arrington and Lyman, "Mormon Church and Nevada Gold Mines."

78. For a thoughtful overview of Mormon-Indian historiography and a call to recognize such complexities in the intercultural relations between these two groups, see Ronald W. Walker, "Toward a Reconstruction of Mormon and Indian Relations, 1847–1877," *BYU Studies* 29 (Fall 1989): 23–42.

79. Whittaker, "Mormons and Native Americans," 33–64.

80. Walker, "Toward a Reconstruction," 33. See also Floyd A. O'Neil and Stanford J. Layton, "Of Pride and Politics: Brigham Young as Indian Superintendent," *Utah Historical Quarterly* 46 (Summer 1978): 241.

81. For details of Young's earlier policy, see Howard A. Christy, "Open Hand and Mailed Fist: Mormon-Indian Relations in Utah, 1847–52," *Utah Historical Quarterly* 46 (Summer 1978): 216–35.

82. Quoted in Walker, "Toward a Reconstruction," 35.

83. Ibid.

84. Brigham Young, 8 May 1853, *Journal of Discourses*, vol. 1 (London: LDS Booksellers Depot, 1855), 105–6.

85. Book of Mormon, Helaman 2:11.

86. Helaman 11:25.

87. 3 Nephi 4:1.

88. Mormon 1:18.

89. Helaman 2:13.

90. For a detailed examination of the robbers as cultural discourse, see W. Paul Reeve, "'As Ugly as Evil' and 'As Wicked as Hell': Gadianton Robbers and the Legend Process among the Mormons," *Journal of Mormon History* 27 (Fall 2001): 125–49.

91. Wilford Woodruff, *Wilford Woodruff's Journal, 1833–1898*, vol. 4, ed. Scott G. Kenney, (Midvale, Utah: Signature Books, 1983), 26; Journal History, 16 May 1851, 1. The Journal History account recorded the event this way: Young "wished to have sufficient men there [Parowan] to be secure from the children of the Gadianton robbers who had infested the mountains for more than a thousand years and had lived by plundering all the time."

92. Journal History, 6 April 1853, 3.

93. Heber C. Kimball, 16 December 1860, *Journal of Discourses*, vol. 8 (London: LDS Booksellers Depot, 1861), 258.

94. John Taylor, 9 November 1881, *Journal of Discourses*, vol. 23 (London: LDS Booksellers Depot, 1883), 17.

95. Elder Marion J. Shelton, Harmony, Washington Co., Utah, to George A. Smith, Salt Lake City, Journal History, 18 December 1858, 2–3. For other examples of Latter-day Saints linking Native Americans of the Great Basin region to Gadianton robbers, see Journal History, 30 July 1853, 2; 21 December 1854, 5; Robert S. McPherson, "Of Papers and Perception: Utes and Navajos in Journalistic Media, 1900–1930," *Utah Historical Quarterly* 67 (Summer 1999): 201; and John Alton Peterson, *Utah's Black Hawk War* (Salt Lake City: University of Utah Press, 1998), 172.

96. Corbett, "History of the Muddy Mission," 124–25. For other examples of Mormons whipping Paiutes, see Martha C. Knack, *Boundaries Between: The Southern Paiutes, 1775–1995* (Lincoln: University of Nebraska Press, 2001), 91–92; *Deseret News*, 4 September 1852, quoted in J. Cecil Alter, "The Mormons and the Indians: News Items and Editorials, from the Mormon Press," *Utah Historical Quarterly* 12 (January–April 1944): 49–68.

97. Hebron Ward Historical Record, vol. 1, 29, 31.

98. Erastus Snow to John D. L. Pearce, Meltiar Hatch, and Samuel F. Lee, in Journal History, 27 August 1864, 1–3; Bleak, "Annals," vol. A, 170–71.

99. Peterson, *Utah's Black Hawk War,* 218–24, 245–48.

100. Hebron Ward Historical Record, vol. 1, 25. A similar inspection and muster took place at Clover Valley and Panaca. See Journal History, 31 August 1865, 2. See also Daniel H. Wells, Lieutenant General, Nauvoo Legion, Salt Lake City, to Erastus Snow, Brigadier General, St. George, Journal History, 3 May 1866, 3–5, for additional evidence of a military footing in southern Utah. The tradition of a local militia was well entrenched prior to the Black Hawk War, but that conflict led to a heightened military readiness.

101. Ibid., vol. 2, 1–2. A militia unit had existed at Shoal Creek previously, but it largely lay dormant until this reorganization.

102. Huntsman, Diary, vol. 1, 36.

103. Journal History, 11 March 1866, 1.

104. Hebron Ward Historical Record, vol. 1, 29. Erastus Snow to John D. L. Pearce, Meltiar Hatch, and Samuel F. Lee, in Journal History, 27 August 1864, 1–3; Bleak, "Annals," vol. A, 170–71.

105. Peterson, *Utah's Black Hawk War*, 256–59; Brigham Young, Salt Lake City, to Erastus Snow and the Bishops and Saints of Washington and Kane Counties, 2 May 1866, in Bleak, "Annals," vol. A, 226–29.

106. Hebron Ward Historical Record, vol. 1, 78–82.

107. Ibid., vol. 1, 6–7, 8, 29.

108. Huntsman, Diary, vol. 1, 12–13.

109. Hebron Ward Historical Record, vol. 1, 82.

110. Ibid., vol. 1, 33–34.

111. Ibid., vol. 1, 86.

112. Ibid., vol. 2, 57.

113. Brigham Young, on occasion, did lament the hand of the Saints in the hardships that Utah's Native Americans experienced. See O'Neil and Layton, "Of Pride and Politics," 241–42 and n.34.

114. Juanita Brooks, "Indian Relations on the Mormon Frontier," *Utah Historical Quarterly* 12 (January–April 1944): 1–48; Juanita Brooks, *Quicksand and Cactus: A Memoir of the Southern Mormon Frontier* (Logan: Utah State University Press, 1992), 47–48; Juanita Brooks, *On the Ragged Edge: The Life and Times of Dudley Leavitt* (Salt Lake City: Utah State Historical Society, 1973), 93–97. For additional analysis of Mormon-Indian marriages as well as Indian foster children taken in by Mormons, see Sondra Jones, *The Trial of Don Pedro León Luján: The Attack against Indian Slavery and Mexican Traders in Utah* (Salt Lake City: University of Utah Press, 2000), 100–104.

115. Bleak, "Annals," vol. B, 422.

116. Orrilla Woods Hafen, Mary R. Edwards, and Elbert B. Edwards, comps., *The Woods Family of Clover Valley, Nevada, 1869–1979* (Boulder City, Nev.: Woods Family Genealogical Committee, 1979), 8–10.

117. In 1874, St. George authorities organized a United Order effort at Hebron. Brigham Young had recently launched the communal movement as a last-ditch attempt to achieve self-sufficiency through a variety of cooperative enterprises. While there were several different levels of participation, generally those involved in orders consecrated all or part of their properties to the Church, with the aim of becoming economically and socially equal. United Order participants were encouraged to use only material goods produced within the order, which in some cases were inferior to items available in commercial markets—or among Paiutes. In southern Utah, the effort to avoid importing leather led to the production of wooden-bottomed shoes, with "strong cloth" for the uppers. Brigham Young told women at St. George that using the shoes would not only save the Saints money but would be especially helpful during the scorching southern Utah summers when the ground became heated. For the United Order effort in general, see Leonard J. Arrington, Feramorz Y. Fox, and Dean L. May, *Building the City of God: Community and Cooperation among the Mormons* (1976; reprint, Urbana:

University of Illinois Press, 1992). For Young's advice on wooden-bottomed shoes, see ibid., 157–58; and Bleak, "Annals," vol. B, 260.

118. Huntsman, Diary, vol. 1, 78.

119. John Lewis Pulsipher, *The Life and Travels of John Lewis Pulsipher, 1884–1963: The Autobiography of a Southern Nevada Pioneer* (N.p., n.d.), 4. See also Hunt, *Memories of the Past*, 23, 40.

120. Walker, "Toward a Reconstruction," 37.

121. Pulsipher, *Life and Travels*, 4, 20; Brooks, *Quicksand and Cactus*, 84–85.

122. Anthony W. Ivins, Journal, 201–5, Utah State Historical Society Library, Salt Lake City; Anthony W. Ivins, "Traveling over Forgotten Trails: A Mystery of the Grand Canyon Solved," *Improvement Era* 27 (1924): 1017–25; Inter-Tribal Council of Nevada, *Nuwuvi: A Southern Paiute History* (Salt Lake City: University of Utah Printing Service, 1976), 113–14; Knack, *Boundaries Between*, 131.

123. Quoted in Knack, *Boundaries Between*, 137.

124. The government survey did not make it to Shivwits until after the Indian policy again had changed, and therefore the allotment process bypassed the Shivwits. See Knack, *Boundaries Between*, 137.

125. Ivins, Journal, 204; Inter-tribal Council of Nevada, *Nuwuvi*, 109–18; Knack, *Boundaries Between*, 136–39.

126. Huntsman, Diary, vol. 2, 29–30; John Lewis Pulsipher, *Life and Travels*, 20, 22.

127. The key was that in the Paiute case it was Mormon men marrying Indian women, while in the other case it would be male miners marrying Mormon women.

Chapter 6: "The Out-Post of Civilization"

1. *Pioche Daily Record*, 4, 6 July 1873; 4 July 1874.

2. *Pioche Daily Record*, 4 July 1873; 7 July 1874.

3. "New York Letter," *Pioche Daily Record*, 17 December 1872.

4. *Pioche Weekly Record*, 26 May 1877. By 1900, Pioche's population had fallen to 242. It was made Lincoln County seat in 1871, a role that helped keep the town alive.

5. Laurie F. Maffly-Kipp, *Religion and Society in Frontier California* (New Haven, Conn.: Yale University Press, 1994), 130.

6. Only forty-two families lived at Pioche in 1870, in a population that totaled over 1,100 people. The camp was home to over a thousand white males and a mere eighty-three females. James W. Hulse, *Lincoln County, Nevada, 1864–1909: History of a Mining Region* (Reno: University of Nevada Press, 1971), 22; Michael Bourne, "Early Mining in Southwestern Utah and Southeastern Nevada, 1864–1873: The Meadow Valley, Pahranagat, and Pioche Mining Rushes" (Master's thesis, University of Utah, 1973), 142–43; Carolyn Grattan-Aiello, "The Chinese Community of Pioche, 1870–1900," *Nevada Historical Society Quarterly* 39 (Fall 1996): 201–15.

7. Dean L. May, *Three Frontiers: Family, Land, and Society in the American West, 1850–1900* (Cambridge: Cambridge University Press, 1994), 75–80.

8. Maffly-Kipp, *Religion and Society*, 130–31.

9. David Brion Davis, "Some Themes of Counter-Subversion: An Analysis of Anti-Masonic, Anti-Catholic, and Anti-Mormon Literature," *Mississippi Valley Historical Review* 47 (September 1960): 209–10.

10. See, for example, *Ely Record*, 1, 13, 21 September 1872; *Pioche Daily Record*, 1 December 1872; 28 January, 9 February, 19, 22, 27 March, 2, 4, 10 May, 25 April, 12 June, 26 July, 17 September 1873; 23, 24, 25, 27 January, 10 February, 21 June 1874; 5, 7, 27 May, 1, 2, 3 June 1875; Hulse, *Lincoln County*, 24–25; Mel Gorman, "Chronicle of a Silver Mine: The Meadow Valley Mining Company of Pioche," *Nevada Historical Society Quarterly* 29 (Summer 1986): 78; Bourne, "Early Mining," 142, 151–52; Franklin A. Buck, *A Yankee Trader in the Gold Rush: The Letters of Franklin A. Buck*, comp. Katherine A. White (Boston: Houghton Mifflin Co., 1930), 233–34, 235, 237, 246.

11. *Pioche Daily Record*, 26 July 1873 (quoting the *Virginia Enterprise*).

12. *Pioche Daily Record*, 8, 10 March 1874; see also *Pioche Daily Record*, 9 January, 8 February 1873.

13. On filth, see *Pioche Daily Record*, 4 October 1872; 15 February, 16, 19 April 1873; 1, 7 May 1875. There was renewed concern about the physical condition of the town in 1890 when the newspaper ran an article titled "Some Cold Facts about the Filthy State of the Town," *Pioche Weekly Record*, 29 March 1890.

14. Hulse, *Lincoln County*, chap. 8; Bourne, "Early Mining," 137; Myron Angel, *History of Nevada* (Oakland, Calif.: Thompson and West, 1881), 487; James W. Hulse, "Boom and Bust Government in Lincoln County, Nevada, 1866–1909," *Nevada Historical Society Quarterly* 1 (November 1957): 65–80.

15. Hulse, *Lincoln County*, 23; Gorman, "Chronicle of a Silver Mine," 72, 75–76, 79.

16. Paul Dean Proctor and Morris A Shirts, *Silver, Sinners, and Saints: A History of Old Silver Reef, Utah* (N.p.: Paulmar, Inc., 1991), 47–49; *Pioche Weekly Record*, 13 April 1878. For additional information on the connection between Pioche and Silver Reef, see W. Paul Reeve, "Silver Reef and Southwest Utah's Shifting Mining Frontier," in *From the Ground Up: The History of Mining in Utah*, ed. Colleen Whitely (Logan: Utah State University Press, 2006), 250–71.

17. Gorman, "Chronicle of a Silver Mine," 81–82; Hulse, *Lincoln County*, 31–33; Bourne, "Early Mining," 156; Ronald W. Walker, *Wayward Saints: The Godbeites and Brigham Young* (Urbana: University of Illinois Press, 1998), 334–35.

18. Buck, *Yankee Trader*, 260.

19. *Pioche Daily Record*, 21 September 1872.

20. Buck, *Yankee Trader*, 233.

21. *Pioche Daily Record*, 3 June 1875.

22. Hulse, *Lincoln County*, 28.

23. Davis, "Some Themes of Counter-Subversion," 205, 208–9.

24. *Pioche Daily Record*, 28 March, 24 April 1873.

25. Rossiter W. Raymond, *Statistics of Mines and Mining in the States and Territories West of the Rocky Mountains*, U.S. Treasury Department, annual report (Washington, D.C.: Government Printing Office, 1873), 300; George M. Wheeler and Daniel W. Lockwood, *Preliminary Report upon a Reconnaissance through Southern and Southeastern Nevada, Made in 1869*, U.S. Army, Engineer Department (Washington, D.C.: Government Printing Office, 1875), 54; U.S. House, 39th

Cong., 1st Sess., Committee on the Territories, *The Condition of Utah*, House report No. 96, serial set 1272, 13.

26. *Daily Union Vedette*, 10 April 1866.

27. On the Utah War, see Norman F. Furniss, *The Mormon Conflict, 1850–59* (New Haven, Conn.: Yale University Press, 1960); Donald R. Moorman and Gene A. Sessions, *Camp Floyd and the Mormons: The Utah War* (Salt Lake City: University of Utah Press, 1992); Richard D. Poll and William P. MacKinnon, "Causes of the Utah War Reconsidered," *Journal of Mormon History* 20 (Fall 1994): 16–44; William P. MacKinnon, "The Buchanan Spoils System and the Utah Expedition: Careers of W. M. F. Magraw and John M. Hockaday," *Utah Historical Quarterly* 31 (Spring 1963): 127–50. On the Mountain Meadows Massacre, see Juanita Brooks, *The Mountain Meadows Massacre* (Norman: University of Oklahoma Press, 1962); Juanita Brooks, *John Doyle Lee: Zealot, Pioneer Builder, Scapegoat*, 3d ed. (Salt Lake City: Howe Brothers, 1984); and Will Bagley, *Blood of the Prophets: Brigham Young and the Massacre at Mountain Meadows* (Norman: University of Oklahoma Press, 2002).

28. *Pioche Daily Record*, 27 September, 5, 8 October 1872; *Pioche Weekly Record*, 23 July 1881; Anna Jean Backus, *Mountain Meadows Witness: The Life and Times of Bishop Philip Klingensmith* (Spokane, Wash.: Arthur H. Clark Co., 1996), 217–22, 231.

29. *Pioche Daily Record*, 19, 22 December 1872; 15 June 1875; Inez Smith, "Biography of Charles Wesley Wandell," *Journal of History* 3 (October 1910): 462–63; Marjorie Newton, *Hero or Traitor: A Biographical Study of Charles Wesley Wandell* (Independence, Mo.: Herald Publishing House, 1992), 42–52; Charles W. Wandell, Sydney, Australia, to Joseph Smith III, 26 September 1874, 3, Henry A. Stebbins Papers, box P24, file no. 28, Community of Christ Archives, Independence, Mo.; Charles W. Wandell, Turlock, Calif., to Joseph Smith III, 25 May 1873, Henry A. Stebbins Papers, box P24, file no. 25, Community of Christ Archives, Independence, Mo. Wandell believed that Brigham Young started a conspiracy against him while he lived at Pioche. Wandell alleged that Young instructed Mormon teamsters who traded at Pioche to circulate a report that Wandell was himself a participant in the Mountain Meadows Massacre. It was to protect his reputation as an elected official of Lincoln County that Wandell wrote the letters charging Young with the massacre. In 1873, Wandell abandoned the Salt Lake City Church to join the Reorganized Church of Jesus Christ of Latter Day Saints. Wandell's evidence against Brigham Young perished in a fire at the Reorganized Church's Herald Publishing House in 1907, making it impossible to verify his accusations.

30. *Pioche Daily Record*, 25 May, 23 July, 1 August 1875; 29, 30 September 1876; Brooks, *Mountain Meadows Massacre*, 191–98.

31. Brooks, *Mountain Meadows Massacre*, 206; *Pioche Weekly Record*, 24 March 1877. The "synopsis," printed in small type, filled nearly a full news page.

32. *Pioche Daily Record*, 11 January 1876.

33. Madsen, *Glory Hunter*, 183–84, 197–98, 200, 202–11; *Pioche Daily Record*, 26, 28 September 1872.

34. Madsen, *Glory Hunter*, 65, 161–62, 227–31; U.S. House, 39th Cong., 1st Sess., Committee on the Territories, *The Condition of Utah*, House Report No. 96, serial set 1272, 10–14.

35. Walker, *Wayward Saints*, 334–35; John M. Townley, *Conquered Provinces: Nevada Moves Southeast, 1864–1871*, Charles Redd Monographs in Western History No. 2 (Provo, Utah: Brigham Young University Press, 1973), 63 n.117.

36. *Pioche Daily Record*, 30 March, 18, 19, 30 April 1873. For additional reports of trade goods from Utah, see *Pioche Daily Record*, 21, 26 September 1872; 8 February, 23 March, 2, 11, 12, 13, 30 April 1873; 16 January 1874; 1 August 1876; 25 August 1877; 28 June 1884; Jack R. Mathews, "Mule Skinners and Bull Whackers: An Archeological Study of Two Historic Wagon Roads in Southeast Nevada" (Master's thesis, University of Nevada at Las Vegas, 1992), 35–37; and William R. Palmer, "Early Day Trading with the Nevada Mining Camps," *Utah Historical Quarterly* 26 (October 1958): 353–68.

37. Mathews and Palmer chronicle Mormon trade at Pioche past the turn of the century. Mathews, "Mule Skinners"; Palmer, "Early Day Trading." Mathews documents other avenues of supply for Pioche, from San Francisco, Salt Lake City, and the East (25–34).

38. *Pioche Daily Record*, 21 September 1872; *Pioche Weekly Record*, 25 August 1877; Mathews, "Mule Skinners," 44; Palmer, "Early Day Trading," 356; Orson Welcome Huntsman, Diary of Orson W. Huntsman, typescript, vol. 1, 94, L. Tom Perry Special Collections Library, Harold B. Lee Library, Brigham Young University, Provo, Utah.

39. Mathews, "Mule Skinners," 44; Huntsman, Diary, vol. 2, 33. See also *Pioche Daily Record*, 13 April 1873.

40. Journal History of the Church of Jesus Christ of Latter-day Saints (chronology of typed entries and newspaper clippings, 1830 to the present), 4 April 1871, 2; 4 April 1874, 3; 9 April 1874, 3; 25 May 1874, 3; 2 June 1874, 12; 6 June 1874, 2 (hereafter cited as Journal History), Family and Church History Department, Church of Jesus Christ of Latter-day Saints, Salt Lake City; Thomas G. Alexander, "Federal Authority versus Polygamic Theocracy: James B. McKean and the Mormons, 1870–1875," *Dialogue: A Journal of Mormon Thought* 1 (Autumn 1966): 85–100.

41. Bourne, "Early Mining," 68–69; James W. Abbott, "The Story of Pioche," in *The Arrowhead: A Monthly Magazine of Western Travel and Development* (Los Angeles: San Pedro, Los Angeles, and Salt Lake Railroad, 1907), 6; Hulse, *Lincoln County*, 18–19; Charles Gracey, "Early Days in Lincoln County," in *First Biennial Report of the Nevada Historical Society, 1907–1908* (Carson City: State Printing Office, 1909), 108; *White Pine Daily News* (Hamilton/Treasure City, Nev.), 28 July 1870; John L. Considine, "The Birth of Old Pioche," *Sunset: The Pacific Monthly* 54 (January 1925): 29.

42. *Pioche Weekly Record*, 28 June 1884; 2 June 1883.

43. Huntsman, Diary, vol. 1, 118–19; Hebron Ward Historical Record, vol. 3, 145–47, microfilm, Historical Department, Church Archives, Church of Jesus Christ of Latter-day Saints, Salt Lake City. The *Pioche Daily Record* frequently carried advertisements announcing the Sherwood lumber yard at Pioche (see, for example, 15 February 1873).

44. Buck, *Yankee Trader*, 234–36.

45. *Pioche Weekly Record*, 11 November 1882; 27 April 1893.

46. Edward Leo Lyman, *Political Deliverance: The Mormon Quest for Utah Statehood* (Urbana: University of Illinois Press, 1986), 22–23.

47. *Pioche Weekly Record*, 25 February 1882.

48. *Pioche Weekly Record*, 13 May 1882.

49. *Pioche Weekly Record*, 1 September 1877.

50. *Pioche Weekly Record*, 9 January 1896.

51. The Pioche press often failed to distinguish between Paiutes and Shoshones; it simply labeled members of both tribes "Indians." It is impossible, therefore, to trace a definitive Paiute stance at Pioche, but the arguments made here still apply. Whether Shoshone or Paiute, the prevailing bias against "Indians" was the same. See Martha C. Knack, *Boundaries Between: The Southern Paiutes, 1775–1995* (Lincoln: University of Nebraska Press, 2001), 105.

52. George W. Arnold, Pioche, Nev., to Gideon, [ca. 1870], manuscript, MSS 12, Special Collections, Lied Library, University of Nevada at Las Vegas. For a similar sentiment about clearing the land of Indians so that it would be "open for the passage of prospectors and adventurers," see *Pioche Daily Record*, 19 November 1872.

53. *Pioche Daily Record*, 17 December 1874.

54. For an elaboration of this idea, see "Murders by Indians," *Pioche Daily Record*, 17 December 1874.

55. *Tri-Weekly Ely Record* (Pioche, Nev.), 11 September 1872.

56. *Pioche Daily Record*, 26 September 1872.

57. *Pioche Daily Record*, 26 March 1873.

58. *Pioche Daily Record*, 17 August 1873.

59. *Pioche Daily Record*, 24 June 1874.

60. Robert C. Euler, *Southern Paiute Ethnohistory*, University of Utah Anthropological Papers Number 78 (Salt Lake City: University of Utah Press, 1966), 77–78. Euler notes an 1871 U.S. army reconnaissance warning of this band. In addition to the reported murders listed below, see *Pioche Daily Record*, 28 May 1875, for an example of presumed Indian involvement when a miner was missing. See *Pioche Daily Record*, 17 December 1874, for stories of Indian murder under the headlines: "Rumored Massacre," "The Hiko Murderers," "Murders by Indians," and "Request for Aid."

61. *Pioche Daily Record*, 17 December 1874.

62. *Pioche Daily Record*, 17, 19, 23, 24 December 1874; 15 January 1875; David Krause, Captain, 14th Infantry, to 2 Leiut. R. A. Hovell, Post Adjutant, Fort Cameron, Utah, 15 January 1875; W. W. Bishop, Pioche, Nev., to Commander, U.S. Troops, Fort Cameron, Beaver, Utah, 14 January 1875, microfilm roll 541, National Archives, Letters Received by the Office of Indian Affairs, Nevada Superintendency, 1874–75 (hereafter cited as OIA-NV).

63. J. M. Schofield, Major General, Headquarters, Military Division of the Pacific, San Francisco, to General W. T. Sherman, Commanding U.S. Army, St. Louis, 13 September 1875; W. S. Rosencrans, Cherry Creek, Nev., to Major General Schofield, San Francisco, 4 September 1875; J. M. Schofield, San Francisco, to General Rosencrans, Cherry Creek, Nev., 4 September 1875; J. M. Schofield, San Francisco, to General Sherman, St. Louis, 6 September 1875; Captain E. V. Sumner, Cavalry Camp, near Camp Halleck, Nev., to Lieut. H. E. Tutherly, 1st Cavalry, Acting Adjutant, 24 September 1875, microfilm roll 541, OIA-NV.

64. Ibid.; see also Journal History, 11 September 1875, 2.

65. *Pioche Daily Record*, 7 September 1875.

66. *Pioche Daily Record,* 14 May 1876.

67. *Pioche Weekly Record,* 22 July 1882.

68. *Pioche Weekly Record,* 7, 14 April 1883.

69. *Pioche Weekly Record,* 18 May 1878; 5, 12 December 1895.

70. *Pioche Weekly Record,* 25 October 1879.

71. *Pioche Weekly Record,* 16 August 1890. For additional discussion of inter-ethnic violence at Pioche, see Knack, *Boundaries Between,* 101–9.

72. Martha C. Knack, "Newspaper Accounts of Indian Women in Southern Nevada Mining Towns, 1870–1900," *Journal of California and Great Basin Anthropology* 8.1 (1986): 86–87. "A White Outrage upon Indians," *Pioche Daily Record,* 15 December 1872. See "Attempted Outrage," *Pioche Daily Record,* 19 December 1872, for an example of attitudes toward a white rapist. The outcry in this case was no doubt worse because the sexual assault was committed against a girl of about twelve years of age.

73. Knack, *Boundaries Between,* 106.

74. *Pioche Daily Record,* 10 May 1873.

75. *Pioche Daily Record,* 20 April 1873, 22 August 1875; *Pioche Weekly Record,* 5 March 1881; 4 February 1882.

76. *Pioche Daily Record,* 27 March 1873; *Pioche Weekly Record,* 12 February 1881.

77. For a Pioche business directory listing seventeen of the town's seventy-six businesses as either saloons, breweries, or liquor stores, see *Pioche Daily Record,* 2 June 1875. For samples of liquor advertisements, see *Pioche Daily Record,* 8 February 1873, 27 May 1875. For articles on public intoxication, see *Pioche Daily Record,* 27 May, 2 June 1875.

78. *Pioche Daily Record,* 8 February 1873; Buck, *Yankee Trader,* 260.

79. Prucha, *The Great Father: The United States Government and the American Indians,* vols. 1 and 2 (Lincoln: University of Nebraska Press, 1984), 19–20, 309–14, 334, 653–55.

80. *Pioche Weekly Record,* 7 April 1877; 4 February 1882. See also *Pioche Daily Record,* 21, 27 November 1872, for a similar argument about selling guns to Indians.

81. *Pioche Weekly Record,* 29 November 1890; 27 April 1893.

82. See *Pioche Daily Record,* 9 February 1873, for an account of a miner robbing a Shoshone of his cash.

83. *Pioche Weekly Record,* 4 February 1882.

84. Buck, *Yankee Trader,* 273, 276.

85. Maffly-Kipp, *Religion and Society,* 115.

Chapter 7: "Dead and Dying in the Sagebrush"

1. Don D. Fowler and Catherine Fowler, *Anthropology of the Numa: John Wesley Powell's Manuscripts on the Numic People,* Smithsonian Contributions to Anthropology 14 (Washington, D.C.: Smithsonian Institution, 1971), 61.

2. John Wesley Powell, *The Exploration of the Colorado River and Its Canyons* (1895; reprint, New York: Dover, 1961), 322.

3. Fowler and Fowler, *Anthropology of the Numa,* 123.

4. Ibid., 61. Due to the nature of some of Powell's notes regarding this incident,

Fowler and Fowler question whether Powell actually saw the three women, or if such ritualistic notions of sacrifice were merely described to him by the Paiutes. See ibid., 61, 123, 162, and 283 n.16.

5. Tom F. Driver, *Liberating Rites: Understanding the Transformative Power of Ritual* (Boulder, Colo.: Westview Press, 1998), 93 and chaps. 7 and 8.

6. *Pioche Daily Record,* 23 March 1873.

7. *Pioche Daily Record,* 3 April 1873.

8. *Pioche Daily Record,* 3 April 1873.

9. *Pioche Daily Record,* 19 April 1873.

10. *Pioche Daily Record,* 17, 19 August 1873.

11. Edward Palmer, *Notes on the Utah Utes by Edward Palmer, 1866–1877,* ed. R. F. Heizer, Anthropological Papers Number 17, May 1954 (Salt Lake City: University of Utah Press, 1954), 4.

12. Isabel T. Kelly, "Southern Paiute Shamanism," *Anthropological Records* 2.4 (Berkeley: University of California Press, 1939), 151–67 (for herbal remedies, see 153 n.7). William R. Palmer, "Pahute Indian Medicine," *Utah Historical Quarterly* 10 (January–October 1942): 1–13, offers an informal description of Paiute medical practices in the early twentieth century, albeit one that is framed in paternalistic tones.

13. Kelly, "Southern Paiute Shamanism."

14. Quoted in ibid., 155.

15. Ibid., 153, 156, 157, 159, 160–61, 164–65.

16. Fowler and Fowler, *Anthropology of the Numa,* 59–61.

17. Ibid.

18. Juanita Brooks, ed., *Journal of the Southern Indian Mission: Diary of Thomas D. Brown,* Western Text Society No. 4 (Logan: Utah State University Press, 1972), 22–23.

19. A. J. Barnes to Edward P. Smith, 11 September 1875, *Annual Report of the Commissioner of Indian Affairs* (Washington, D.C.: Government Printing Office, 1875), 337–38.

20. Ibid., 337.

21. Brooks, *Journal of the Southern Indian Mission,* 42; Robert J. Franklin and Pamela A. Bunte, *The Paiute* (New York: Chelsea House, 1990), 41, 96; Isabel T. Kelly and Catherine S. Fowler, "Southern Paiute," in *Great Basin,* ed. Warren L. D'Azevedo, vol. 11 of *Handbook of North American Indians,* ed. William C. Sturtevant (Washington, D.C.: Smithsonian Institution, 1986), 380; Barnes to Smith, 11 September 1875, 337; Palmer, *Notes on the Utah Utes,* 5; Isabel T. Kelly, *Southern Paiute Ethnography* (1964; reprint, New York: Garland Publishing, 1976), 95, 102. Kelly suggests that in some bands cremation "was reserved for a little-esteemed person."

22. Barnes to Smith, 11 September 1875, 337–38.

23. Brooks, *Journal of the Southern Indian Mission,* 42.

24. *Pioche Weekly Record,* 7 April 1883.

25. *Pioche Weekly Record,* 25 October 1879.

26. Henry H. Lee, "The Murder of George Rogers," in *A Century in Meadow Valley, 1864–1964,* ed. Ruth Lee and Sylvia Wadsworth (Salt Lake City: Deseret News Press, 1966), 21.

27. Franklin and Bunte, *The Paiute*, 79; Levi Johnson, Cry Songs, 2 April 1980, Kanosh, Utah, tape recording, Special Collections, Gerald R. Sherratt Library, Southern Utah University, Cedar City.

28. William R. Palmer, "Utah Indians," 99–106, typescript, Palmer Collection, box 36, Special Collections, Gerald R. Sherratt Library, Southern Utah University, Cedar City.

29. The Doctrine and Covenants of the Church of Jesus Christ of Latter-day Saints, 42:43–44.

30. Lester E. Bush Jr., *Health and Medicine among the Latter-day Saints: Science, Sense, and Scripture* (New York: Crossroad Publishing Co., 1993), 69–107; Thomas J. Wolfe, "Steaming Saints: Mormons and the Thomsonian Movement in Nineteenth-Century America," in *Disease and Medical Care in the Mountain West: Essays on Region, History, and Practice*, ed. Martha L. Hildreth and Bruce T. Moran (Reno: University of Nevada Press, 1998), 18–28. For examples of herbal remedies practiced by Clover Valley Mormons, see Orrilla Woods Hafen, Mary R. Edwards, and Elbert B. Edwards, comps., *The Woods Family of Clover Valley, Nevada, 1869–1979* (Boulder City, Nev.: Woods Family Genealogical Committee, 1979), 12. For Mormon women healers, see Margaret K. Brady, *Mormon Healer and Folk Poet: Mary Susannah Fowler's Life of "Unselfish Usefulness"* (Logan: Utah State University Press, 2000); and Donna Toland Smart, ed., *Mormon Midwife: The 1846–1888 Diaries of Patty Bartlett Sessions* (Logan: Utah State University Press, 1997).

31. Carrie Elizabeth Laub Hunt, *Memories of the Past and Family History* (Salt Lake City: Utah Printing Co., 1968), 60.

32. Book of Mormon, Mosiah 4:26.

33. John Pulsipher, "The Journal of John Pulsipher," 93–94, typescript, L. Tom Perry Special Collections, Harold B. Lee Library, Brigham Young University, Provo, Utah.

34. Hunt, *Memories of the Past*, 60.

35. Bush, *Health and Medicine*, 180.

36. Hebron Ward Historical Record, vol. 1, 37–38, microfilm, Historical Department, Church Archives, Church of Jesus Christ of Latter-day Saints, Salt Lake City.

37. Ibid., vol. 1, 39–42.

38. Ibid., vol. 1, 42–43.

39. Ibid., vol. 1, 43–46.

40. Ibid., vol. 1, 46–47.

41. Ibid., vol. 1, 47–49.

42. Ibid., vol. 1, 49–53.

43. Orson Welcome Huntsman, Diary of Orson W. Huntsman, typescript, vol. 1, 16–17, L. Tom Perry Special Collections Library, Harold B. Lee Library, Brigham Young University, Provo, Utah.

44. Hebron Ward Historical Record, vol. 1, 102–4 (emphasis added).

45. Pulsipher, "Journal," 97.

46. Quoted in Juanita Brooks, *On the Ragged Edge: The Life and Times of Dudley Leavitt* (Salt Lake City: Utah State Historical Society, 1973), 128. For other accounts of Mormon intervention on behalf of a Paiute left behind, see Angus M.

Woodbury, "A History of Southern Utah and its National Parks," *Utah Histori-cal Quarterly* 12 (July–October, 1944): 111–209; and Palmer, *Notes on the Utah Utes*, 4.

47. Lee, "Murder of George Rogers," 21.

48. Hebron Ward Historical Record, vol. 3, 50–51; Huntsman, Diary, 84.

49. Corbett, "History of the Muddy Mission," 124–25.

50. Leu Wanna Bunker and Josie Walker, "Sarah Ann Browning Lang Bunker," in *The Bunker Family History*, ed. Josephine B. Walker (N.p.: Edward Bunker Family Association, 1957), 99.

51. Hebron Ward Historical Record, vol. 2, 57; Hunt, *Memories of the Past*, 23–24.

52. Duane A. Smith and Donald C. Brown, *No One Ailing Except the Physician: Medicine in the Mining West, 1848–1919* (Boulder: University Press of Colorado, 2001), xi–xv.

53. James W. Hulse, *Lincoln County, Nevada, 1864–1909: History of a Mining Region* (Reno: University of Nevada Press, 1971), 28; *Pioche Daily Record*, 24 September, 13 November 1872; 23 January 1873.

54. *Pioche Daily Record*, 4 September, 5 October 1872; 21 January 1873 (piles are hemorrhoids).

55. *Pioche Weekly Record*, 9, 16 July 1881; 27 April 1893; 9 January 1896.

56. *Pioche Daily Record*, 9 January 1873; 2 August 1876; *Pioche Weekly Record*, 12 January 1889.

57. Hulse, *Lincoln County*, 28; *Pioche Daily Record*, 21 January 1873; Charles A. Sumner, *A Trip to Pioche: Being a Sketch of Recent Frontier Travel* (San Francisco: Bacon and Co. Book and Job Printers, 1873), 12.

58. Theodore A. Ross, *The Illustrated History of Odd Fellowship: A Documentary and Chronological History of the Origin, Rise, and Progress of the Independent Order of Odd Fellows throughout the World* (New York: Ross History Co., 1913), ii, 523, 590; Rev. Aaron B. Grosh, *The Odd-Fellow's Manual: Illustrating the History, Principles, and Government of the Order, and the Instructions and Duties of Every Degree, State, and Office in Odd-Fellowship; with Directions for Laying Corner-Stones; Dedicating Cemeteries, Chapels, Halls, and Other Public Edifices; Marshalling Funeral and Other Processions; Forms for Petitions, Reports, etc. Also, Odes, with Music, for Various Occasions* (Philadelphia: H. C. Peck and Theo. Bliss, 1853), 222–23, 360–61, 365–68, 374.

59. *Pioche Daily Record*, 1 January 1873; 13 February 1874.

60. Anna Layton, Evan Blythin, and Martha Lauritzen, eds., "Diary of a Wood-cutter: December 1, 1872 to January 17, 1873," *Nevada Historical Society Quarterly* 40 (Winter 1997): 408.

61. Ibid., 408–9.

62. Ibid., 409–10.

63. Ibid., 409–13.

64. *Pioche Daily Record*, 13 November 1872; 3 May, 12 June 1873. See also *Pioche Daily Record*, 19 March 1873, for a suicide at Pioche.

65. *Pioche Daily Record*, 21 January 1873; Sumner, *Trip to Pioche*, 12; James W. Abbott, "The Story of Pioche," in *The Arrowhead: A Monthly Magazine of Western Travel and Development* (Los Angeles: San Pedro, Los Angeles, and Salt Lake Railroad, 1907), 7–8; "Who Lies Yonder in Boot Hill: Actual Known Obituaries of

Those Buried in Pioche Boot Hill," typescript, Lincoln County Museum, Pioche, Nevada. Hulse calls the legend concerning violent deaths at Pioche before one of a natural cause unfounded. It nonetheless persisted from the early days to the present and varies in number from seventy-two to seventy-nine. Hulse, *Lincoln County*, 24.

66. *Pioche Daily Record*, 21 January 1873; *Pioche Weekly Record*, 27 April 1893; 9 January 1896; Hafen, Edwards, and Edwards, *Woods Family*, 12.

67. *Pioche Weekly Record*, 31 March 1883.

Chapter 8: Transformations

1. Orson Welcome Huntsman, Diary of Orson W. Huntsman, typescript, vol. 3, 11–14, L. Tom Perry Special Collections Library, Harold B. Lee Library, Brigham Young University, Provo, Utah.

2. "St. George Shaken Up," *Salt Lake Tribune*, 18 November 1902; *Lincoln County Record* (Pioche, Nev.), 21 November 1902.

3. Huntsman, Diary, vol. 3, 11–14.

4. W. Paul Reeve, "Cattle, Cotton, and Conflict: The Possession and Dispossession of Hebron, Utah," *Utah Historical Quarterly* 67 (Spring 1999): 173–75; Eagle Valley Ward, St. George Stake, manuscript history and historical reports, microfilm, Historical Department, Church Archives, Church of Jesus Christ of Latter-day Saints, Salt Lake City (hereafter cited as CA); Clover Valley Branch, Moapa Stake, manuscript history, microfilm, CA; Orilla Woods Hafen, Mary R. Edwards, and Elbert B. Edwards, comps., *The Woods Family of Clover Valley, Nevada, 1869–1979* (Boulder City, Nev.: Woods Family Genealogical Committee, 1979), 24.

5. Huntsman, Diary, vol. 3, 11–14; Newell R. Frei, "History of Pioneering on Shoal Creek" (Master's thesis, Brigham Young University, 1932), 102–7. For a more complete description of factors leading to the abandonment of Hebron, see W. Paul Reeve, *A Century of Enterprise: The History of Enterprise, Utah, 1896–1996* (Enterprise, Utah: City of Enterprise, 1996), 3–30; and Reeve, "Cattle, Cotton, and Conflict."

6. Reeve, *Century of Enterprise*, chaps. 1–3. For changes in Mormonism during this period, see Thomas G. Alexander, *Mormonism in Transition: A History of the Latter-day Saints, 1890–1930* (Urbana: University of Illinois Press, 1986).

7. *Lincoln County Record*, 27, 30 January, 3 February 1905.

8. *Lincoln County Record*, 7 July 1905. See also *Lincoln County Record*, 6 July 1900 and 8 July 1904 for similar celebrations.

9. *Pioche Daily Record*, 4, 6, July 1873; 4 July 1874.

10. *Pioche Weekly Record*, 1 February 1900.

11. *Lincoln County Record*, 8 July 1904; 3 February 1905.

12. *Lincoln County Record*, 6 January 1905.

13. *Lincoln County Record*, 3 February 1905.

14. *Lincoln County Record*, 24 February 1905.

15. *Lincoln County Record*, 10 February, 30 June, 3 November 1905.

16. *Lincoln County Record*, 29 December 1905.

17. Prince Consolidated Mining Company Reorganization Committee, *Pioche History as It Relates to the Prince Mine* (Salt Lake City: N.p., 1923), special col-

lections, J. Willard Marriott Library, University of Utah, Salt Lake City; James W. Hulse, "'The Camp That Came Back': The Combined Metals Reduction Company and the Revival of Pioche, 1912–1958," *Nevada Historical Society Quarterly* 42 (Fall 1999): 160–68. For examples of the way in which Pioche is popularly remembered, see Miner Mike, "The Story of Pioche," *Utah Farmer*, 25 November 1946, 22–23; 14 December 1946, 25; Don Ashbaugh, *Nevada's Turbulent Yesterday: A Study in Ghost Towns* (Los Angeles: Westernlore Press, 1963), 21–37; Vernon Jeffcott, "Tales of Pioche," *Utah Humanities Review* 2 (April 1948): 192–93; Willie Arthur Chalfant, *Gold, Guns, and Ghost Towns* (Stanford, Calif.: Stanford University Press, 1947), 80–86; John L. Considine, "The Pistoleers of Old Pioche, *Sunset: The Pacific Monthly* 53 (December 1924): 24–25; John L. Considine, "The Birth of Old Pioche," *Sunset: The Pacific Monthly* 54 (January 1925): 29, 56, 58; and John L. Considine, "How Zink Barnes Corrupted Pioche," *Sunset: The Pacific Monthly* 54 (February 1925): 40, 60.

18. Inter-Tribal Council of Nevada, *Nuwuvi: A Southern Paiute History* (Salt Lake City: University of Utah Printing Service, 1976), 103–6; Martha C. Knack, *Boundaries Between: The Southern Paiutes, 1775–1995* (Lincoln: University of Nebraska Press, 2001), 130–79.

19. *Lincoln County Record*, 30 January 1905.

20. Robert C. Euler, *Southern Paiute Ethnohistory*, University of Utah Anthropological Papers Number 78 (Salt Lake City: University of Utah Press, 1966), 96.

21. William R. Palmer, "Utah Indians," 94–95, typescript, Palmer Collection, box 36, Special Collections, Gerald R. Sherratt Library, Southern Utah University, Cedar City.

22. Powell, *Exploration of the Colorado*, 323.

23. *Pioche Daily Record*, 22 September 1874.

24. David J. Weber, "*The Legacy of Conquest*, by Patricia Nelson Limerick: A Panel of Appraisal," *Western Historical Quarterly* 20 (August 1989): 316.

25. Theodore Roosevelt, *Fear God and Take Your Own Part* (New York: George H. Doran Co., 1916), 357–76.

26. See Frank Van Nuys, *Americanizing the West: Race, Immigrants, and Citizenship, 1890–1930* (Lawrence: University Press of Kansas, 2002).

27. Knack, *Boundaries Between*, 244–68.

28. See Elliot West, *Contested Plains: Indians, Goldseekers, and the Rush to Colorado* (Lawrence: University Press of Kansas, 1998), 33–58 (esp. 57), for eloquent descriptions of the frontier that influenced this rendering.

29. Hebron Ward Historical Record, vol. 2, 57, microfilm, Historical Department, Church Archives, Church of Jesus Christ of Latter-day Saints, Salt Lake City.

30. Franklin A. Buck, *A Yankee Trader in the Gold Rush: The Letters of Franklin A. Buck*, comp. Katherine A. White (Boston: Houghton Mifflin Co., 1930), 236.

31. Quoted in James E. McCarty, "The Center of the Universe: A Ceremony at Pipe Spring Sweat Lodge" (Master's thesis, University of Nevada at Las Vegas, 1995), 1–12.

32. James W. Hulse, "The Afterlife of St. Mary's County; or, Utah's Penumbra in Eastern Nevada," *Utah Historical Quarterly* 55 (Summer 1987): 236–49; Hulse, "'The Camp That Came Back,'" 167.

33. Book of Mormon, 2 Nephi 26:33.

SELECTED BIBLIOGRAPHY

Abbreviations

CA   Church Archives, Family and Church History Department, Church of Jesus Christ of Latter-day Saints, Salt Lake City

FHL   Family History Library, Church of Jesus Christ of Latter-day Saints, Salt Lake City

JWML   J. Willard Marriott Library, University of Utah, Salt Lake City

LCC   Lincoln County Courthouse, Pioche, Nev.

OIA-NV   National Archives, Letters Received by the Office of Indian Affairs, Nevada Superintendency

OIA-UT   National Archives, Letters Received by the Office of Indian Affairs, Utah Superintendency

USHS   Utah State Historical Society Library, Salt Lake City

Primary

NEWSPAPERS

American Journal of Mining, Milling, Oil-Boring, Geology, Mineralogy, Metallurgy, etc. (New York)
Daily Union Vedette (Salt Lake City)
Deseret Evening News (Salt Lake City)
Deseret News (Salt Lake City)
Deseret Weekly News (Salt Lake City)
Latter-day Saints' Millennial Star (Liverpool, U.K.)
Lincoln County Record (Pioche, Nev.)
Mining and Scientific Press (San Francisco)
Pioche (Nev.) Daily Record
Pioche (Nev.) Weekly Record
Rio Virgen Times (St. George, Utah)
St. George (Utah) Union
Tri-Weekly Ely Record (Pioche, Nev.)
Utah Farmer (Salt Lake City)
Weekly Ely Record (Pioche, Nev.)
White Pine Daily News (Hamilton/Treasure City, Nev.)

LETTERS

Arnold, George W., Pioche, Nev., to Gideon, [ca. 1870]. Manuscript. MSS 12. Special Collections. Lied Library, University of Nevada at Las Vegas.

Barnes, A. J., Moapa River Reserve, to Edward P. Smith, Commissioner of Indian Affairs, Washington, D.C., 11 September 1875. *Annual Report of the Commissioner of Indian Affairs.* Washington, D.C.: Government Printing Office, 1875. 838–40.

———, St. George, Utah, to Edward P. Smith, Commissioner of Indian Affairs, Washington D.C., 17 November 1874, 19 January 1875. Microfilm Roll 541. OIA-NV.

———, St. Thomas, Nev., to Edward P. Smith, Washington, D.C., 3, 20 December 1874, 19 January 1875. Microfilm Roll 541. OIA-NV.

Bateman, C. A., Pyramid Lake Reserve, Nev., to Hon. E. P. Smith, Commissioner of Indian Affairs, 10 September 1875. *Annual Report of the Commissioner of Indian Affairs.* Washington, D.C.: Government Printing Office, 1875. 840–44.

Bishop, W. W., Pioche, Nev., to Commander, U.S. Troops, Fort Cameron, Beaver, Utah, 14 January 1875. Microfilm Roll 541. OIA-NV.

Bonelli, Daniel, St. Thomas, Nev., to E. P. Smith, Commissioner of Indian Affairs, Washington, D.C., 10, 20 September, 5, 23 October 1874. Microfilm Roll 541. OIA-NV.

———, to George A. Smith, 30 April 1864. Brigham Young Collection, Office Files, 1832–78. Microfilm. Reel 40, Box 29, Folder 17. CA.

Buck, Franklin A. *A Yankee Trader in the Gold Rush: The Letters of Franklin A. Buck.* Comp. Katherine A. White. Boston: Houghton Mifflin Co., 1930.

Bunker, Edward, Santa Clara, to Brigham Young, Salt Lake City, 20 January 1864. Brigham Young Collection, Office Files, 1832–78. Microfilm. Reel 40, Box 29, Folder 17. CA.

Clum, H. R., Acting Commissioner of Indian Affairs, to C. Delano, Secretary of the Interior, 7 March 1873. Holograph Photocopies. Maryellen Vallier Sadovich Collection, Manuscript x45, Folder 3. Special Collections. Lied Library, University of Nevada at Las Vegas.

Cram, Daniel, Assistant Special Detective, Salt Lake City, to George H. Williams, U.S. Attorney General, Washington D.C., 8 December 1874. Microfilm Roll 541. OIA-NV.

Delano, C., Secretary of the Interior, to Ulysses S. Grant, 12 March 1873. Holograph Photocopy. Maryellen Vallier Sadovich Collection, Manuscript x45, Folder 3. Special Collections. Lied Library, University of Nevada at Las Vegas.

Doty, James Duane, and Amos Reed, to O. H. Irish, 7 September 1864. Microfilm Roll 901. OIA-UT.

Durkee, Governor Charles, Salt Lake City, to President Andrew Johnson, Washington, D.C., 18 May 1866. Microfilm. Vol. 2, No. 629. U.S. Department of State, State Department Territorial Papers, Utah Series.

Fenton, R. N., Pioche, Nev., to H. Douglas, Superintendent Indian Affairs of Nevada, 22 September 1870. *Report of Commissioner of Indian Affairs.* House Exec. Doc. No. 1, 1870, Serial Set 1449, 577–78.

———, St. Thomas, Nev., to F. S. Parker, Washington, D.C., 14 October 1869. *Report of Commissioner of Indian Affairs.* House Exec. Doc. No. 37, 1869, Serial Set 1414, 645–46.

Foster, J. C., Register, U.S. Land Office, Pioche, Nev., to C. Delano, Secretary of the Interior, Washington D.C., 23 September 1874. Microfilm Roll 541. OIA-NV.

Geib, Henry P., M.D., Physician to Pai-Ute Reservation, to E. P. Smith, Washington, D.C., 26 October 1874. Microfilm Roll 541. OIA-NV.

Ingalls, G. W., to E. P. Smith, Washington, D.C., 25 January 1874. Microfilm Roll 541. OIA-NV.

Irish, O. H., Salt Lake City, to William P. Dole, Washington, D.C., 9 September 1864, 22 November 1864, 15 May 1865. Microfilm Roll 901. OIA-UT.

Irish, O. H., Salt Lake City, to William P. Dole, Washington, D.C., 26 September 1864. *Report of Commissioner of Indian Affairs.* House Exec. Doc. No. 1, 38th Cong., 2d Sess., Serial Set 1220. 312–15.

Krause, Captain David, 14th Infantry, to 2 Lieut. R. A. Hovell, Post Adjutant, Fort Cameron, Utah, 15 January 1875. Microfilm Roll 541. OIA-NV.

Letter from the Acting Secretary of the Interior, Relative to the Condition of the Pi-Ute Indians. 42d Cong., 3d Sess., 1873, House Ex. Doc. No. 66, Serial Set 1565, 2–3.

Petition, Meadow Valley, Washington Co., Utah Territory, to O. H. Irish, Salt Lake City, Utah, 27 August 1864. Microfilm Roll 901. OIA-UT.

Petition, Panaca City, Utah Territory, to James D. Doty, Governor of Utah, Salt Lake City, 28 April 1865. Microfilm Roll 901. OIA-UT.

Powell, Charles F., St. George, Utah Territory, to H. R. Clum, Acting Commissioner of Indian Affairs, Washington, D.C., 20 October 1871. *Report of Commissioner of Indian Affairs, 1871.* Washington, D.C.: Government Printing Office, 1872.

Rosencrans, W. S., Cherry Creek, Nev., to Major General Schofield, San Francisco, 4 September 1875. Microfilm Roll 541. OIA-NV.

Sale, Thomas C. W., Meadow Valley, Utah Territory, to O. H. Irish, Salt Lake City, 18 November 1864, 15 December 1864, 4 May 1865, 19 May 1865. Microfilm Roll 901. OIA-UT.

Schofield, Major General J. M., Headquarters Military Division of the Pacific, San Francisco, to General Rosencrans, Cherry Creek, Nev., 4 September 1875. Microfilm Roll 541. OIA-NV.

———, Headquarters Military Division of the Pacific, San Francisco, to General W. T. Sherman, Commanding U.S. Army, St. Louis, 6, 13 September 1875. Microfilm Roll 541. OIA-NV.

Smith, George A., Salt Lake City, to William H. Hooper, Washington, D.C., 24 January 1869. Historian's Office, Letterpress Copybooks. Vol. 2, p. 764. CA.

Snow, Erastus, St. George, to Brigham Young, Salt Lake City, 19 June 1864. Brigham Young Collection, Office Files, 1832–78. Microfilm. Reel 55, Box 42, Folder 18. CA.

Spencer, James E., to Commissioner of Indian Affairs, 30 August 1880. *Report of Commissioner of Indian Affairs.* 46th Cong., 3d Sess., House Exec. Doc. No. 1, 1880, Serial Set 1959, 247–48.

Sumner, Captain E. V., Cavalry Camp, near Camp Halleck, Nev., to Lieut. H. E. Tutherly, 1st Cavalry, Acting Adjutant, 24 September 1875. Microfilm Roll 541. OIA-NV.

Wandell, Charles W., Sydney, Australia, to Joseph Smith III, 26 September 1874. Henry A. Stebbins Papers, Box P24, File 28. Community of Christ Archives, Independence, Mo.

————, Turlock, Calif., to Joseph Smith III, 25 May 1873. Henry A. Stebbins Papers, Box P24, File 25. Community of Christ Archives, Independence, Mo.

Young, Brigham, Salt Lake City, to Edward Bunker, 6 February 1864. Brigham Young Collection, Outgoing Correspondence. CA.

MANUSCRIPTS: DIARIES, JOURNALS, AND PAPERS

Bleak, James G. "Annals of the Southern Utah Mission." Vols. A and B. Typescript. Special Collections. JWML.

Clover Valley Branch, Moapa Stake. Manuscript history. Microfilm. CA.

Durkee, Charles. "Governor's Message," 11 December 1865. Governors' Messages to the Utah Legislature, 1851–76. USHS.

Eagle Valley Ward, St. George Stake. Manuscript History and Historical Reports. Microfilm. CA.

Hebron Ward Historical Record. 2 vols. Microfilm. CA.

Hebron Ward Historical Record, 1872–97. Vol. 3. Holograph Photocopy. Enterprise Branch, Washington County Library, Enterprise, Utah.

Huntsman, Orson Welcome. Dairy of Orson W. Huntsman. Typescript. L. Tom Perry Special Collections Library. Harold B. Lee Library, Brigham Young University, Provo, Utah.

Ivins, Anthony W. Journal. Holograph. USHS.

Johnson, Levi. Cry Songs, 2 April 1980. Kanosh, Utah. Tape recording. Special Collections. Gerald R. Sherratt Library, Southern Utah University, Cedar City.

Journal History of the Church of Jesus Christ of Latter-day Saints (chronology of typed entries and newspaper clippings, 1830 to the Present). Family and Church History Department, Church of Jesus Christ of Latter-day Saints, Salt Lake City.

Journal of Discourses. 26 vols. London: LDS Booksellers Depot, 1855–86.

"Journal of Stephen Vandiver Jones, April 21, 1871–December 14, 1872." Ed. Herbert E. Gregory. *Utah Historical Quarterly* 16–17 (1948–49): 19–174.

Layton, Anna, Evan Blythin, and Martha Lauritzen, eds. "Diary of a Woodcutter: December 1, 1872, to January 17, 1873." *Nevada Historical Society Quarterly* 40 (Winter 1997): 403–14.

Palmer, William R. "Utah Indians." Typescript. Palmer Collection. Box 36. Special Collections. Gerald R. Sherratt Library, Southern Utah University, Cedar City.

Panaca Ward, Uvada Stake. Manuscript History and Historical Reports. Microfilm. CA.

Prince Consolidated Mining Company Reorganization Committee. *Pioche History as It Relates to the Prince Mine.* Salt Lake City, 1923. Special Collections. JWML.

Pulsipher, John. "The Journal of John Pulsipher." Typescript. L. Tom Perry Special Collections. Harold B. Lee Library, Brigham Young University, Provo, Utah.

Raymond and Ely vs. The Kentucky Mining Co.: Judge Beatty's Decision. Pioche: Record Publishing Co., 1873. Nevada Historical Society, Reno.

Spring Valley Branch, Panaca Ward, Uvada Stake. Manuscript History and Historical Reports. Microfilm. CA.

Sumner, Charles A. *A Trip to Pioche: Being a Sketch of Recent Frontier Travel.* Delivered at Dashaway Hall, 17 August 1873. San Francisco: Bacon and Co. Book and Job Printers, 1873.

Tillohash, Toney. Interview by Kay Fowler, 16 June 1967. No. 119. Transcript. Doris Duke Oral History Project. Special Collections. JWML.

"Who Lies Yonder in Boot Hill: Actual Known Obituaries of Those Buried in Pioche Boot Hill." Typescript. Lincoln County Museum, Pioche, Nev.

Woodruff, Wilford. *Wilford Woodruff's Journal, 1833–1898.* 9 vols. Typescript. Ed. Scott G. Kenney. Midvale, Utah: Signature Books, 1983–85.

GOVERNMENT DOCUMENTS

Annual Report of the State Mineralogist of the State of Nevada for 1866. Carson City: Joseph E. Eckley, State Printer, 1867.

"Articles of Agreement and Convention Made and Concluded at Pinto Creek," 18 September 1865. Photocopy of Holograph. Ronald L. Holt Papers. Box 3, Folder 9, Special Collections. JWML.

Congressional Globe. 39th Cong., 1st Sess. Washington, D.C.: F. and J. Rives, 1866.

Congressional Globe. 40th Cong., 3d Sess. Washington, D.C.: F. and J. Rives and George A. Bailey, 1869.

Court Judgement Record. Book 445. Vol. A, 1868–79. County Clerk's Office. LCC.

Court Order Book. Book B. Vol. 2. County Clerk's Office. LCC.

"Extension of Boundaries, Speech of Hon. William H. Hooper, of Utah, Delivered in the House of Representatives, February 25, 1869." *Congressional Globe and Appendix.* 40th Cong., 3d Sess., pt. 3. Appendix. Washington, D.C.: F. and J. Rives and George A. Bailey, 1869.

Fifth District Court. Washington County. Probate Records. Book A, 1856–67. Microfilm. Series 3168, Reel 1. Utah State Archives, Salt Lake City.

Grant, Ulysses S. Executive Orders, 12 March 1873, 12 February 1874. Holograph Photocopies. Maryellen Vallier Sadovich Collection. Manuscript x45, Folder 3. Special Collections. Lied Library, University of Nevada at Las Vegas.

Lincoln County Tax Roll, 1868–70. Treasurer's Office. LCC.

Muddy or Moapa Indian Reservation. Resolution of the Legislature of the State of Nevada, 4 February 1875. 43d Cong., 2d Sess., Misc. Doc. No. 61, 1–2.

Powell, J. W., and G. W. Ingalls. *Report of Special Commissioners J. W. Powell and G. W. Ingalls on the Condition of the Ute Indians of Utah; the Paiutes of Utah, Northern Arizona, Southern Nevada, and Southeastern California; the Northwestern Shoshones of Idaho and Utah; and the Western Shoshones of Nevada; and Report Concerning Claims of Settlers in the Mo-a-pa Valley, Southeastern Nevada.* In *Annual Report of the Commissioner of Indian Affairs,* 1873. Serial Set 1601, 437–42.

Raymond, Rossiter W. *Statistics of Mines and Mining in the States and Territories West of the Rocky Mountains.* U.S. Treasury Department, Annual Report. Washington, D.C.: Government Printing Office, 1872, 1873.

"Resolution of the Legislature of the State of Nevada, in Favor of the Passage of a Law Fixing as the Eastern Boundary of the State of Nevada the Thirty-Seventh Degree of Longitude West from Washington." 38th Cong., 2d Sess., Senate Misc. Doc. No. 43., 24 February 1865, Serial Set 1210.

"Territory of Nevada." 35th Cong., 1st Sess., House Report No. 375, 12 May 1858, Serial Set 966, 4.

U.S. Army, Engineer Department. *Preliminary Report upon a Reconnaissance through Southern and Southeastern Nevada, Made in 1869,* by George M. Wheeler and Daniel W. Lockwood. Washington, D.C.: Government Printing Office, 1875.

U.S. District Court, Utah (Second District). *Report of the Grand Jury of the Second District of Utah Territory, September Term, 1859.* Carson Valley: Printed at the Office of the Territorial Enterprise, 1859. Beinecke Library, Yale University, New Haven, Conn.

U.S. House of Representatives. *The Condition of Utah.* 39th Cong., 1st Sess. Committee on the Territories. House Report No. 96, Serial Set 1272.

U.S. Treasury Department. *Statistics of Mines and Mining in the States and Territories West of the Rocky Mountains.* 1st Annual Report of Rossiter W. Raymond, U.S. Commissioner of Mining Statistics. 40th Cong., 3d Sess., 1868, House Ex. Doc. No. 54.

U.S. Treasury Department. *Statistics of Mines and Mining in the States and Territories West of the Rocky Mountains.* 2d Annual Report of Rossiter W. Raymond, U.S. Commissioner of Mining Statistics. 41st Cong., 2d Sess., 1869, House Ex. Doc. No. 207.

War of the Rebellion: A Compilation of the Official Records of the Union and Confederate Armies. Series 1, Vol. 50, Pt. 2. Washington, D.C.: Government Printing Office, 1897.

Secondary

Abbott, James W. "The Story of Pioche." In *The Arrowhead: A Monthly Magazine of Western Travel and Development.* Los Angeles: San Pedro, Los Angeles, and Salt Lake Railroad, [1907]. 3–11.

Alder, Douglas D., and Karl F. Brooks. *A History of Washington County: From Isolation to Destination.* Salt Lake City: Utah State Historical Society and Washington County Commission, 1996.

Alexander, Thomas G. "Federal Authority versus Polygamic Theocracy: James B. McKean and the Mormons, 1870–1875." *Dialogue: A Journal of Mormon Thought* 1 (Autumn 1966): 85–100.

Alley, John R. Jr. "Prelude to Dispossession: The Fur Trade's Significance for the Northern Utes and Southern Paiutes." *Utah Historical Quarterly* 50 (Spring 1982): 104–23.

Alter, J. Cecil. "The Mormons and the Indians: News Items and Editorials, from the Mormon Press." *Utah Historical Quarterly* 12 (January–April 1944): 49–68.

Angel, Myron. *History of Nevada.* Oakland, Calif.: Thompson and West, 1881.

Arrington, Leonard J. "Abundance from the Earth: The Beginnings of Commercial Mining in Utah." *Utah Historical Quarterly* 31 (Summer 1963): 192–219.

———. *Great Basin Kingdom: An Economic History of the Latter-day Saints, 1830–1900.* 1958; reprint, Lincoln: University of Nebraska Press, 1966.

Arrington, Leonard J., and Edward Leo Lyman. "The Mormon Church and Nevada Gold Mines." *Nevada Historical Society Quarterly* 41 (Fall 1998): 191–205.

Arrington, Leonard J., and Richard Jensen. "Panaca: Mormon Outpost among the Mining Camps." *Nevada Historical Society Quarterly* 18 (Winter 1975): 207–16.

Arrington, Leonard J., Feramorz Y. Fox, and Dean L. May. *Building the City of God: Community and Cooperation among the Mormons.* 1976; reprint, Urbana: University of Illinois Press, 1992.

Ashbaugh, Don. *Nevada's Turbulent Yesterday: A Study in Ghost Towns.* Los Angeles: Westernlore Press, 1963.

Backus, Anna Jean. *Mountain Meadows Witness: The Life and Times of Bishop Philip Klingensmith.* Spokane, Wash.: Arthur H. Clark Co., 1996.

Bagley, Will. *Blood of the Prophets: Brigham Young and the Massacre at Mountain Meadows.* Norman: University of Oklahoma Press, 2002.

Bakken, Gordon Morris. *Rocky Mountain Constitution Making, 1850–1912.* New York: Greenwood Press, 1987.

Bancroft, Hubert Howe. *History of Nevada, Colorado, and Wyoming, 1540–1888.* San Francisco: History Company Publishers, 1890.

Bourne, John Michael. "Early Mining in Southwestern Utah and Southeastern Nevada, 1864–1873: The Meadow Valley, Pahranagat, and Pioche Mining Rushes." Master's thesis, University of Utah, 1973.

Bowers, Michael W. *The Nevada State Constitution: A Reference Guide.* Westport, Conn.: Greenwood Press, 1993.

Brady, Margaret K. *Mormon Healer and Folk Poet: Mary Susannah Fowler's Life of "Unselfish Usefulness."* Logan: Utah State University Press, 2000.

Brightman, George F. "The Boundaries of Utah." *Economic Geography* 16 (January 1940): 87–95.

Brooks, Juanita. "Indian Relations on the Mormon Frontier." *Utah Historical Quarterly* 12 (January–April 1944): 1–48.

———. *John Doyle Lee: Zealot, Pioneer Builder, Scapegoat.* 3d ed. Salt Lake City: Howe Brothers, 1984.

———. *Mountain Meadows Massacre.* Norman: University of Oklahoma Press, 1962.

———. *On the Ragged Edge: The Life and Times of Dudley Leavitt.* Salt Lake City: Utah State Historical Society, 1973.

———. *Quicksand and Cactus: A Memoir of the Southern Mormon Frontier.* Logan: Utah State University Press, 1992.

———, ed. *Journal of the Southern Indian Mission: Diary of Thomas D. Brown.* Western Text Society No. 4. Logan: Utah State University Press, 1972.

Brown, James Stephens. *Life of a Pioneer: Being the Autobiography of James S. Brown.* Salt Lake City: G. Q. Cannon, 1900.

Bufkin, Donald. "The Lost County of Pah-Ute." *Arizoniana: The Journal of Arizona History* 5 (Summer 1964): 1–11.

Bush, Lester E. Jr. *Health and Medicine among the Latter-day Saints: Science, Sense, and Scripture.* New York: Crossroad Publishing, 1993.

Bushman, Richard Lyman. *Making Space for the Mormons.* Leonard J. Arrington Mormon History Lecture Series No. 2. Logan: Utah State University Press, 1997.

Cannon, Donald Q. "Angus M. Cannon: Frustrated Mormon Miner." *Utah Historical Quarterly* 57 (Winter 1989): 36–45.

Chalfant, Willie Arthur. *Gold, Guns, and Ghost Towns.* Stanford, Calif.: Stanford University Press, 1947.

Chidester, David, and Edward T. Linenthal, eds. *American Sacred Space.* Bloomington: Indiana University Press, 1995.

Christian, Lewis Clark. "Mormon Foreknowledge of the West." *BYU Studies* 21 (Fall 1981): 403–15.

Christy, Howard A. "Open Hand and Mailed Fist: Mormon-Indian Relations in Utah, 1847–52." *Utah Historical Quarterly* 46 (Summer 1978): 216–35.

Considine, John L. "The Birth of Old Pioche." *Sunset: The Pacific Monthly* 54 (January 1925): 29, 56, 58.

———. "How Zink Barnes Corrupted Pioche." *Sunset: The Pacific Monthly* 54 (February 1925): 40, 60.

———. "The Pistoleers of Old Pioche, *Sunset: The Pacific Monthly* 53 (December 1924): 24–25.

Corbett, Pearson H. *Jacob Hamblin: The Peacemaker.* Salt Lake City: Deseret Book Co., 1968.

Corbett, Pearson Starr. "A History of the Muddy Mission." Master's thesis, Brigham Young University, 1968.

Cuch, Forrest S., ed. *A History of Utah's American Indians.* Salt Lake City: Utah State Division of Indian Affairs/Utah State Division of History, 2000.

Dalin, David G., and Charles A. Fracchia. "Forgotten Financier: François L. A. Pioche." *California Historical Quarterly* 53 (Spring 1974): 17–24.

Davis, David Brion. "Some Themes of Counter-Subversion: An Analysis of Anti-Masonic, Anti-Catholic, and Anti-Mormon Literature." *Mississippi Valley Historical Review* 47 (September 1960): 205–24.

Davis, Samuel P., ed. *The History of Nevada.* 2 vols. Reno: Elms Publishing Co., 1913.

Del Papa, Frankie Sue, ed. *Political History of Nevada.* 9th ed. Carson City: State Printing Office, 1990.

Driver, Tom F. *Liberating Rites: Understanding the Transformative Power of Ritual.* Boulder, Colo.: Westview Press, 1998.

Dyal, Donald Henriques. "The Agrarian Values of Mormonism: A Touch of the Mountain Sod." Ph.D. dissertation, Texas A&M University, 1980.

Eliade, Mircea. *The Sacred and the Profane: The Nature of Religion, the Significance of Religious Myth, Symbolism, and Ritual within Life and Culture.* Trans. Willard R. Trask. New York: Harper and Row, 1961.

Ellsworth, S. George. *Mormon Settlement on the Muddy.* Ogden, Utah: Weber State College Press, 1987.

Euler, Robert C. *The Paiute People.* Phoenix: Indian Tribal Series, 1972.

———. *Southern Paiute Ethnohistory.* University of Utah Anthropological Papers No. 78. 1966; reprint, Salt Lake City: University of Utah Press, 1973.

Faragher, John Mack. "The Frontier Trail: Rethinking Turner and Reimagining the American West." *American Historical Review* 98 (February 1993): 106–17.

Fish, Joseph. "History of Enterprise and Its Surroundings." Typescript in possession of Kay Reeve, Hurricane, Utah.

Fleming, L. A. "The Settlements on the Muddy, 1865 to 1871: 'A Godforsaken Place.'" *Utah Historical Quarterly* 35 (Spring 1967): 147–72.

Foner, Eric. *Reconstruction: America's Unfinished Revolution, 1863–1877.* New York: Harper and Row, 1988.

Forbes, Jack D., ed. *Nevada Indians Speak.* Reno: University of Nevada Press, 1967.

Fowler, Don D., and Catherine Fowler. *Anthropology of the Numa: John Wesley Powell's Manuscripts on the Numic People.* Smithsonian Contributions to Anthropology 14. Washington, D.C.: Smithsonian Institution, 1971.

———. "Notes on the History of the Southern Paiutes and Western Shoshonis." *Utah Historical Quarterly* 39 (Spring 1971): 95–113.

Francaviglia, Richard V. *Hard Places: Reading the Landscape of America's Historic Mining Districts.* Iowa City: University of Iowa Press, 1991.

Franklin, Robert J., and Pamela A. Bunte. *The Paiute.* New York: Chelsea House, 1990.

Furniss, Norman F. *The Mormon Conflict, 1850–59.* New Haven, Conn.: Yale University Press, 1960.

Gates, Paul W. *The Jeffersonian Dream: Studies in the History of American Land Policy and Development.* Ed. Allan G. Bogue and Margaret Beattie Bogue. Albuquerque: University of New Mexico Press, 1996.

Gibson, Arrell Morgan. *The American Indian: Prehistory to the Present.* Lexington, Mass.: D.C. Heath and Co., 1980.

Gorman, Mel. "Chronicle of a Silver Mine: The Meadow Valley Mining Company of Pioche." *Nevada Historical Society Quarterly* 29 (Summer 1986): 69–88.

Gracey, Charles. "Early Days in Lincoln County." In *First Biennial Report of the Nevada Historical Society, 1907–1908.* Carson City, Nev.: State Printing Office, 1909.

Grattan-Aiello, Carolyn. "The Chinese Community of Pioche, 1870–1900." *Nevada Historical Society Quarterly* 39 (Fall 1996): 201–15.

Grosh, Rev. Aaron B. *The Odd-Fellow's Manual: Illustrating the History, Principles, and Government of the Order, and the Instructions and Duties of Every Degree, State, and Office in Odd-Fellowship; with Directions for Laying Corner-Stones; Dedicating Cemeteries, Chapels, Halls, and Other Public Edifices; Marshalling Funeral and Other Processions; Forms for Petitions, Reports, etc. Also, Odes, with Music, for Various Occasions.* Philadelphia: H. C. Peck and Theo. Bliss., 1853.

Hafen, Orrilla Woods, Mary R. Edwards, and Elbert B. Edwards, comps. *The Woods Family of Clover Valley, Nevada, 1869–1979.* Boulder City, Nev.: Woods Family Genealogical Committee, 1979.

Hinckley, Gordon B. "This Great Millennial Year." *Ensign* 30 (November 2000): 67–71.

Holt, Ronald L. *Beneath These Red Cliffs: An Ethnohistory of the Utah Paiutes.* Albuquerque: University of New Mexico Press, 1992.

Hulse, James W. "The Afterlife of St. Mary's County; or, Utah's Penumbra in Eastern Nevada." *Utah Historical Quarterly* 55 (Summer 1987): 236–49.

———. "Boom and Bust Government in Lincoln County, Nevada, 1866–1909." *Nevada Historical Society Quarterly* 1 (November 1957): 65–80.

———. "'The Camp That Came Back': The Combined Metals Reduction Company and the Revival of Pioche, 1912–1958." *Nevada Historical Society Quarterly* 42 (Fall 1999): 160–68.

———. *Lincoln County, Nevada: 1864–1909: History of a Mining Region.* Reno: University of Nevada Press, 1971.

———. *The Nevada Adventure: A History.* 6th ed. Reno: University of Nevada Press, 1990.

———. *The Silver State: Nevada's Heritage Reinterpreted.* 2d ed. Reno: University of Nevada Press, 1998.

Hunt, Carrie Elizabeth Laub. *Memories of the Past and Family History.* Salt Lake City: Utah Printing Co., 1968.

Inter-Tribal Council of Nevada. *Nuwuvi: A Southern Paiute History.* Salt Lake City: University of Utah Printing Service, 1976.

Ivins, Anthony W. "Traveling over Forgotten Trails: A Mystery of the Grand Canyon Solved." *Improvement Era* 27 (1924): 1017–25.

Jackson, W. Turrentine. *Treasure Hill.* Tuscon: University of Arizona Press, 1963.

Jeffcott, Vernon. "Tales of Pioche." *Utah Humanities Review* 2 (April 1948): 192–93.

Jeffredo-Warden, Louise V. "Perceiving, Experiencing, and Expressing the Sacred: An Indigenous Southern Californian View." In *Over the Edge: Remapping the American West.* Ed. Valerie J. Matsumoto and Blake Allmendinger. Berkeley: University of California Press, 1999. 329–38.

Johnson, David Alan. *Founding the Far West: California, Oregon, and Nevada, 1840–1890.* Berkeley: University of California Press, 1992.

Jones, Sondra. "Saints or Sinners? The Evolving Perceptions of Mormon-Indian Relations in Utah Historiography." *Utah Historical Quarterly* 72 (Winter 2004): 19–46.

———. *The Trial of Don Pedro León Luján: The Attack against Indian Slavery and Mexican Traders in Utah.* Salt Lake City: University of Utah Press, 2000.

Jorgensen, Joseph G. "Land Is Cultural, So Is a Commodity: The Locus of Differences among Indians, Cowboys, Sod-Busters, and Environmentalists." *Journal of Ethnic Studies* 12 (Fall 1984): 1–21.

Kappler, Charles J., comp. and ed. *Indian Affairs: Laws and Treaties.* Vol. 1. Washington, D.C.: Government Printing Office, 1904.

Kelly, Isabel T. "Southern Paiute Bands." *American Anthropologist* 36 (1934): 548–60.

———. *Southern Paiute Ethnography.* 1964; reprint, New York: Garland Publishing Inc., 1976.

———. "Southern Paiute Shamanism." *Anthropological Records* 2.4. Berkeley: University of California Press, 1939. 151–67.

Kelly, Isabel T., and Catherine S. Fowler. "Southern Paiute." In *Great Basin.* Ed. Warren L. D'Azevedo. Vol 11 of *Handbook of North American Indians.* Ed. William C. Sturtevant. Washington, D.C.: Smithsonian Institution, 1986. 368–97.

Knack, Martha C. *Boundaries Between: The Southern Paiutes, 1775–1995.* Lincoln: University of Nebraska Press, 2001.

———. "Newspaper Accounts of Indian Women in Southern Nevada Mining Towns, 1870–1900." *Journal of California and Great Basin Anthropology* 8.1 (1986): 83–98.

———. "Nineteenth-Century Great Basin Indian Wage Labor." In *Native Ameri-*

cans and Wage Labor: Ethnohistorical Perspectives. Ed. Alice Littlefield and Martha C. Knack. Norman: University of Oklahoma Press, 1996. 144–76.

———. "Utah Indians and the Homestead Laws." In *State and Reservation: New Perspectives on Federal Indian Policy.* Ed. George Pierre Castile and Robert L. Bee. Tucson: University of Arizona Press, 1992. 63–91.

Lamar, Howard R. "Statehood for Utah: A Different Path." *Utah Historical Quarterly* 39 (Fall 1971): 307–27.

Larson, Andrew Karl. *"I Was Called to Dixie," the Virgin River Basin: Unique Experiences in Mormon Pioneering.* Salt Lake City: Deseret News Press, 1961.

Larson, Gustive O. *The "Americanization" of Utah for Statehood.* San Marino, Calif.: Huntington Library, 1971.

Lee, Henry H. "The Murder of George Rogers." In *A Century in Meadow Valley, 1864–1964.* Ed. Ruth Lee and Sylvia Wadsworth. Salt Lake City: Deseret News Press, 1966. 21.

Limerick, Patricia Nelson. *The Legacy of Conquest: The Unbroken Past of the American West.* New York: W. W. Norton and Co., 1987.

Limerick, Patricia Nelson, Clyde A. Milner II, and Charles E. Rankin, eds. *Trails toward a New Western History.* Lawrence: University Press of Kansas, 1991.

Long, Lloyd K. "Pioche, Nevada, and Early Mining Developments in Eastern Nevada." Master's thesis, University of Nevada at Las Vegas, 1975.

Ludlow, Daniel H., ed. *Encyclopedia of Mormonism.* New York: Macmillan, 1992.

Lyman, Edward Leo. *Political Deliverance: The Mormon Quest for Utah Statehood.* Urbana: University of Illinois Press, 1986.

MacKinnon, William P. "The Buchanan Spoils System and the Utah Expedition: Careers of W. M. F. Magraw and John M. Hockaday." *Utah Historical Quarterly* 31 (Spring 1963): 127–50.

———. "'Like Splitting a Man up His Backbone': The Territorial Dismemberment of Utah, 1850–1896." *Utah Historical Quarterly* 71 (Spring 2003): 100–124.

Madsen, Brigham D. *Glory Hunter: A Biography of Patrick Edward Connor.* Salt Lake City: University of Utah Press, 1990.

Madsen, David B. "Dating Paiute-Shoshoni Expansion in the Great Basin." *American Antiquity* 40 (January 1975): 82–86.

Maffly-Kipp, Laurie F. *Religion and Society in Frontier California.* New Haven, Conn.: Yale University Press, 1994.

Martineau, LaVan. *Southern Paiutes: Legends, Lore, Language, and Lineage.* Las Vegas: KC Publications, 1992.

Mathews, Barbara S. "The Boundary Tax Dispute." In *A Century in Meadow Valley, 1864–1964.* Ed. Ruth Lee and Sylvia Wadsworth. Salt Lake City: Deseret News Press, 1966. 9–15.

Mathews, Charles P. "The Death of Railroad Jim." In *A Century in Meadow Valley, 1864–1964.* Ed. Ruth Lee and Sylvia Wadsworth. Salt Lake City: Deseret News Press, 1966. 21.

Mathews, Jack R. "Mule Skinners and Bull Whackers: An Archeological Study of Two Historic Wagon Roads in Southeast Nevada." Master's thesis, University of Nevada at Las Vegas, 1992.

May, Dean L. *Three Frontiers: Family, Land, and Society in the American West, 1850–1900.* Cambridge: Cambridge University Press, 1994.

McCormack, Patricia. "Native Homelands as Cultural Landscapes: Decentering the Wilderness Paradigm." In *Sacred Lands: Aboriginal World Views, Claims, and Conflicts.* Occasional Publication Series No. 43. Ed. Jill Oakes, Rick Riewe, Kathi Kinew, and Elaine Maloney. Alberta: Canadian Circumpolar Institute and University of Manitoba, Dept. of Native Studies, 1998. 25–32.

McPherson, James M. *Battle Cry of Freedom: The Civil War Era.* New York: Ballantine, 1989.

McPherson, Robert S. "Of Papers and Perception: Utes and Navajos in Journalistic Media, 1900–1930." *Utah Historical Quarterly* 67 (Summer 1999): 196–219.

Meinig, D. W. "American Wests: Preface to a Geographical Interpretation." *Annals of the Association of American Geographers* 62 (June 1972): 159–84.

Michaelsen, Robert S. "Dirt in the Court Room: Indian Land Claims and American Property Rights." In *American Sacred Space.* Ed. David Chidester and Edward T. Linenthal. Bloomington: Indiana University Press, 1995. 43–96.

Moorman, Donald R., and Gene A. Sessions. *Camp Floyd and the Mormons: The Utah War.* Salt Lake City: University of Utah Press, 1992.

Morgan, Dale L., ed. "The Reminiscences of James Holt: A Narrative of the Emmett Company, Part II." *Utah Historical Quarterly* 23 (April 1955): 151–79.

Mortensen, A. R., ed. *Utah's Dixie: The Cotton Mission.* Salt Lake City: Utah State Historical Society, 1961.

Newton, Marjorie. *Hero or Traitor: A Biographical Study of Charles Wesley Wandell.* Independence, Mo.: Herald Publishing House, 1992.

Older, Fremont, and Cora M. Older. *George Hearst: California Pioneer.* Los Angeles: Westernlore, 1966.

O'Neil, Floyd A., and Stanford J. Layton. "Of Pride and Politics: Brigham Young as Indian Superintendent." *Utah Historical Quarterly* 46 (Summer 1978): 236–50.

Palmer, Edward. *Notes on the Utah Utes by Edward Palmer, 1866–1877.* Ed. R. F. Heizer. Anthropological Papers No. 17. Salt Lake City: University of Utah Press, 1954.

Palmer, William R. "Early Day Trading with the Nevada Mining Camps." *Utah Historical Quarterly* 26 (October 1958): 353–68.

———. "Pahute Indian Government and Laws." *Utah Historical Quarterly* 2 (April 1929): 35–42.

———. "Pahute Indian Medicine." *Utah Historical Quarterly* 10 (January–October 1942): 1–13.

Parshall, Ardis E. "Marysvale: Mormons, Miners, and Methodists." Paper presented at the Mormon History Association Conference, Cedar City, Utah. May 2001.

Peterson, John Alton. *Utah's Black Hawk War.* Salt Lake City: University of Utah Press, 1998.

Poll, Richard D. "The Americanism of Utah." *Utah Historical Quarterly* 44 (Winter 1976): 76–93.

———. "The Legislative Antipolygamy Campaign." *BYU Studies* 26.4 (1986): 107–21.

Poll, Richard D., and William P. MacKinnon. "Causes of the Utah War Reconsidered." *Journal of Mormon History* 20 (Fall 1994): 16–44.

Porter, Kirk H., and Donald Bruce Johnson, comps. *National Party Platforms, 1840–1956.* Urbana: University of Illinois Press, 1956.

Powell, Allan Kent, ed. *Utah History Encyclopedia.* Salt Lake City: University of Utah Press, 1994.

Powell, John Wesley. *The Exploration of the Colorado River and Its Canyons.* 1895; reprint, New York: Dover, 1961.

Proctor, Paul Dean, and Morris A. Shirts. *Silver, Sinners, and Saints: A History of Old Silver Reef, Utah.* N.p.: Paulmar, Inc., 1991.

Prucha, Francis Paul. *The Great Father: The United States Government and the American Indians.* 2 vols. Lincoln: University of Nebraska Press, 1984.

Pulsipher, John Lewis. *The Life and Travels of John Lewis Pulsipher, 1884–1963: The Autobiography of a Southern Nevada Pioneer.* N.p., n.d.

Queen, Rolla Lee. "Historical Archaeology and Historic Preservation at Candelaria and Metallic City, Nevada." Master's thesis, University of Nevada at Reno, 1987.

Reeve, W. Paul. "'As Ugly as Evil' and 'As Wicked as Hell': Gadianton Robbers and the Legend Process among the Mormons." *Journal of Mormon History* 27 (Fall 2001): 125–49.

———. "Cattle, Cotton, and Conflict: The Possession and Dispossession of Hebron, Utah." *Utah Historical Quarterly* 67 (Spring 1999): 148–75.

———. *A Century of Enterprise: The History of Enterprise, Utah, 1896–1996.* Enterprise, Utah: City of Enterprise, 1996.

———. "Silver Reef and Southwest Utah's Shifting Mining Frontier." In *From the Ground Up: The History of Mining in Utah.* Ed. Colleen Whitley. Logan: Utah State University Press, 2006. 250–71.

Reisner, Marc. *Cadillac Desert: The American West and Its Disappearing Water.* New York: Penguin, 1987.

Ronda, James P. "Coboway's Tale: A Story of Power and Places along the Columbia." In *Power and Place in the North American West.* Ed. Richard White and John M. Findlay. Seattle: Center for the Study of the Pacific Northwest and University of Washington Press, 1999. 3–22.

Ross, Theodore A. *The Illustrated History of Odd Fellowship: A Documentary and Chronological History of the Origin, Rise, and Progress of the Independent Order of Odd Fellows throughout the World.* New York: Ross History Co., 1913.

Rush, Philip S. "The Strange Story of F. L. A. Pioche." Typescript. Lincoln County Museum, Pioche, Nevada.

Sapir, Edward. "Song Recitative in Paiute Mythology." *Journal of American Folklore* 23 (October–December 1910): 455–72.

Shirts, Morris A., and Kathryn H. Shirts. *A Trial Furnace: Southern Utah's Iron Mission.* Provo, Utah: Brigham Young University Press, 2001.

Smart, Donna Toland, ed. *Mormon Midwife: The 1846–1888 Diaries of Patty Bartlett Sessions.* Logan: Utah State University Press, 1997.

Smith, Duane A., and Donald C. Brown. *No One Ailing Except the Physician: Medicine in the Mining West, 1848–1919.* Boulder: University Press of Colorado, 2001.

Smith, Inez. "Biography of Charles Wesley Wandell." *Journal of History* 3 (October 1910): 462–63.

Smith, Joseph Jr. *History of the Church of Jesus Christ of Latter-day Saints.* 7 vols. 2d ed. Ed. B. H. Roberts. Salt Lake City: Deseret Books, 1971.

Telling, Irving. *A Preliminary Study of the History of Ramah, New Mexico.* N.p., n.d. FHL.

Townley, John M. *Conquered Provinces: Nevada Moves Southeast, 1864–1871.* Charles Redd Monographs in Western History No. 2. Provo, Utah: Brigham Young University Press, 1973.

Turner, Frederick Jackson. *The Frontier in American History.* New York: Henry Holt and Co., 1921.

Van Hoak, Stephen P. "And Who Shall Have the Children? The Indian Slave Trade in the Southern Great Basin, 1800–1865." *Nevada Historical Society Quarterly* 41 (Spring 1998): 3–25.

———. "Waccara's Utes: Native American Equestrian Adaptations in the Eastern Great Basin, 1776–1876." *Utah Historical Quarterly* 67 (Fall 1999): 309–30.

Walker, Josephine B., ed. *The Bunker Family History.* N.p.: Edward Bunker Family Association, 1957.

Walker, Ronald W. "Toward a Reconstruction of Mormon and Indian Relations, 1847–1877." *BYU Studies* 29 (Fall 1989): 23–42.

———. *Wayward Saints: The Godbeites and Brigham Young.* Urbana: University of Illinois Press, 1998.

Weber, David J. "*The Legacy of Conquest,* by Patricia Nelson Limerick: A Panel of Appraisal." *Western Historical Quarterly* 20 (August 1989): 313–16.

Weber, David J., and Jane M. Rausch, eds. *Where Cultures Meet: Frontiers in Latin American History.* Wilmington, Del.: Scholarly Resources Inc., 1994.

West, Elliott. *The Contested Plains: Indians, Goldseekers, and the Rush to Colorado.* Lawrence: University Press of Kansas, 1998.

White, Richard. *"It's Your Misfortune and None of My Own": A New History of the American West.* Norman: University of Oklahoma Press, 1991.

Whitney, Orson F. *History of Utah.* 4 vols. Salt Lake City: George Q. Cannon, 1892–1904.

Whittaker, David J. "Danites." In *Encyclopedia of Mormonism.* Vol. 1. Ed. Daniel H. Ludlow. New York: Macmillan, 1992. 356–57.

———. "Mormons and Native Americans: A Historical and Bibliographical Introduction." *Dialogue: A Journal of Mormon Thought* 18 (Winter 1985): 33–64.

Williamson, Naida R. "William Haynes Hamblin, 1830–1872." Typescript. FHL.

Wolfe, Thomas J. "Steaming Saints: Mormons and the Thomsonian Movement in Nineteenth-Century America." In *Disease and Medical Care in the Mountain West: Essays on Region, History, and Practice.* Ed. Martha L. Hildreth and Bruce T. Moran. Reno: University of Nevada Press, 1998. 18–28.

Worster, Donald. *A River Running West: The Life of John Wesley Powell.* New York: Oxford University Press, 2001.

———. *Rivers of Empire: Water, Aridity, and the Growth of the American West.* New York: Pantheon Books, 1985.

INDEX

against, 98–99, 100, 111; and miners, spiritual defense against, 90–99;
and miners, trade with, 95–97, 111;
and mining policy, 46, 99–100, 111,
195n69, 195n76, 195n77; and polygamy, 34–35; and record keeping,
19–20, 32; and sacred space, 15–20,
90, 159, 173n24, 173n25; and
Southern Paiute abandonment of
elderly, 148, 156, 165, 205n46; and
Southern Paiutes, defense against,
104–7; and Southern Paiutes, intermarriage with, 104, 108, 111–12,
198n127; and Southern Paiutes,
mass baptism of, 75–77, 108; and
Southern Paiutes, trade with, 109,
112. *See also* Brigham Young: mining policy
Moroni (Southern Paiute): as band
leader, 65; and conciliatory policy
toward whites, 72–73; and Huntsman, Orson W, moccasins for, 109;
and Mormons, confrontation with,
14; and Pioche, founding of silver
at, 22, 24, 29, 49, 174n47, 175n51
Morrill Act (1862), 35
Mountain Meadows Massacre, 76,
119–21, 185n9, 188n55
Muddy Mission: abandonment of,
54, 90, 111, 183n72, 191n19; and
miners, defense against, 88; and
Southern Paiutes, 11, 71, 73–74,
104–5, 149
Muddy Valley Reservation. *See
Moapa Reservation*

Ná-guts, 65
Navajos, 49, 72
Nebeker, John, 87, 88
Nevada: boundary shift, 37, 38, 44–
47, 57; statehood, 37–38; territorial
formation, 36–37, 61
Nichols, F. C., 150
Nichols, W. T., 70
Northern Paiutes, 81

Ocean Grandmother, 12, 49
Okus: execution of, 2, 74; and Rogers,
George, burial of body with rocks,

143, 149; and Rogers, George, murder of, 1–2, 72–73
Old Spanish Trail, 39, 53, 119

Pahranagat Mining District: and
Blasdel, Henry Goode, interest in,
40–41; and boundary shift, 44–47;
disappointing results from, 40,
44–45, 47, 181n49; discovery and
organization of, 33, 38–39, 179n22;
and Durkee, Charles, interest in,
41–43, 47; and location, uncertainty
of, 33, 39–40; miners move from,
27; and Mormons, relationship
with, 61, 67, 88, 94, 95, 119; and
ore shipments from, 44; and Southern Paiutes, relationship with, 33,
38, 67, 70–71, 72, 75, 78, 129
Panaca, Nevada: and boundary tax
dispute, 88–90; founding of, 25, 87;
and miners, relationship with, 85,
87–88, 90, 97–100, 111, 125, 126,
158–59; and Okus/Rogers deaths,
1–2, 148–49; and Southern Paiutes,
relationship with 11, 50–51, 69–70,
106
Parowan, Utah, 15, 103
Peterson, John Alton, 69
Pikyavit, Bennjamin, 166
Pinto, Utah, 95
Pioche, François Louis Alfred, 27–28,
32, 116, 176n79
Pioche, Nevada: and absentee capitalists, 8, 116–17; and booster press,
160–61; and boundary tax dispute,
88–90; cemetery at, 151, 154; decline of, 159–60; demographics of,
93, 115, 198n4, 198n6; earthquake
at, 157; filth at, 116, 163, 199n13;
founding story, 4, 21–28, 32, 49,
174n46, 174n47, 175n51, 175n52;
as haven for those disgruntled with
Mormonism, 121–22; Independent
Order of Odd Fellows at, 150, 151–
53, 154; as Indian agent headquarters, 54; and Indian extermination,
call for, 130–31; and individualism,
117–18, 134; as Lincoln County
seat, 116, 159–60, 198n4; Masonic

W. PAUL REEVE is an assistant professor of history at the University of Utah.

The University of Illinois Press
is a founding member of the
Association of American University Presses.

Composed in 9.5/12.5 Trump Mediaeval
by Jim Proefrock
at the University of Illinois Press
Manufactured by Thomson-Shore, Inc.

University of Illinois Press
1325 South Oak Street
Champaign, IL 61820-6903
www.press.uillinois.edu